The Enterprise Engineering Series

Enterprise Engineering is an emerging discipline for coping with the challenges (agility, adaptability, etc.) and the opportunities (new markets, new technologies, etc.) faced by contemporary enterprises, including commercial, nonprofit and governmental institutions. It is based on the paradigm that such enterprises are purposefully designed systems, and thus they can be redesigned in a systematic and controlled way. Such enterprise engineering projects typically involve architecture, design, and implementation aspects.

The Enterprise Engineering series thus explores a design-oriented approach that combines the information systems sciences and organization sciences into a new field characterized by rigorous theories and effective practices. Books in this series should critically engage the enterprise engineering paradigm, by providing sound evidence that either underpins it or that challenges its current version. To this end, two branches are distinguished: Foundations, containing theoretical elaborations and their practical applications, and Explorations, covering various approaches and experiences in the field of enterprise engineering. With this unique combination of theory and practice, the books in this series are aimed at both academic students and advanced professionals.

Jörg Ziemann

Fundamentals of Enterprise Architecture Management

Foundations for Steering
the Enterprise-Wide Digital System

 Springer

Jörg Ziemann
Institut für Wirtschaftsinformatik
University of Hannover
Hannover, Germany

ISSN 1867-8920   ISSN 1867-8939   (electronic)
The Enterprise Engineering Series
ISBN 978-3-030-96733-8   ISBN 978-3-030-96734-5   (eBook)
https://doi.org/10.1007/978-3-030-96734-5

This Springer imprint is published by the registered company Springer Nature Switzerland AG
The registered company address is: Gewerbestrasse 11, 6330 Cham, Switzerland

Foreword

Enterprise Architecture Management (EAM) is a "hot topic" because it addresses the core of enterprise digitalization: how to design the digital ecosystem "in the large" to meet strategic and operational business requirements. EAM is applied in disruptive situations, where fast, large-scale changes of the digital landscape need to be architected. EAM is also applied in the everyday life of an enterprise, where the multitude of continuous, iterative digitalization efforts spread over the enterprise must form a coherent big picture.

Today, the importance of an efficient, customer-oriented digital ecosystem is obvious. It is also clear that this ecosystem must be stable and secure against cybercrime. However, what is the best way to reach such goals? What does the process of shaping the highly complex and dynamic enterprise-wide digital ecosystem look like? Clearly, there must be a balance between central and decentral activities. On the one hand, ambitious, innovative target pictures for large parts of the digital enterprise must be centrally coordinated. Central optimization and standardization are also needed to leverage economies of scale and to keep the enterprise-wide digital ecosystem lean. On the other hand, there must be room for creativity and context sensitivity in the local digitalization departments.

EAM provides a set of methods, artifacts, and tools to address these challenges. Given the huge importance of EAM, it is good that Jörg Ziemann took on the challenge to write a comprehensive book on EAM, as the books published so far have either been too distant from today's practical challenges and solutions or they lacked a clear, comprehensive description of EAM. This book aims to close this gap. Regardless of your role or responsibility, this book provides you with introductions, formal definitions, process descriptions, strategic EAM parameters, goals, and a framework for measuring EAM's success.

I wish you an enjoyable and enriching reading experience!

Lufthansa Group, Hamburg, Germany Thomas Rückert
December 15, 2021

Preface

The disruptions in the last years have clearly illustrated that every large enterprise needs a comprehensive method for business digitalization. The quality of the digital ecosystem is vital both for the CEO and the CIO, and business and IT jointly must *plan, steer, and control the enterprise-wide digital ecosystem.* This activity, known as Enterprise Architecture Management (EAM), is described in this book.

Goals of the Book and Target Audience

For my university lecture, I missed having a textbook that would cover the topic of EAM comprehensively and that would be scientifically rigorous and practically relevant. Similarly, in my role as Senior Enterprise Architect inside large international companies, I missed a comprehensive, precise description of EAM that plainly addresses questions like: How can you derive EAM goals for your individual enterprise, fitting to its business model? What does the corresponding, optimal EAM implementation in the enterprise look like, e.g., the EAM capabilities, processes, and tools? What is a realistic way of measuring the success of your EAM activities? This book aims at closing this gap, being a fundamental handbook for scholars, business managers, architects, and other professionals engaged in enterprise digitalization and the enterprise-wide IT landscape. Accordingly, the goals of this book are:

- *Comprehensive:* The goal is a comprehensive, rather high-level overview of Enterprise Architecture Management (EAM) addressing all topics relevant in the practice of EAM.
- *Holistic:* Many EAM books stem from IT practitioners and pursue a bottom-up approach. On the other hand, some academic EAM books pursue a top-down approach and come from a strategic business perspective. This book combines both aspects, connecting strategic and operational aspects of EAM.

- *Scientifically precise, practically relevant,* i.e., addressing EAM with scientific rigor combined with knowledge gained in many years of practice as a senior enterprise architect in different large enterprises. This book describes EAM core concepts clearly and thoroughly, based on an extensive state-of-the-art review and real-life experiences.
- *Established concepts and current trends:* The focus of this book is on established EAM concepts that have been proven in real-life enterprises. However, current trends are also addressed, for instance, how EAM relates to disruptive digitalization and to lean, agile methods.

This book focuses on two groups:

- *EAM scholars:* The fields of IT strategy, enterprise digitalization, and EAM are highly relevant for scholars of business information systems or enterprise digitalization. In this vein, the book addresses advanced bachelor or master students of Business Information Systems, Business Administration, or Computer Science. It aims to be a scientifically sound, clear textbook on the topic of EAM.
- *EAM practitioners:* EAM remains a highly relevant but challenging topic for practitioners. Though the general idea of EAM today is understood, a precise, applicable description of how exactly to configure EAM to the requirements of a specific company is missing. Thus, this book also aims at practitioners in the field of IT strategy and EAM that need a reliable, scientifically rounded, and practical proven state-of-the-art description of essential EAM methods.

Though the experiences of both groups are different, there is an overlap between them regarding the need of a clear, proven description of this complex matter.

Structure and Content of This Book

Note that the topic of this book is Enterprise Architecture *Management*, not Enterprise Architecture. Regarding Enterprise Architecture, a lot of work exists including mature EA frameworks like TOGAF. What is lacking is a precise description of Enterprise Architecture Management. This book is neither about detailed individual architecture methods nor artifacts, like application maps, roadmaps, or architecture principles. It will cover such artifacts on a high level but will leave detailed descriptions to books specializing on these topics.

Figure 1 provides an overview of the context and the main topics of this book. Topics adjacent to EAM are displayed on the left-hand side. Starting from the top, the business model and the enterprise strategy provide the parameters for shaping EAM. EAM on the other hand plans and controls the Enterprise Architecture, while the Enterprise Architecture represents the fundamental structure of the enterprise-wide digital ecosystem. We will describe the topics above and below EAM only as far as necessary to understand EAM and its shaping. The right-hand side of Fig. 1

displays the four core parts of the book, which follow a typical development lifecycle: First, the requirements and context of EAM are addressed, i.e., strategic and tactical EAM parameters. Second, core elements of an EAM implementation are described, e.g., EAM processes and tools. And third, closing the cycle, we address the evaluation of EAM. These topics will be described in five chapters:

Enterprise Architecture Management in a nutshell: The first chapter provides a overview of Enterprise Architecture Management. It addresses questions like: What does EAM mean, what is the history of EAM, why do enterprises need EAM, what are its goals, and how is it related to digitalization? Further topics include the consequences of a laissez-faire approach in a complex enterprise-wide digital eco-system, which is not steered but emerges "organically." Afterward, we address a related question: Is there a middle ground between unmanaged chaos and exuberant, all-controlling central steering and planning of the digital ecosystem landscape? The chapter concludes with a short overview of essential EAM standards and literature.

Enterprise Architecture in a nutshell: The previous chapter introduced EAM, including its objective to establish and maintain a "good" Enterprise Architecture. Delving deeper into the latter concept, this chapter provides an overview of Enter-prise Architecture. We start with clarifying basic terminology, like "system," "archi-tecture," and the difference between Enterprise Architecture (EA) and Enterprise Architecture Management (EAM). We also revisit the concept of system complexity and how it relates to parameters like standardization of the IT landscape. Afterward, we provide a short summary of existing EA frameworks and methods for structuring the digital ecosystem into layers and views. Next, basic principles for structuring socio-technical systems are laid out, like the forming of hierarchies and aligning the structures of organizational and digital systems. Finally, we describe core parameters of the Enterprise Architecture. These include, for example, the degree of standard-ization, centralization, and integration of the ecosystem, but also the desired degree of innovativeness, risk appetite, outsourcing, as well as cost and quality priorities.

Strategic and tactical context of EAM: This third chapter addresses the strategic and tactical context of the EAM capability in an enterprise. To provide a basis for the following sections, first essential terms in the context of enterprise strategy and tactics are defined. Afterward, core parameters of the business strategy and the business operations of an enterprise are sketched out. These include classic strategy parameters, like cost focus, quality focus, or the market coverage of an enterprise. More operational parameters include the degree of business process integration, process standardization, and innovation within an enterprise. When these overarch-ing enterprise parameters are clarified, we describe the parameters of the EAM capability itself. These include the scope of the EAM capability, its allocation, its stance toward standardization, and its planning horizon. In the following synthesis, we correlate the parameters for the enterprise strategy, the operative enterprise, and the EAM capability. The last section describes the operative, organizational context of EAM. Here, we discuss the general shape of the IT organization (e.g.,

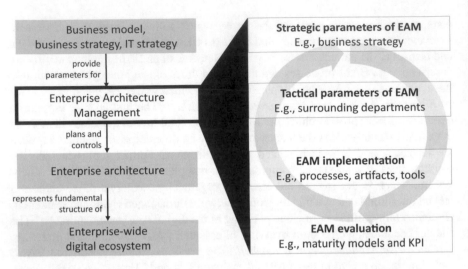

Fig. 1 Context and main topics of the book

centralized vs. decentralized) as well as fundamental tasks of the IT organization. Next, the individual capabilities of the IT organization being most relevant for EAM are described.

EAM implementation: After the clarification of the strategic, tactical, and operative parameters, this chapter specifies the detailed goals, processes, functions, artifacts, roles, and tools of EAM. Thus, after revisiting EAM goals, an EAM process framework is described that provides a comprehensive overview of EAM processes and functions. On the one hand, this consists of the EAM cube with the core EAM processes (envisioning, specifying, implementing, and evaluating architectures on all enterprise levels and for all technical domains). On the other hand, it encompasses supporting processes for enabling and steering the EAM capability. Each process type and its practical implementation are described in detail. Next, we describe EAM artifacts. After a classification of artifacts along various dimensions, we describe how to create coherent collections of principles. Further artifacts described include, for example, maps of the digital ecosystem, target architectures, and roadmaps. In a similar vein the tools as well as the EAM organization and roles required to fulfill the EAM processes and capabilities are described.

EAM evaluation: The previous chapters covered the definition, design, and implementation of Enterprise Architecture Management. Now, we close the circle by describing how to evaluate EAM in a specific enterprise. The chapter starts by laying out core terminology, like "metric" and "strategic performance measurement system." Afterward, we describe and relate core measuring areas in the context of EA and EAM. Following these areas, the chapter comprises three major sections: 1. evaluating individual digital systems, 2. evaluating the enterprise-wide digital ecosystem, and 3. evaluating the Enterprise Architecture Management capability. For each area, we describe existing measurement systems, like EAM maturity models. Subsequently, we condense and extend the state of the art into a coherent set of metrics. Each set is also illustrated in the form of a comprehensive EAM cockpit.

Acknowledgments First of all, special thanks go to the reviewers of this book. Konstantin Reidel, Sergiy Nevstruyev, Jamie Yates, and Jonathan Fuentes from Accenture used their Enterprise Architecture Management skills to give valuable feedback for which I am most grateful. My dear former colleague Rüdiger Gruschka also provided brilliant advice for improving the book.

A big thank you goes out to Professor Michael Breitner and his Institute of Computer Science for Business Administration at the University of Hannover. Since 2016, he has given me the opportunity to create and present the Enterprise Architecture Management lecture, which was the basis for this book. From the same institute, Diana Srynnikova and Felix Bäßmann helped greatly in preparing and finishing the script. Many thanks also to Ralf Gerstner and Petra Steinmüller from Springer for their support and the excellent guidance during the evolution of this book. It was a great experience to work with them.

I am also grateful for the amazing colleagues that since 2010 have inspired and taught me about Enterprise Architecture Management in the never-boring reality of large enterprises. Among many others, from Talanx Systeme AG, this includes Ralf Konwalinka and Axel Perk and, from the Lufthansa Group, Carsten Breithaupt and Didier Arnold. Heartfelt thanks also go to Thomas Rückert, Christine Krämer, Marina Küffner, and Christina Koch from Lufthansa for their support with the book.

Finally, I would like to thank the authors of all the excellent books in the context of Enterprise Architecture Management (see also the reference section). They represent an enormous body of condensed experience and theoretical concepts that have been a great basis and inspiration for this book.

Hannover, Germany   Jörg Ziemann

Contents

About the Author

Jörg Ziemann is a Senior Enterprise Architect, university lecturer, and author. More than 15 years of practical and academic experience with Enterprise Architecture Management and enterprise digitalization have given him the chance to become familiar with these topics from various angles. He studied Business Information Systems at the University of Göttingen, the University of California (Irvine), and the University of Hamburg. In parallel, he gained practical experience in several industrial companies, including Volkswagen de Mexico and IT start-ups. After his studies, he took a position as researcher and international project manager at the German Research Center for Artificial Intelligence (DFKI). Working for 6 years on European research projects, he specialized on the topic of cross-enterprise business process digitalization. In this context, the University of Saarbrücken awarded him a doctorate for his thesis "Architecture of Interoperable Information Systems."

Returning to industry afterward, he worked for 8 years as a senior enterprise architect and project lead in the finance industry. There he was responsible for various enterprise digitalization areas, including business process digitalization, business service integration, and identity and access management. Since 2018, he has been a senior enterprise architect for the Lufthansa Group, responsible for the fields of Internet of Things, data analytics, and EAM strategy of the Lufthansa Group.

Since 2016, he is a lecturer for "Enterprise Digitalization and Enterprise Architecture Management" at the University of Hannover. He was a reviewer for several conferences and journals as well as for IT research projects for European agencies. He has published more than 40 scientific and industrial articles and is an experienced international conference speaker.

List of Abbreviations

AIOS	Architecture of Interoperable Information Systems
API	Application Programming Interface
ATAM	Architecture Tradeoff Analysis Method
CEO	Chief Executive Officer
CIO	Chief Information Officer
COTS	Commercial off-the-Shelf
CSF	Critical Success Factors
EA	Enterprise Architecture
EAM	Enterprise Architecture Management
ERP	Enterprise Resource Planning
GUI	Graphical User Interface
IaaS	Infrastructure as a Service
IoT	Internet of Things
JSON	JavaScript Object Notation
KPI	Key Performance Indicator
ODS	Operational Data Store
OKR	Objectives and Key Results
PaaS	Platform as a Service
SaaS	Software as a Service
SLA	Service-Level Agreement
SOA	Service-Oriented Architecture
SQL	Structured Query Language
XML	Extensible Markup Language

Chapter 1
EAM in a Nutshell

This chapter provides a comprehensive overview of Enterprise Architecture Management. It addresses questions like: What does EAM mean, what is the history of EAM, why do enterprises need EAM, what are its goals, and how is it related to digitalization? Further topics include the consequences of a laissez-faire approach in a complex enterprise-wide digital ecosystem, which is not steered but emerges "organically." We also address the related question: if there is a middle ground between unmanaged chaos and exuberant, all-controlling central steering and planning of the digital ecosystem landscape. The chapter concludes with a short overview of essential EAM standards and literature.

1.1 The Idea of EAM

Enterprises have used information technology for more than five decades. Originally, IT was primarily a tool for making enterprises more efficient, i.e., for "doing things right." However, the digital disruption of traditional business models in the last years impressively adjusted this perception: Today, it is clear that digitalization is also essential for making the business more effective—for "doing the right things." In other words, not only the Chief Information Officer (CIO) but also the Chief Executive Officer (CEO) of a large enterprise needs to have a good understanding of the enterprise-wide digital ecosystem and its capabilities. They do not need to know the bits and bytes of every application in their organization, but they should have a high-level overview and must be able to answer questions, regarding, for example:

- *Fulfilment of functional and non-functional requirements:* Does the digital ecosystem offer a seamless customer experience on the frontend? Does the backend

J. Ziemann, *Fundamentals of Enterprise Architecture Management*, The Enterprise Engineering Series, https://doi.org/10.1007/978-3-030-96734-5_1

provide for an integrated data landscape and for highly automated business processes? Are the IT systems stable, available, secure, fast, and of high usability?

- *Chaos or order:* Does the enterprise-wide digital ecosystem have a simple structure, or does it rather resemble a chaotic "spaghetti ball" that nobody can understand and control? Is it full of redundant services and technologies or rather a lean ecosystem with a controlled amount of technology standards? Can the enterprise easily prove to auditors that the IT landscape is compliant with external regulations?
- *System agility and interoperability:* Can the enterprise adjust and extend existing digital functions easily? Can it efficiently integrate new internal functions, services of a B2B-partner, or new functions from mergers and acquisitions? Can it efficiently carve out internal functions, for example, if parts of the enterprise are sold?
- *Future-proof or outdated:* Are the technologies innovative enough to keep and expand competitive advantages for the company? Or—the other extreme—are too many new, fancy technologies pursued that do not address the core requirements of the business but instead lead to an overly complex, inflexible, and hard-to-maintain overall system?
- *Cost-efficiency and sourcing:* Are the costs for developing, changing, and maintaining the digital ecosystem adequate to the services delivered? Does the enterprise have an optimal ratio of in-house development versus IT services sourced from external providers?

The high-level overview that answers these strategic questions is called Enterprise Architecture (EA). It resembles the fundamental elements of the digital enterprise landscape and their relationships. Only with transparency of the Enterprise Architecture are the planning, steering, and controlling of the enterprise-wide digital ecosystem possible. This activity, also known as *Enterprise Architecture Management (EAM)*, is described in this book.

EAM Focuses on the Strategic Development of Digital Landscapes

A metaphor often used for EAM is that of city or landscape architecting: Like a city planner, an enterprise architect must think strategically and plan a complete landscape of systems. Naturally, instead of quarters, train stations, urban residences, and parks, the enterprise architect designs a landscape consisting of business domains, large applications, middleware, and IT infrastructure. Now, some cities have been planned on a drawing table; others have grown organically. In this vein, Nilsson and Gil (2019) describe a spectrum of organically grown versus planned cities, including, for example, Venice and Tokyo (self-organized, grown), New York (high degree of planning), and Brasilia (very high degree of planning).

For better or for worse, the IT landscapes of large enterprises have developed rather organically via decades and thus rather resemble the "morphological structure" of the city on the right of Fig. 1.1 (Algier). Now, from a touristic perspective, a city with many narrow-curved streets might be charming. However, from a practical perspective, *the digital landscape of a large enterprise should rather not be designed to be mysterious*, but to be transparent and maintained easily, i.e., resembling the city outline on the left of Fig. 1.1 (Krefeld). Since in practice you hardly ever design an enterprise-wide digital ecosystem on a green field, a major task for an enterprise architect is the iterative transformation of the grown landscape toward a simpler, harmonized structure. *Relating to the metaphor of landscape architecting,* Fig. 1.2

Fig. 1.1 Layout of a planned city and an organically grown city. © Gerhard Curdes/Public Domain CC BY-SA 3.0

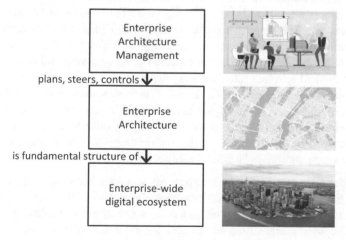

Fig. 1.2 EAM plans, steers, and controls the Enterprise Architecture. © From top: Shutterstock/Unitone Vector, Shutterstock/Ink Drop, Tim Reckmann/PublicDomain CC-BY-SA-3.0

illustrates the terms of EAM, EA, and *enterprise-wide digital ecosystem*, while the text below provides working definition of these key concepts.

> **Working Definition of EAM and Underlying Terms**
> - *Enterprise Architecture Management:* Planning, steering, and controlling of the Enterprise Architecture.
> - *Enterprise Architecture:* The fundamental structure of the enterprise-wide digital ecosystem, comprising its core elements and the relationships between those as well as the relationships to the environment.
> - *Enterprise-wide digital ecosystem:* The enterprise-wide digital ecosystem comprises the enterprise-wide information technology, i.e., all software and hardware used in the enterprise.

EAM Means the Business-Driven Design of the Enterprise-Wide Digital Ecosystem

Generally, three different scopes of Enterprise Architecture Management are viable:

1. *All digital and non-digital parts of the enterprise:* Here, the scope of EAM would be the strategic planning, steering, and controlling of the complete enterprise, including enterprise parts that have nothing to do with IT.
2. *All enterprise parts with digitalized business processes:* Going beyond software and hardware, here also machines and human actors in the (partially) digitalized business processes would be object to the EAM activities. This scope is chosen by classic business information systems science. The aim is to optimize a *socio-technical system*, where human and digital actors both must be considered to achieve a holistic enterprise digitalization. Aier and Schönherr (2006, p. 3) in this vein wrote that Enterprise Architecture comprises "the combination of organizational, technical, and psychosocial aspects during planning and development of socio-technical business information systems."
3. *Only the digital ecosystem:* Here, EAM activities only focus on the digital ecosystem. This comprises digital actors (applications running on computers), data and information, as well as the underlying IT infrastructure. Note that since architecture always incorporates the requirements of the customer, also this narrow scope comprises "business architecture."

Now, the term *Enterprise* Architecture Management suggests that the scope of EAM is the complete enterprise, including the non-digital enterprise elements. Without any doubt, an approach where business and IT are conceptualized together from the beginning has strong advantages for enterprise digitalization and would save many efforts spent today on the alignment of IT and business. Accordingly, EAM literature has demanded since decades that EAM should be allocated to the business organization to comprehensively address enterprise digitalization [e.g., Broadbent and Kitzis (2005), Ahlemann et al. (2011)]. However, the origins of the term Enterprise Architecture lay in the 1980s, when information system implementations had increased in complexity, and an architectural approach was needed to ensure the enterprise-wide system coherency. At this time, Scheer (1984) developed the idea of IT-oriented business administration, Zachman (1987) issued his often-cited framework for Enterprise Architecture, and in 1989, the National Institute of Standards and Technology published the NIST Enterprise Architecture Model [cp. Kotusev (2016)]. Among others, this led to the Architecture of Integrated Information Systems, where "enterprise modeling" is the basis of integrated enterprise systems (Scheer, 2000). Due to its IT-based origins, "Enterprise Architecture" became largely synonymous to enterprise-wide architecture of the IT landscape [cp. also Korhonen et al. (2016)].

And in the reality of today's enterprises, business strategy and IT strategy are often still disjoint disciplines. In these cases, the IT is seen as a service provider separated from the "real business." However, this depends on the business model of the enterprise: If you take, for example, a successful global online retailer or an equally successful global movie streaming platform, here IT and business might be indistinguishable. But even in business models with a high degree of digital services and processes like the insurance industry, IT and business are often still addressed as largely disjoint organizations.

To sum it up, the concept of EAM today is used predominantly in and for the digital world. At least in enterprises that do not have a completely digital business model, EAM is positioned in or near the IT department, architecting the enterprise-wide IT landscape. Normally, other departments are responsible for architecting and optimizing the business, like departments for business strategy, marketing, and business process optimization [cp. Khosroshahi et al. (2015)]. The digital focus of EAM also becomes clear when looking at *job advertisements* for "Enterprise Architects," which normally refer to architects of the digital ecosystem. Similarly, *EAM tool suites* normally focus on artifacts displaying the IT landscape or on the business capabilities needed for a business-driven digitalization. Accordingly, in the following, the scope of *EAM is confined to the third option mentioned above,* i.e., *the digital actors and resources of the enterprise*, as displayed in the bold-framed boxes of Fig. 1.3. Again, these digital elements today often implement a huge part of core business processes—thus, our focus on the digital ecosystem does by no means indicate that EAM is separated from the business. On the contrary, *EAM needs to be the trusted advisor and partner of "the business" for designing a suitable digital landscape.*

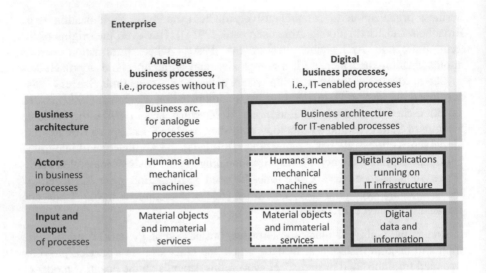

Fig. 1.3 EAM means the business-driven design of the digital ecosystem

1.2 Complexity Management as Core EAM Goal

1.2.1 Enterprise IT Landscapes Are Complex

Large enterprises consist of many business and IT elements that are closely interlinked and change all the time. In other words, large enterprises are extraordinarily complex. As an example, we have a look at a typical insurance company, the fictional "BEI group." The BEI is an international insurance group with 30,000 employees and millions of customers worldwide. It is headquartered in Cologne, Germany. The core company was founded in the year 1920, though by mergers and acquisitions, new parts were added. The group is diversified over the six business units displayed in Fig. 1.4, and each unit is instantiated as a separate legal enterprise.

The following areas contribute to the complexity of the BEI group:

Large Number of Interlinked Business Functions
A main reason for the complexity of the digital ecosystem is the complexity of the underlying business ecosystem. It starts on the highest level: A large enterprise consists of many business domains and legal organizations, for example, in the case of the BEI group, the six business units displayed in Fig. 1.4. In each of these exist many departments that fulfill different business capabilities, many product variations, business processes, and roles. Now, one might think that even a large business unit can be structured in the form of a couple of vertical business departments (e.g., purchasing, manufacturing, sales) and maybe some cross-cutting, horizontal product-oriented departments (e.g., product a, product b, and product c). However,

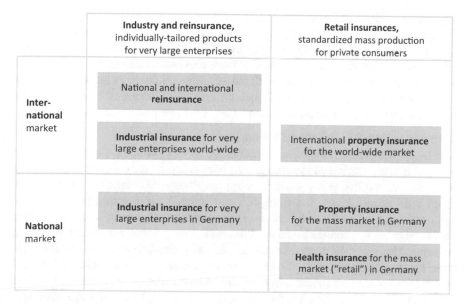

Fig. 1.4 BEI's business model addresses six insurance types

the reality is usually not as straightforward, and in an enterprise with 100,000 employees, even colleagues who have been employed there for years would be struggling to understand the intricacies of its organizational structure and who exactly is responsible for what. Other than the organizational structures, soft factors influence the shape of the digital ecosystem, like heterogenous stakeholders, different cultures, and contradicting interests inside the same enterprise; examples for such conflicting interests are short-term success versus long-term sustainability and local department vs. global, enterprise-wide interests.

Market Pressure
Though the exact amount differs among industries, there is constant pressure on all enterprises to become more efficient and more effective, which results in continuous change requirements on an enterprise's digital ecosystem. Examples for increasing efficiency are the introduction of process automation measures (like service orchestration or robotics process automation); the replacement of a large, self-developed legacy inventory application with a commercial off-the-shelf (COTS) product from a large vendor; or the replacement of paper-based B2B data exchanges with digital messaging. Examples for measures to increase effectivity are business changes like renewing customer interactions by establishing a digital B2C portal, but also mergers and acquisitions (M&A) or the merging of business units inside an enterprise.

Complex and Changing Regulations
Some industries are heavily regulated, for example, public administrations, the finance industry, or the aviation industry. An example for a finance industry-specific

regulation is SEPA ("Single Euro Payments Area"), which was implemented in the Eurozone countries in 2014. Examples for general regulations are the Sarbanes-Oxley Act and, more recently, the "General Data Protection Regulation" (GDPR), which was implemented in 2018. Each of these regulations affects many IT systems, which must be adapted to comply with the new regulations. This induces very large and expensive projects. And the more complex and nontransparent the digital ecosystem of an enterprise is, the more expensive these projects are.

Large Number of Interlinked IT Systems

Generally, the IT landscape of large enterprises is very complex, since it consists of many different, interlinked systems grown over many decades. For example, the IT landscape of the BEI group comprises approximately 1000 applications that stem from 5 different decades and from different internal and external providers. The applications are based on different IT development standards, follow different architectural styles, and are based on different infrastructure elements and operating systems. The applications are interlinked via many physical and logical dependencies, for example, business applications exchanging data with each other or business applications relying on shared infrastructure elements like servers. Besides business applications, over the decades, the BEI group established various large databases that feed the business applications. And on top of the core business IT systems, many supporting systems exist, for example, large repositories to administer users and provide roles and rights.

Fast-Changing Technologies

Today, the most prominent catalysator for enterprise changes are the current digital technology developments, also captured under the acronym SMAC (Social, Mobile, Analytics, and Cloud). Impressed by companies like Amazon or Google, in the last years, every large enterprise has been testing where to apply new technologies like Big Data, artificial intelligence (AI), Internet of Things (IoT), XaaS (different cloud service models), DevOps, Micro Services, and so on.

Heterogenous Stacks of Legacy Technology

In large, traditional enterprises, you will often find core business applications that are older than 30 years. In some industries, this is stimulated by long product lifespans. For instance, the policies and contracts of a health insurance company must be stored for many decades. But it also goes for basically any other industry: Some decades ago, all these large enterprises engaged in huge investments for mainframe systems, like IBM z/OS or Siemens BS2000. Some years later, they invested in large Enterprise Resource Planning Systems, for example, SAP R/3. Currently, these big companies are rearchitecting their applications to make them cloud-ready and migrate them to hosting providers like Microsoft or Amazon. All these big systems brought their own development stacks (e.g., COBOL, ABAP, Java) and infrastructure stacks: proprietary databases, application integration solutions, identity, and access management systems. Why do these systems have such a long lifetime? On the one hand, because they represent huge investments; on the other hand, even today they are reliable, and their performance is not necessarily worse than those of current solutions. Note that besides the software and hardware of these different technology stacks, you also need people to maintain, change, and extend these stacks. Thus, significant costs result for maintaining IT systems that are based on different technology stacks but have strong functional overlaps.

Even in small enterprises, the complexity of processes, products, product versions, customers, applications, and technology stacks fast emerge into chaos, if these artifacts are not systematically managed. In a large enterprise—like an international retail insurance company—the complexity of the enterprise-wide digital ecosystem is obviously much higher.

1.2.2 Complexities' Negative Impact at a Small Enterprise

A main characteristic of complex situations is the *lack of transparency*: A decision-maker has no way to intuitively grasp the network of circular causalities, no possibility to model and predict the impact of decisions. Instead, in such situations, managers must deal with potentially large surprises and side effects [cp. also Feess (2021)]. Practical examples of negative results stemming from overly complex IT systems are easy to find.

For instance, around the year 2000, in a large German city, there was a small IT start-up with ca. ten employees. The founder was a former government official and had good sales contacts to academies for fire brigades and the police force. He sold a simple, Microsoft Access and Visual Basic-based database to administer, for example, courses, registrations, and teachers. Due to the plain product, he did not need highly qualified software engineers. The customers were satisfied, and the company made good profits. Then, the fast demise happened in three steps:

1. *Too fast growth:* The number of customers and product variations increased steadily. Since the owner wanted to expand fast, he focused on sales and quick, cheap application development. Housekeeping activities like a systematic product management were neglected. It worked well before without "administrative overhead"—so why change anything now?
2. *First struggles with complexity:* Due to the increasing number of product variations combined with changing staff, the company lost overview of the code and dependencies between products for the various customers. The number of software errors increased, and the customer satisfaction decreased. Instead of "doing the right things" by setting up an ordering system, the company tried running faster and increased the output of software quantity. Since costs had to stay the same, they hired more interns as programmers.
3. *Panic:* Not surprisingly, the code quality further decreased, while the staff turnover further increased. In a last attempt of reacting to quality complaints from frustrated customers, the owner decided to change the development basis. Thus, the main engineers were busied migrating code from Visual Basic to Java. This migration never finished, due to the bankruptcy of the enterprise.

1.2.3   Impact of Organic Growth in Large Enterprises

In the daily life of companies with 10,000 or more employees, problems of the size described above occur frequently. They might not lead to bankruptcy but are still very costly. For example, Hesse (2017) named the following problems of the IT landscape in German banks: (1) organic, chaotic growth, and unmanaged evolution ("Wildwuchs"); (2) too many outdated legacy applications; and (3) the lack of a clear strategic objective. Further real-life examples of complexities' negative effects are:

Difficult System Analysis and Troubleshooting in Complex Digital Ecosystems
A frequent example revealing a lack of transparency are IT incidents where the network is not performing as it should. A recent B2E-example is a collaboration tool from a major vendor, used by employees to communicate during home office. This had worked well for 2 months, and then significant service interruptions occurred. A comparable incident occurred a couple of years ago in another large company in a B2C-example: The customer uses the web portal; the web portal uses the so-called Enterprise Service Bus (the companies' internal application integration platform) to access an application in the backend, for example, to retrieve the customer insurance policy. Now, timeouts occurred because some system was answering too slowly. In these cases, the CIO established task forces with ten highly skilled internal and external experts. These typically must work for many weeks or even months, until the exact cause of the problem is identified and fixed. Analyzing todays multi-layered, multi-vendor IT systems is not trivial; and since usually the products of at least two major vendors are involved, finger-pointing and extensive escalation rounds at the CIO level are the consequences.

A valid question in this context is: To what level of detail should you document your system, and how much "documentation" should you produce only on demand, ad hoc, when an incident occurs? At least for mission-critical systems, the short answer is that there should be more documentation available than you normally will find in today's average enterprise. However, to reduce the need for extensive documentation, the overall system should be architected so clean and simple that it is easy to understand and analyze, also in case of incidents.

Vulnerabilities Induced by a Complex Digital Ecosystem
The need for transparent, easy to understand system landscapes and system development mechanisms also becomes clear with security incidents. In the year 2020, a major global incident was caused by a malware inserted into a well-known, trusted application to manage large organizational networks. This software was used by thousands of large enterprises, including key American business and governmental organizations. The hackers gained access by putting their malware into updates of this software, and when the customer updated their systems, they also imported the malware. At this time, nobody knew the exact extent of the security breach and which components had been infiltrated. This case also illustrates some typical symptoms in the context of EAM:

1. *Short-term profits higher prioritized than thorough system building:* After the incident became public, it turned out that the CEO of the software company had been focusing on short-term profit and cutting down on security: "an accountant by training and a former chief financial officer, every part of the business was examined for cost savings and common security practices were eschewed because of their expense. His approach helped almost triple [the software vendors] annual profit margins" (Sanger et al., 2021).
2. *(Security) architecture measures only addressed after governmental pressure:* Even though the software was previously installed throughout federal networks, the company addressed security only under threat of penalty from a new European privacy law. Only then did they hire their first chief information officer and installed a vice president of security architecture.
3. *Untransparent venue of software and untransparent system landscape:* The customers have not been aware that the software was maintained in Eastern Europe. Many did not even know they have been using this software at all (cp. Sanger et al., 2021).

Large enterprises today have thousands of different business applications, and digital services are produced and sourced internationally via complex supply chains. In addition, the possibility to easily obtain cloud services in these days increases fast sourcing and the opaqueness of what lies beneath the sourced service. And obviously, only one infiltrated application suffices to contaminate the entire digital ecosystem. EAM helps to address these challenges in two ways: first, by establishing clear rules and standards for sourcing digital services and second, by creating an Enterprise Architecture that induces a simple, well-structured digital ecosystem. The second point not only reduces vulnerabilities but also supports an efficient analysis of the digital ecosystem once it is contaminated.

Redundant Applications in an Untransparent Digital Ecosystem
If a large enterprise has various product-oriented business units in parallel, for example, life insurance and property insurance, both need similar applications. For example, both need an application for Customer Relationship Management. Thus, from a corporate perspective, the business units have redundant applications, fulfilling the same business function. This happens also on a smaller scale in the context of supporting applications. A real-life example was an application with a complex function for enterprise security, where nobody really knew for which processes it still was needed. However, nobody wanted to be responsible for pulling the plug to a potentially security-relevant system. Only after a thorough, company-internal investigation, it was confirmed that the capability was indeed redundant and thus the costs of the €100,000 p.a. for this service could be saved.

Redundant   Application   Management   Capabilities   in   Untransparent Landscapes
The enterprise in the next example was making good profits for decades and comprised 15 different business units. Each business unit needed a tool to plan and monitor the attendance of employees. On the positive side, they all bought the

same product from the same vendor. On the negative side, they all did this independent from each other; thus, no economies of scale and scope could be leveraged: The vendor could negotiate expansive contracts with each business unit separately, each business unit had to employ its own experts for business changes and technical administration, and most of the business units used different infrastructure (databases, servers) in various data centers. Now, in the times of high profits, the business units also valued their independence highly; they appreciated the "uncomplicated" way of just talking to the vendor and purchase, for example, some 100 licenses in addition. However, after a sudden worldwide plunge of revenues, the central architecture management capability got a stronger mandate and harmonized the product policies. Thus, they established a central competence center, which bundled license purchasing and management as well as application management. Moreover, the infrastructure was consolidated at one cloud provider. Other than significantly lower costs, the quality of the services was improved due to the specialization of the employees, and the complexity of the system architecture was reduced.

1.2.4   Complexity Reduces the Agility of the Digital Ecosystem

In a curve comparable to the one shown in Fig. 1.5, Murer et al. (2011, p. 16) illustrate that *enterprise agility* decreases with the increase of business functions, if the landscape is not managed by EAM. Complementary to this, Niemann (2006, p. 56) illustrates that the "share of non-productive activities" rises exponentially to the degree of "IT heterogeneity." He argues that in a complex, heterogenous digital ecosystem, the IT spends too much time and money on managing redundant systems and complex dependencies.

Table 1.1 summarizes stereotypical effects of EAM on the digital landscape. The categories on the left represent typical Enterprise Architecture layers. Though this

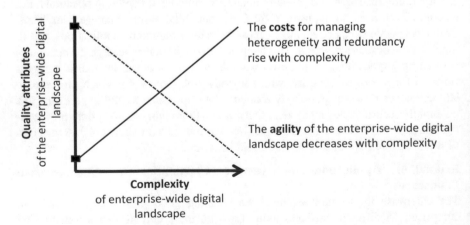

Fig. 1.5 Rising complexity induces lower agility and higher costs

Table 1.1 Exemplary EAM effects in different areas

Architecture area	*Results of laissez-faire approach,* i.e., unmanaged evolution and organic growth of the enterprise-wide digital ecosystem	*Results of EAM,* i.e., managed evolution of the enterprise-wide digital ecosystem
Business applications	Too high heterogeneity and redundancy of business applications. Example: Each of ten business units has its own customer relationship management application	Lean set of standard business applications. Example: Each of the ten business units uses the same type of customer relationship management application, from the same vendor
Systems structure	Technically cut, too fine-grained system elements, leading to a high number of system elements and dependencies	Digital system boundaries and other digital elements follow business domains, systems are layered into hierarchies, and coarse-grained modules reduce system complexity
Business data	Unclear data ownerships, the same information is managed at redundant places and not synchronized, and correlating information across business units is difficult	Right degree of central and decentral information management solutions, single sources of truths correlated with business ownerships, and enterprise-wide information is easy to gather
Application integration	Integration based on bilateral contracts and local solutions results in a multitude of message syntaxes and many heterogenous and untransparent dependencies	Enterprise-wide harmonized business semantics and technical standards—also for access control—reduce the landscape's complexity and increase the quality of individual connections
Infrastructure	A high heterogeneity and redundancy of IT infrastructure elements induce high costs and complexity. Example: Using SQL databases from ten different vendors, provided by six different cloud vendors	Small set of standard infrastructure elements. Example: Using SQL databases from only two different vendors, run on the enterprise clouds provided by three major vendors
Development and sourcing	Many different technology stacks for system development and sourcing. Example: Many programming languages, heterogenous deployment pipelines, and cloud service providers	Small set of development and sourcing standards. Example: Using two development frameworks and deployment pipelines
Overall effect	**Heterogenous landscape, many elements and dependencies, high complexity, low transparency, high costs, and low overall agility**	**Homogenous landscape, well-structured, fewer elements and dependencies, lower system complexity and costs, higher economies of scale and scope, and higher agility**

selection of categories is not exhaustive, it suffices to illustrate the effects of organic growth versus the effects of evolution controlled by EAM. The bottom line is that for large digital ecosystems, organic growth leads to a too heterogenous landscape, too many elements and dependencies, high complexity, low transparency, high costs, and low agility of the overall system. If, on the other hand, the IT landscape of a large enterprise is systematically steered by EAM, this will result in a *homogenous, well-structured landscape with fewer elements and dependencies, lower system*

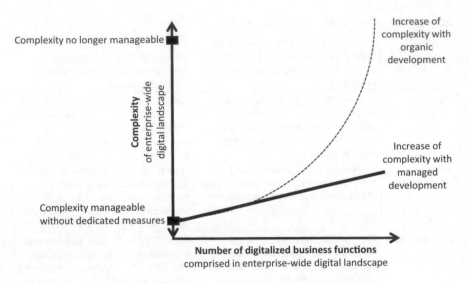

Fig. 1.6 EAM tames complexity despite a rising number of digital functions

complexity and costs, higher economies of scale and scope, and a higher agility of the overall landscape.

1.2.5   EAM Must Keep Complexity in Check

Figure 1.6 is a typical curve of EAM and illustrates that enterprise complexity rises exponentially to the number of digital functions. If, on the other hand, the IT landscape is managed, complexity rises much slower. In the case of "unmanaged evolution," the individual, federated units of the enterprise are not aligned via central standards. Extremely put, every IT department or project can choose freely which technologies to use. Likewise, every business department can choose, independent from the rest of the company, which business applications it wants to acquire. In the case of managed evolution, the enterprise-wide digital landscape is centrally planned, steered, and controlled by EAM. Note that also in this "managed" scenario, complexity does rise with a growing digital landscape, at least due to the increased number of business functions. However, here, EAM ensures that the amount of technical system elements and dependencies between the technical elements increases much less than in the unmanaged scenario.

This is accomplished foremost by the enterprise-wide harmonization and standardization of digital systems: the usage of only a few standard solutions induces a more homogenous digital landscape. An example for standardization of system elements is to use only two types of business intelligence solutions in the enterprise instead of ten different types. Note that with standardization, we not only control the increase of system *elements*, but we also control the increase of *dependencies* between these elements. An example for reducing the number of dependencies is using a standardized infrastructure for application integration. In the unmanaged scenario, each application has individual contracts and technical means to exchange data with other applications; you have bilateral, so-called point-to-point agreements. With a standardized application integration, all applications use the same syntax for cross-application communication, the same patterns to ensure reliability of data transmission, the same service-level agreements (like about speed of transmission, response times, or system availability), and possibly also the same physical platform for exchanging messages.

1.3   EAM Needs to Balance Local and Global Interests

Despite having generally positive effects, also standardization and homogenization of the enterprise-wide ecosystem need to be applied in a healthy dose: if they are overdone and too few digital standards are allowed in the enterprise, too high coordination costs will occur, and the level of redundancy becomes too low. Another classic trap is trying to standardize digital products when the overlaying business requirements are too heterogenous. For example, the two business units A and B both engage in business process automation. However, unit A has primarily complex, knowledge intensive processes that it addresses with a specialized process engine (for "case management"). Business unit B on the other hand has primarily highly repetitive, simple processes that are addressed with another type of process engine (for "service orchestration"). Trying to get rid of this perceived redundancy by allowing only one of these process engines or a generalized standard will not work; here, two specialized products are needed. We will discuss the balance between standardization and redundancy below in more detail.

Between Monoculture and Jungle

Before delving into the digital world, we have a look at a more tangible, traditional example: in agricultural systems, the question of "portfolio heterogeneity" has been discussed for centuries. A monoculture, for example, is efficient to maintain, and large machines like tractors can be used for harvesting crops. On the other hand, a monoculture is not organic and thus harder to "enforce": Fertilizers must be used, to foster the crops you want, and fungicides, to keep plants away that do not fit in your portfolio. In addition, the mono cropping leads to greater vulnerability against diseases: one virus can destroy the complete field since all plants expose the same weakness. A jungle by contrast develops organically without any human effort and produces a great biodiversity. However, from a harvesting and maintenance perspective, you need many different specialized tools to address the different plants, and you could not access the plants as easily as in monoculture. A compromise

Fig. 1.7 Monoculture, polyculture, and jungle. © From left: Shutterstock/oticki, Shutterstock/Pixeljoy, Shutterstock/Petr Muckstein

between monoculture and jungle is a polyculture, where a controlled amount of diversity is cultivated (Fig. 1.7).

As an enterprise architect in practice, sooner or later you will encounter stakeholders that like their "jungle"; they do not want to be bothered by central standards and prefer local autonomy over global alignment. One answer to that is the following: there is no right or wrong, and the optimal degree of global standardization and centralization depends on the individual enterprise and inside the enterprise again on the individual area. For example, a project endowed with improving a *core business* area by creating a new digital customer platform will typically obtain more creative freedom and autonomy than projects that adapt an application for a highly *standardized support process* (like the payroll process).

Without any doubt, there needs to be a balance between local autonomy and global harmonization. The discussion of alignment versus autonomy in sociotechnical systems obviously has been led on different levels for centuries. For example, the laissez-faire movement in the eighteenth century argued that the market is a self-regulating system and thus should be competitive and free of regulations. In the same vein, Adam Smith used the metaphor of the "invisible hand of the market" as an argument against regulation; the self-interested behavior of individuals would in the end lead to a desirable overall system. In analogy to that, one could trust in the *invisible hand of the enterprise* that provides for an optimally structured digital ecosystem without any central IT governance. One could believe that "emergent design" inside the local departments will provide for an overall optimized enterprise. And to be clear, too much central governance *can* have negative effects, for example, the risk of slow, bottle-necked processes, bad alignment with local business departments, as well as restricted creativity and motivation of the local highly skilled developers.

Central Governance Enables Local Autonomy and Self-Organization
Intuitively, it seems that with an increasing number of centrally prescribed rules, the autonomy and the freedom of the local individual decrease. However, in society, a critical number of rules are needed to enable individual freedom. From the perspective of the overall population, anarchy is rather limiting the freedom of the individual instead of making it possible. Thus, contrary to intuition, *central governance and local autonomy are not mutually exclusive*. This concept is as old as the ten

commandments that prescribed basic behavioral rules to enable a joint life in society. Today traffic rules enable us to drive safely anywhere we want, syntax rules enable us to express anything we want, and the strict standards of the Internet led to an explosion of worldwide creativity and productivity. For one individual, it might be timesaving to ignore red traffic lights and other traffic rules (at least, when the others do stick to the rules). However, for the overall population, the disadvantages of such behavior would outweigh the benefits of lawless driving [cp. also Hoogervorst (2009, p. 103)].

Which Enterprises Should Do Enterprise Architecture Management?
Only enterprises that want to go out of business appreciate an IT systems landscape that is chaotic, untransparent, and expensive to maintain and to change. Generally, enterprises need to leverage the advantages of central standards to increase transparency, improve cross-department interoperability, reduce redundancies, and achieve enterprise-wide economies of scope and economies of scale. Central coordination and governance are needed to ensure that the digital ecosystem of an enterprise is not a collection of locally optimized silos, but a globally coherent, optimized system. In this context, Tamm et al. (2011) state that companies profiting most from EAM are those "with a complex IT environment, whose business model favors high levels of organization-wide standardization and integration." Unfortunately, today's high level of digitalization induces a "complex IT environment" in basically every large enterprise.

Thus, the question is not whether enterprise-wide coordination of the digital landscape generally is needed; the question is *to what extent* coordination is needed. Unfortunately, answering this is challenging, as indicated by the century-old discussion on the balance of local autonomy and global coordination in the context of social and economic systems. In the endeavor to address this problem with mathematical models, variations of Fig. 1.8 have been displayed by various authors, for

Fig. 1.8 Balancing local autonomy and global coordination

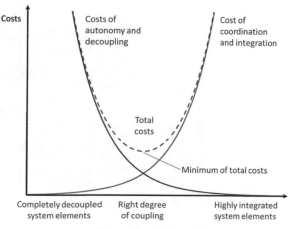

example, by Frese et al. (2019, p. 102). As they also state, even though this model illustrates one point of balance, in practice, it is hard to assess the exact values of these curves. However, on a more coarse-grained level, models exist that at least roughly indicate for what kind of business model and enterprise which level of standardization and integration is needed; we will come back to this in Sect. 3.2.

1.4   EAM and Digitalization

Since EAM is about managing the enterprise-wide digital ecosystem, it comes as no surprise that EAM and digitalization are highly intertwined. Imagine you hire an architect to design a complex system for you; you will expect that he applies all current, modern technologies to design an efficient system optimal for your needs. Now imagine your system is already 5 years old and new building technologies entered the market; you will expect from your architect that he tells you how to enhance your system with these new technologies. Similarly, an enterprise architect ensures that the digital ecosystem is optimal for the strategic and operative business requirements of the enterprise. The enterprise architect also ensures a lasting, permanent alignment, so that the mapping between requirements and architecture stays optimal via the course of time, changing technologies, and requirements.

Figure 1.9 relates EAM to the following concepts:

- *Business model digitalization* means that the business model is changed significantly toward an increased usage of digital technologies. For example, a traditional car insurance decides to get rid of its insurance brokers and sell insurance policies online only.

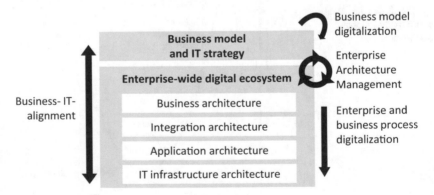

Fig. 1.9 EAM in the context of digitalization and business-IT-alignment

- *Enterprise and business process digitalization* means that the requirements of a given business model are increasingly being implemented with digital means. For example, the traditional car insurance strategically decides not to change its insurance broker organization and its core processes. However, it wants to make these processes faster and cheaper. To this aim, it introduces business process engines that digitalize processes currently performed by insurance clerks. Note that in the efficiency-effectivity dichotomy, business model digitalization is about effectivity and "doing the right things" on the business strategy level. From the perspective of business strategy, enterprise digitalization on the other hand is about "doing things right." Ross et al. (2019, p. 39) use a similar distinction between "digitization" (referring to enterprise digitalization) and "digitalization" (referring to business model digitalization).
- *Business-IT-alignment* means to continuously ensure a fit between business requirements and IT implementation. As described above, this is a classic architecture task. Business-IT-alignment must be ensured on different levels of granularity: On the strategic level, the enterprise (IT) architecture must fit to the business model. On an operative level, individual digital systems must fit to the requirements of the business functions they implement. Figure 1.9 illustrates this aligning, "bridging" role, where EAM is positioned between business model and the enterprise-wide digital ecosystem. In other words, EAM is that part of the IT strategy that transmits the fundamental, strategic business requirements to the fundamental, strategic characteristics into the enterprise-wide digital ecosystem.

In the context of digitalization, exemplary tasks of an enterprise architect are:

- Understand the *business model* and point out opportunities for improvement by making use of current technology. Based on this, identify, plan, and implement the optimal *degree of digitalization* of the company suitable to the business model.
- Ensure the *agility* and the *efficiency* of the overall digital ecosystem, e.g., by setting standards to maintain a lean portfolio of digital products and by developing ambitious target pictures for the application landscape.
- Support the creation of solutions for *business process digitalization*, like business process engines, robotics process automation, or processes digitalized with artificial intelligence.
- Support the creation of enterprise-wide *platforms for central digitalization topics* like Big Data and artificial intelligence.
- Support the creation of *infrastructure platforms for enterprise digitalization*, for example, platforms for application integration, identity and access management, and the software delivery chain (DevOps).

1.5   First Synopsis of EAM Goals

How the Enterprise-Wide Digital Ecosystem Should Not Look Like
Imagine you are the architect of a house. Now it turns out that the house has a leaky roof, the insulation is not suitable to the weather conditions, the cellar cannot cope with the groundwater in the area, and the design of the rooms and windows is not suited to the way people use the house. In consequence, the owner of the house would want to have a chat with you. If you are the chief enterprise architect, both the CIO and the CEO will have a chat with you in case of substantial IT landscape flaws. Coming back to the beginning of this chapter, indicators for such structural, fundamental flaws of the IT landscape include:

- *No coherent overall picture:* The digital ecosystem resembles accidental piecework full of gaps and inconsistencies, both regarding the business applications and the IT infrastructure. The degree of system standardization is much too low, and the degree of heterogeneity too high. The IT landscape is a highly complex, chaotic, untransparent mess. Nobody can say if compliancy rules are fulfilled or not. IT funds are not steered into a well-rounded portfolio of complementary functions.
- *Low system agility and interoperability:* Integrating new IT functions or connecting to B2B-partner systems is slow and expensive, as is the development of new functions.
- *Outdated systems:* There are too many legacy applications; the overall landscape is not modern enough to provide for sufficient digitalization possibilities. Many systems are at their "end of life," resulting in high effort for maintaining them.
- *Insufficient functionality:* Usability, security, and performance of the IT functions do not meet the reasonable expectations of the business. Data quality is bad, and reliable information is expensive to obtain, especially in cross-department scenarios. Instabilities and incidents occur too often, on the application as well as on the infrastructure level.
- *Too high costs for run and change:* Running, maintaining, or changing IT systems is unnecessarily expensive.

Note that already Perks and Beveridge (2003) described similar Enterprise Architecture challenges (e.g., "infrastructure hell," "the problem of incompatible technologies," and "technology anarchy"). And despite the great technology advances in the last decades, for real-life enterprises today, these points remain challenging.

How the Enterprise-Wide Digital Ecosystem Should Look Like
So, the goal of EAM is to ensure that the abovementioned flaws do *not* occur (or to be precise and realistic: that these flaws are kept as small as possible). Correspondingly, we established above that a main EAM goal is to keep the *complexity* of the entire IT landscape low. We need to tame the drive of large digital ecosystems

toward chaos; we do this by creating a well-structured landscape with fewer elements and dependencies. To this end, we apply enterprise-wide, "global" harmonization, for example, by introducing standards for application types and application interoperability. The expected outcome is a homogenous landscape with low system complexity and costs, high economies of scale and scope, as well as a high agility of the digital ecosystem. Let us reiterate that EAM is about the *strategic development and steering of the overall IT landscape.* Accordingly, this must be of the main concern of any companies' chief information officer and today often also of the CEO.

Simply put, the goal of EAM is to ensure that the enterprise is engaged in the iterative development toward reaching and maintaining a "good" overall digital ecosystem. In our context, "good" means that the digital ecosystem is efficient and effective for a specific enterprise. The following chapters will refine this notion. For now, the textbox below summarizes the goals and benefits of EAM.

Preliminary Summary of EAM Goals and Benefits
- Developments in the complex and dynamic enterprise-wide digital ecosystem must be strategically guided toward one coherent target picture. Complementary to short-term, local interests and developments, enterprise-wide coordination and optimization of the digital ecosystem are needed.
- Enterprise Architecture Management is responsible for the iterative and sustainable development and optimization of the enterprise-wide digital ecosystem.
- Benefits for the enterprise are (a) an *effective* and modern IT, where the digital ecosystem fulfills business requirements in an optimal manner, and (b) an *efficient* IT, with relatively low costs for maintaining and changing the digital ecosystem.

1.6   Essential EAM Standards and Literature

Approximately 30 EAM books have been written since the upcoming of the term Enterprise Architecture Management around the year 2000, the early ones mostly by academics that could hardly judge how exactly this knowledge would be applicable in practice. Most of the newer ones were written by IT practitioners, coming rather from a bottom-up perspective. Note that some books carrying "EAM" in their title rather address the topic of Enterprise Architecture, but not Enterprise Architecture *Management*. Here is a small selection of recommendable EAM books: Ross et al. (2006), Murer et al. (2011), Ahlemann et al. (2011), Hanschke (2012), and Rao et al.

Table 1.2 Essential standards in the context of EAM

Standard	References	Area	Description
ArchiMate	Open Group (2020b)	Architecture modeling language	A language for visually describing systems from an architectural standpoint
ARIS	Scheer (2000)	Business architecture	Scheer's classic "Architecture of Integrated Information Systems" provides a thorough basis for business-oriented system design
CEAF	CEAF (2021a)	Practitioner EAM framework	The "California Enterprise architecture framework" is a detailed, practice-proven reference
COBIT	ISACA (2018)	IT governance processes	The main standard for the capabilities and processes inside the IT governance
ISO 25010	ISO (2011)	Metrics for digital systems	The classic standard for quality attributes of digital systems
ISO 42020	IEEE (2019)	Architecture processes	Fairly new standard for generic architecture processes
IT4IT	Open Group (2017)	Capabilities and tools in IT	A reference for the capabilities and the tool chain inside the IT capability of an enterprise
ITIL	ITIL (2019)	IT service processes	The most prominent standard for IT processes in the context of IT infrastructure and service management
O-AA	Open Group (2020a)	Agile architecture development	The new standard "open agile architecture" describes EAM and system creation aligned to the agile paradigm
SAFe	SAFe (2020)	Agile software development	"The scaled agile framework" describes how to apply the agile paradigm for software development in large organizations
TOGAF	Open Group (2020c)	Architecting complex systems	The most prominent standard in the context of EAM, providing a thorough process for developing architectures of complex systems

(2018). In addition to that, Table 1.2 lists the most important standards in the context of EAM. Note that beyond being the object of EAM-focused standards, EAM today is also an explicit part of general IT frameworks like COBIT and ITIL. Thus, though EAM is a comparatively young discipline, today a considerable amount of theoretical background exists for it.

Chapter 2
Enterprise Architecture in a Nutshell

The previous chapter provided an overview of EAM, including its objective, to establish and maintain a "good" Enterprise Architecture. Delving deeper into the latter concept, this chapter provides an overview of Enterprise Architecture. We start with clarifying basic terminology, like "system," "architecture," and the difference between Enterprise Architecture (EA) and Enterprise Architecture Management (EAM). We also revisit the concept of system complexity and how it relates to parameters like standardization of the IT landscape. Afterward, we provide a short summary of existing EA frameworks and methods for structuring the digital ecosystem into layers and views. Next, basic principles for structuring socio-technical systems are laid out, like the forming of hierarchies and aligning the structures of organizational and digital systems. Finally, we describe core parameters of the Enterprise Architecture. These include, for example, the degree of standardization, centralization, and integration of the ecosystem, but also the desired degree of innovativeness, risk appetite, outsourcing, and cost and quality priorities.

2.1 Basic Terms

Figure 2.1 provides an overview of core Enterprise Architecture terms and their relationships. Note that the terms displayed on the left are *generic definitions* of the terms system, architecture, model, and metamodel. They can be used in the context of IT, but also in the context of organizational systems, i.e., enterprises. In the following, we will describe these terms as well as related terms.

© The Author(s), under exclusive license to Springer Nature Switzerland AG 2022   23
J. Ziemann, *Fundamentals of Enterprise Architecture Management*, The Enterprise
Engineering Series, https://doi.org/10.1007/978-3-030-96734-5_2

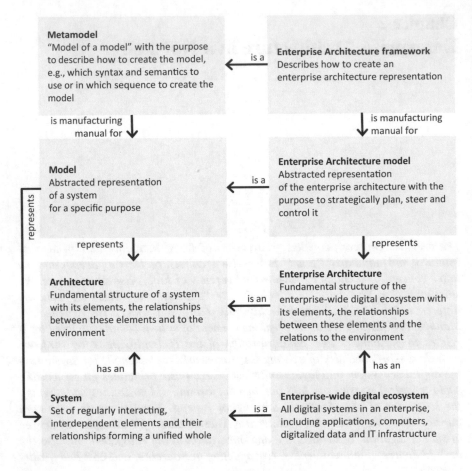

Fig. 2.1 Overview of essential Enterprise Architecture concepts

2.1.1 *System, Architecture, and Related Terms*

System
A system is a set of regularly interacting, interdependent elements and their relationships forming a unified whole. *This can be any kind of system, no matter if technological, social, or biological.* Inside the system, the elements are linked to each other via strong relationships; in IT-architecture terminology, this is called *high internal cohesion*. In contrast, the dependencies to elements outside the system are weaker; in IT terms, there is a *looser coupling* to elements outside the system. The set of relations between the elements of a system is its *structure*. The relationships inside the system stand out quantitatively—higher number of relations—and qualitatively, i.e., a greater productivity of the interactions. These close relationships

constitute a system boundary which distinguishes the system from its environment. A system element is an integral part of a system, which cannot be further decomposed within the totality of the system [compare Gillenkirch (2021)].

Note that there is a certain *subjectivity* in the delimitation of one concrete system, since it is not always objectively possible to say which elements have "closer" relationships among each other than to elements presumably outside the system. An example is the delimitation of a business application: The specification of the boundaries of this "system" is subjective since it depends on the purpose. For example, the application "Contract Management" could include a B2B-gateway to business partners that have the right to change contracts, making the gateway also the responsibility of the owner of the "Contract Management" application. However, if this kind of end-to-end responsibility is not desired, the boundaries of the named application could be defined more narrowly, i.e., excluding the B2B-gateway. In this case, the B2B-gateway is treated as a separate system, owned by a different system owner.

> **A System Is a System Is a System Is a System**
> When experienced IT practitioners read the word "system," they often think of an IT system, like an application or an infrastructure element. However, here we address *systems in the generic sense*. There are, for example, ecological systems, economic system, social systems, and technical systems. There are also socio-technical systems, i.e., enterprises. A house can be seen as a system, an enterprise can be seen as a system, and a computer program can be seen as a system (and all of them have an architecture). Note that also a "system of systems" is a system. Why this high level of genericity? Because enterprise architects need to understand both digital and organizational business systems. They also need to understand very large systems (e.g., an enterprise) as well as smaller systems, e.g., a Customer Relationship Management application.

Architecture

Architecture is the essential structure of a system, comprising its elements and the relationships among the elements as well as the relationships to the environment. This definition is based on these sources:

- The often-cited definition of IEEE 1477 (2007) states: Architecture is the "fundamental organization of a system, embodied in its components, their relationships to each other and the environment, and the principles governing its design and evolution."
- A classic business informatics definition states that an information system architecture "describes the type, the functional properties and the interrelationships among the individual building blocks of the information system" (Scheer, 1999, p. 1).
- In a similar vein, Bass et al. (2006, p. 21) state that "the software architecture of a program or computing system is the *structure* or structures of the system, which

comprise software elements, the externally visible properties of those elements and the relationships among them." They complement their definition with the statement that "architecture is *high-level design*."

At least in the context of EAM, the concept of "architecture" has three additional characteristics:

- *It is not possible to have no architecture:* It is a common misunderstanding that only elaborate complex systems have an architecture. As the definitions above clarify, *every system has an architecture*, even if the architecture is not explicitly described via an architecture model.
- *Subjectivity:* The following definition illustrates that, to a certain degree, architecture is a subjective concept: "The architecture of a system constitutes what is essential about that system considered in relation to its environment. *There is no single characterization of what is essential or fundamental to a system*" (IEEE, 2011).
- *Architecture as a sum of decisions:* Another definition states that an "architecture is the *set of significant decisions* about the organization of a software system, . . ." (Booch et al., 1999). This is relevant, because in the practice of EAM, the architecture of the enterprise-wide digital ecosystem is rather specified by many "small," project-related decisions, standards, and guidelines and seldomly in the form of one "big picture drawing" that captures all system elements and their relationships.

Static Architecture Versus Dynamic Architecting

The definition of the IEEE already indicated that an architecture can comprise both *descriptive,* static, and *constructive,* dynamic aspects: The descriptive aspect tackles static elements of an architecture, e.g., the system elements and their relations, comprising the various levels and views contained in architecture models. The constructive aspect provides methods for the development of the system described by the architecture [compare also Heutschi (2007)].

Architectural Style

An architectural style refers to characteristic features of a group of architectures, characteristics that make systems having this architecture notable or—in the case of buildings—historically identifiable. Such architectural building styles are, for example, Romanesque, Gothic, Baroque, Bauhaus, and Functionalism. Examples of architectural styles for information systems comprise client-server, service-orientation (SOA), event-orientation, or object-orientation.

Dimensions, Stakeholders, Concerns, Viewpoints, and Views

We only bother to create architectural models if the addressed systems are very complex (in the case of a simple system, there is no need to create elaborated models; we can understand it without a model). Enterprise architecture models, for example, depict very complex systems. To reduce this complexity, it is best practice to divide such architecture models along various dimensions that stand orthogonally to each

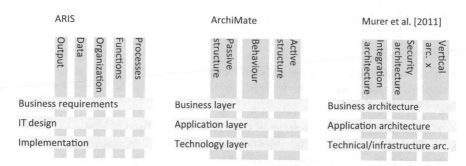

Fig. 2.2   Examples of dimensions and views in architecture frameworks

other. Each dimension represents the system from another viewpoint, and the viewpoint represents the concern of a stakeholder. For example, in medicine, the "stakeholders" orthopedist, surgeon, and neurologist each have different concerns and thus need support for their individual "viewpoints" on the "system" of a patient. Note that instead of view, sometimes the terms layer, tier, or aspect is used. As Fig. 2.2 illustrates, the Architecture of Integrated Information Systems (ARIS, Scheer, 2000), ArchiMate (Open Group, 2020b), and the framework of Murer et al. (2011) all have two dimensions. Let us have a closer look at the dimensions of ARIS:

- The first dimension has three views: business requirements, IT design, and implementation. It supports the concern "model-driven software development" from the viewpoint of the stakeholder "software engineer." Note that these three views completely cover the addressed concern, from top to bottom, so to speak.
- The second dimension has five views: processes, functions, organization, data, and output. This dimension supports the concern "comprehensive coverage of all business process elements." It is important from the viewpoint of the stakeholder product owner. Again, the five views completely cover the concern and address everything that could be part of a business process.

Dimensions and Views Are Used to Structure Complex Systems
- Dimensions of architecture models should stand orthogonally to each other.
- Inside one dimension, the comprised views should be disjoint, complementary, and complete. The views inside one dimension completely cover the concern addressed by the dimension.
- In the terminology of strategy consultants, the views of one dimension should be "Mutually Exclusive and Collectively Exhaustive" (MECE).

2.1.2   Model, Metamodel, and Reference Model

Model

A model is an abstracted representation of a system ("universe of discourse") for a dedicated purpose. According to Stachowiak (1973), models have three main characteristics:

- Illustration property: A model represents natural or artificial objects.
- Reduction property: Only the relevant characteristics are represented.
- Pragmatic property: The relevance of objects is subjectively decided by the model creator, influenced by the time of model creation and by the purpose of the model.

Since models enable an abstracted view on extraordinarily complex systems, they are an important instrument for the analysis and the design of enterprise information systems. It is important to understand that a model does not necessarily have to be expressed in a specific, graphical form but can be represented in any form, also, for example, in a textual form.

Metamodel

A metamodel is "model of a model," where the purpose of the metamodel is to describe how to create the model, e.g., which syntax and semantics to use or in which sequence to create the model. Thus, a metamodel serves as a frame that describes the possibilities and restrictions of model construction. To this purpose, a metamodel specifies the available model building blocks and the possible relationships among them; it can also describe rules for the usage of these building blocks and their relationships. For example, the "Business Process Model and Notation" (BPMN) is formally described with a metamodel in the form of UML class diagrams. These UML diagrams describe the core elements of the BPMN and how these are related [cp. OMG (2011)]. Now, if you want to create a model of a business process using BPMN, this metamodel specifies exactly which elements you can use.

Reference Model

A reference model is a model that can be used as a reference and comparison object in the creation or evaluation of other models or real-world objects. Usually, a reference model has a positive connotation and represents a best practice. In this vein, already Kosiol (1964) spoke of idealized models in contrast to models that depict existing, physical solutions: "idealized models are constructions that represent a wider range of possible real-world situations and serve as prefabricated solution schemes or general recipes for certain classes of decision-making problems to address practical issues." For example, when developing a complex application for the Internet of Things (IoT), you could first look at a reference model that shows how an IoT application is usually developed. Figure 4.10 provides a corresponding example. However, you can also refer negatively to something, in which case the reference model serves as an anti-pattern.

2.1.3 Enterprise Architecture and Related Terms

Enterprise-Wide Digital Ecosystem
The enterprise-wide digital ecosystem is the sum of all digital systems in an enterprise, including applications, computers, digital data, information, and IT infrastructure, simply put, all software and hardware used in the enterprise.

Enterprise Architecture and Enterprise Architecture Management
Based on the definition of architecture from above and the notation that EAM focuses on the digital parts of an enterprise, we define EA as follows: *Enterprise architecture means the fundamental structure of the enterprise-wide digital ecosystem, comprising its elements and the relationships among the elements as well as the relationships to the environment.* Note that this includes the business architecture of the enterprise-wide digital ecosystem (cp. Fig. 1.3 in the introductory chapter). For a comparison of EA definitions, refer, for example, to Rao et al. (2018).

Based on the common understanding of the term "management" and the above-described meaning of EA, we define *Enterprise Architecture Management as the planning, steering, and controlling of the Enterprise Architecture.* The corresponding lifecycle is illustrated in Fig. 2.3. Later, when discussing EAM processes and capabilities in detail, these core functions will be refined.

The relationship between EAM and EA was also illustrated in Fig. 1.2. Again, Enterprise Architecture (EA) and Enterprise Architecture *Management* (EAM) are disjoint concepts. As the definition of EAM suggests, *EA is the object of EAM.* EAM is the activity executed in large enterprises by people who, a bit of a misnomer, are usually called enterprise architects. In basically every large enterprise, the digital ecosystem already exists, and so does the Enterprise Architecture, which represents the fundamental characteristics of it: Unless you work in a start-up company, in

Fig. 2.3 The Enterprise
Architecture Management
lifecycle

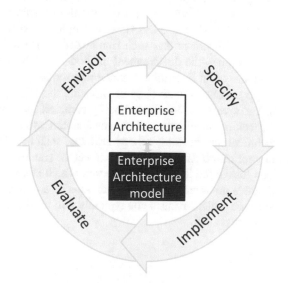

practice, you will not have the chance to develop a new, enterprise-wide digital ecosystem on a green field. Instead, you will try to iteratively develop the existing enterprise-wide digital ecosystem toward a defined direction. In this vein, some authors refer to Enterprise Architecture Management as "managed evolution" [cp. Murer et al. (2011)].

Enterprise Architecture Model
An Enterprise Architecture model is an abstracted representation of the Enterprise Architecture, in other words, a model of the "fundamental structure of the enterprise-wide digital ecosystem." The purpose of this model is to understand and to plan the Enterprise Architecture. Note that in practice you will seldomly find one individual artifact that is called "Enterprise Architecture model." Instead, you will find different models that represent different aspects of the Enterprise Architecture. For example, you will find a business capability model that depicts the business capabilities of an enterprise and thereby describes an important aspect of the business architecture. There are many ways of structuring Enterprise Architecture models, some of them described by classic Enterprise Architecture frameworks; we will address this topic below.

2.1.4   EA Framework and EAM Framework

Enterprise Architecture Framework
The Cambridge Dictionary defines framework as a "system of rules, ideas, or beliefs that is used to plan or decide something." In the context of EAM, the term (enterprise) architecture framework is defined similarly as "*conventions, principles and practices for the description of architectures* established within a specific domain of application and/or community of stakeholders" (IEEE, 2011). The IEEE names DoDAF and TOGAF as examples of such frameworks. The right part of Fig. 2.4 illustrates that such frameworks can support both the dynamic aspect of architecture—the development method—and the static aspect, which describes the structure of an Enterprise Architecture model.

To make this more tangible, imagine the CIO of a large insurance gave you the task to create a new, extraordinarily complex core business application, for example, the central insurance policy management system. Now all kind of information, technical and business-related artifacts, stakeholders, challenges, and tasks appear in your mind. An Enterprise Architecture framework like TOGAF helps you to not "get lost in the jungle" and tells you which steps you might take in which order to produce an architecture and an architecture description for the new system. It also tells you which artifacts you typically will need to describe the architecture and how they are related.

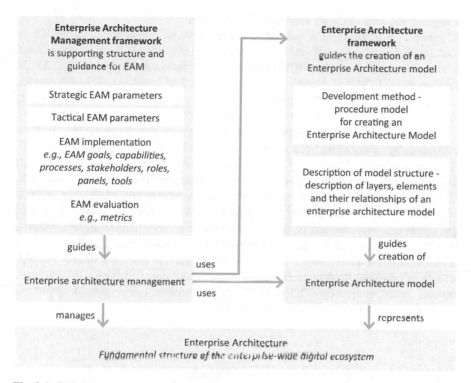

Fig. 2.4 EAM framework vs. EA framework

Enterprise Architecture Management Framework

An EAM framework provides the supporting structure for Enterprise Architecture Management. Unlike an EA framework, the goal here is not to create Enterprise Architecture models, but to provide "a system of rules, ideas, or beliefs" to create or configure the capability of Enterprise Architecture Management. As the left part of Fig. 2.4 illustrates, an EAM framework describes the elements that constitute EAM as well as their relationships, as, for example, EAM goals, capabilities, processes, and roles. An EAM framework could also describe dynamic aspects, i.e., a procedure model for the stepwise development or configuration of EAM inside an enterprise, based on the strategic and tactical parameters that surround EAM.

To make this more tangible, imagine the CIO of a large insurance assigns you as lead of the group-wide Enterprise Architecture Management department. Also, he would like more transparency on core EAM activities, how EAM is integrated with the rest of the organization, what the exact EAM objectives and results are, which steps you plan to improve EAM in the group, and what he can do to support you during these steps as well as in the daily business of the EAM department. An EAM framework provides answers to these questions and relates generic EAM elements to the enterprise-specific environment.

Usage of EA and EAM Frameworks in Practice
In practice, the usage of EA and EAM frameworks in enterprises is astonishingly low. Regarding the usage of *EAM frameworks*, this is explained by the fact that there is no accepted cross-industry EAM framework. What comes closest is TOGAF: In version 9.2. TOGAF addresses some parts of an EAM framework in the section "Architecture Capability Framework" (Open Group, 2020c). This includes, for example, the description of architecture boards and the architecture repository.

In difference to EAM frameworks, a multitude of EA frameworks has been proposed by researchers, practitioners, and standard organizations [see, e.g., Ahlemann et al. (2011, p. 208)]. Nevertheless, in our experience, large enterprises use either none of these frameworks or they use parts of TOGAF; Ahlemann et al. (2011, p. 212) conducted a survey and came to a similar result. TOGAF in practice often has the reputation of being too "theoretic" and too complex. However, if you are confronted with the task of having to architect a very complex system, you are thankful to have a mature, detailed reference like TOGAF that describes possible layers and construction steps. That does not mean that all parts of the TOGAF framework must be implemented in the enterprise or being followed by all projects. Instead, as recommend by TOGAF itself, an enterprise or a large project should use only those parts of TOGAF it deems valuable.

2.2   Typical Layers of EA Frameworks

2.2.1   A Reference Framework for Enterprise Architecture

There Is No Perfect Way of Structuring the Enterprise Architecture
Having in mind that a model is always created for a purpose, it becomes clear that there is no "perfect" system for layering Enterprise Architectures: The way of layering depends on what you want to achieve with your approach of structuring the enterprise-wide digital ecosystem.

Typical Horizontal and Vertical Dimension of EA Frameworks
Figure 2.5 shows typical layers of EA frameworks: business architecture, integration architecture, application architecture, and IT infrastructure architecture. The graphic also illustrates that in the end each architecture layer represents the core elements of real-life elements. Now, what is the purpose, and what is the paradigm behind this structuring? The structure of the four layers supports the goals of IT-business alignment and Service-Oriented Architecture, where the structure of IT components closely follows business structures and elements. Correspondingly, the four vertical lines on the right indicate that business processes, functions, data objects, as well as rights and roles can be deviated from the business organization, over the coarse-grained alignment layer of the integration architecture down to the individual applications.

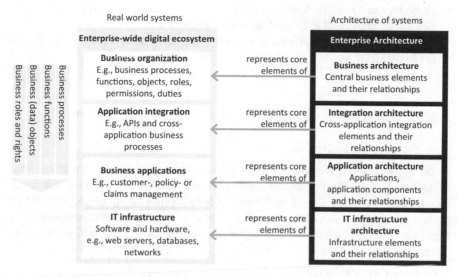

Fig. 2.5 Typical core layers of Enterprise Architecture frameworks

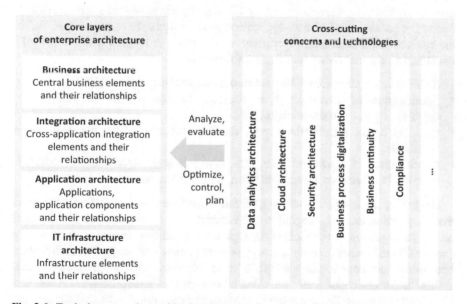

Fig. 2.6 Typical cross-cutting architecture layers

In a similar vein, Fig. 2.6 shows layers orthogonal to the core elements of the enterprise-wide digital ecosystem. These layers are cross-cutting in the sense that they are relevant for various or all the horizontal layers. For example:

- The *cloud architecture* must address the allocation of business applications, of infrastructure elements, and of the middleware components displayed in the integration architecture.

- Business *process digitalization* spans the layers of business architecture, integration architecture, and individual business applications.
- Systems for *security, business continuity, and compliance* need to address all horizontal layers.

2.2.2   Core Layers of Enterprise Architecture Frameworks

Business Architecture
In the layer of *business architecture*, processes, functions (also known as business capabilities), data objects, rights, and roles are defined on the business level, independent from specific IT products or technologies. In practice, here rather global, cross-application elements will be defined. Data structures, business functions, etc. relevant only inside one application on the other hand will be specified rather locally.

Integration Architecture
Based on these business-level specifications described above, in the layer of *integration architecture*, the corresponding IT counterparts are defined. These artifacts follow the coarse-grained, cross-application granularity of the elements specified in the business architecture; however, they are specified to be used inside and by IT systems, i.e., also on code level. Such artifacts are:

- Services descriptions, including foremost interface description (API).
- Specifications of cross-application processes, for example, BPMN models executed via service orchestration engines.
- Business object specifications, e.g., the data structure of the business object "customer."
- Specifications of rights and roles, e.g., "the role sales representative EMEA is permitted to access customer data from the EMEA area."

Regarding the last point—cross-application rights and roles—it should be noted that in practice usually integration architecture and architecture of identity and access management are organized as separate capabilities. However, they play a comparable role, since identity and access management and integration architecture both implement core business elements to enable cross-application services: Integration architecture classically provides a repository of enterprise-wide APIs, services, and processes. To access those, cross-application roles and rights are needed. Comparable to the service repository, these are managed in an enterprise-wide rights and roles repository (for instance, by a service like Microsoft's Active Directory).

Application Architecture
In the context of EAM, application architecture has two facets: First is the architecture of *individual applications*. The system of interest here consists of the elements and relationships of one application: Data objects, processes, functions, rights, and roles are addressed on the application level, i.e., on a more fine-grained level than in

the integration architecture layer. As we will elaborate later in more detail, architecting individual applications is primarily the realm of *solution architects*, not of enterprise architects. However, enterprise architects must provide principles, coaching, and stage gate processes also for the architecture of individual applications. The second facet focuses not on the elements inside an application, but on the development of the *application portfolio*, e.g., if the portfolio is balanced or if it needs to be altered.

Infrastructure Architecture
The lowest layer addresses the enterprise-wide *infrastructure architecture*. This layer addresses, for example, which kind of servers, databases, or operating system are used and if those are obtained as scalable cloud services from a third party or rather hosted in the company's data center.

Data Architecture
Prominent Enterprise Architecture frameworks, like TOGAF, comprise a dedicated layer for data architecture. And obviously data architecture is an important topic in the context of architecting individual systems. For instance, when you architect a new, complex CRM system, you must consider which data will be imported and exported from the system and for which kind of data the system is the "single source of truth" (e.g., customer-related information). Also, on the level of application programming in the last decades, object-orientation was a leading paradigm.

Now, why does Fig. 2.5 *not* comprise a data layer? Because in the last two decades, the leading paradigm for structuring application landscapes was "Service-Oriented Architecture" (SOA). This paradigm focuses on functions and not on data, i.e., the digital landscape was structured along business functions, and only implicitly by data elements, which serve as input and output of business functions. According to this paradigm, there are no operational databases dangling around in the enterprise landscape, accessible by whoever might be interested in it in an uncoordinated manner. Instead, data is always safely stored inside a business application that fulfils a well-defined business function. If you want to access that data, you need to have the rights correlated to the business functions. Then you can access the corresponding business service via a dedicated API offered by the application responsible for this data.

However, due to the rise of Big Data, data analytics, and artificial intelligence in the last years, data again became a prominent element for planning digital landscapes. For example, on the landscape level, we must plan where and for which business areas to implement operational data stores (ODS), data warehouses, data lakes, and the corresponding advanced analytics functionalities.

2.2.3 Exemplary EA Layers in Literature

Figure 2.7 shows a selection of systems for layering Enterprise Architectures, with the layers of the reference architecture on the left. Apart from the top layer, the layers

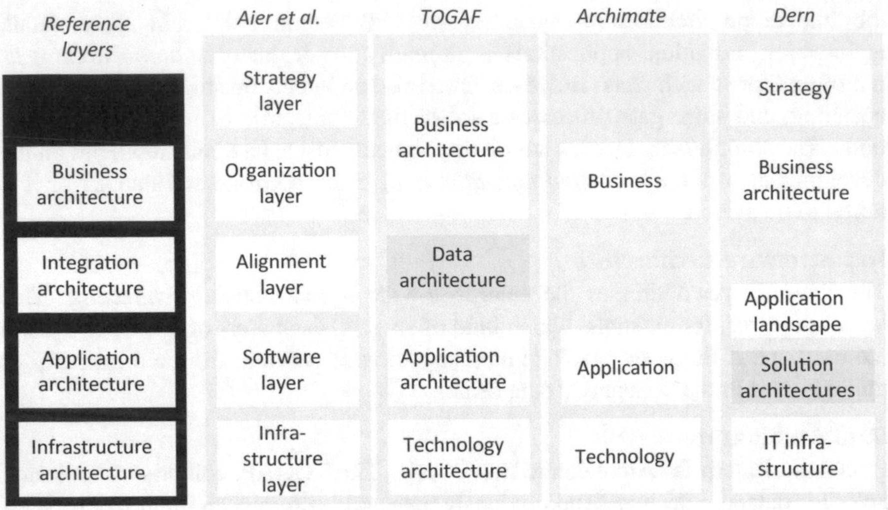

Reference layers	Aier et al.	TOGAF	Archimate	Dern
	Strategy layer	Business architecture		Strategy
Business architecture	Organization layer		Business	Business architecture
Integration architecture	Alignment layer	Data architecture		Application landscape
Application architecture	Software layer	Application architecture	Application	Solution architectures
Infrastructure architecture	Infra-structure layer	Technology architecture	Technology	IT infra-structure

Fig. 2.7 Core EA layers of different authors and frameworks

from Aier et al. (2008) correspond to the reference layers (cp. Fig. 2.7). However, instead of business architecture, they use the term organization layer, and instead of integration architecture, they use the term alignment layer; their "software layer" refers to application architecture. And in addition to the four layers of our reference architecture in Fig. 2.5, they added a strategy layer on top.

TOGAF (Open Group, 2020c) subsumes the description of business strategy in the layer of "business architecture." In contrast to the abovementioned frameworks that support enterprise-wide business-IT-alignment via business functions, TOGAF exhibits a layer for *data architecture*. Note that TOGAF's priority is not the architecture of the enterprise-wide digital ecosystem. Instead, TOGAF is a method for *developing complex architectures for systems of any size*. A typical example of a complex system that requires an elaborate method like TOGAF is a large application for Customer Relationship Management (CRM). Here, clearly an explicit data layer is needed. In this layer, we specify, for example, which data will be owned by the CRM application and which data will be retrieved on-demand from an operational data store or from adjacent master data management systems.

ArchiMate also stems from the Open Group (2020b) and is closely related to TOGAF. Its "core framework" comprises three layers: business, application, and technology. Like TOGAF, by technology, ArchiMate refers to IT infrastructure. As Fig. 2.2 illustrates, ArchiMate has three orthogonal "aspects," which are similar to the "views" of ARIS. The "passive structure aspect" refers to data, which is the object of activities performed by subjects. The "behavior aspect" describes these activities and thus corresponds to the "function" view of ARIS. The "active structure aspect" describes the subjects that execute the activities and thus corresponds to the "organization" view of ARIS.

As also illustrated in Fig. 2.2, Murer et al. (2011, p. 61) proposed the same three layers as ArchiMate. Like ArchiMate, Murer et al. also combine horizontal layers with orthogonal views. However, ArchiMate focuses on the description of large, individual systems. The framework from Murer et al., on the other hand, focuses clearly on managing collections of systems, i.e., on Enterprise Architecture Management in the narrow sense. Therefore, their views address classic cross-cutting, application-spanning aspects like integration architecture and security architecture. Note that they also modeled a "vertical architecture x" to indicate that often further vertical views are needed.

Dern (2009) focuses rather on the architecture management processes and does not provide vertical views for structuring the overall architecture, e.g., for fostering a business-driven alignment of the landscape. Note that his layer of "information architecture" addresses the application landscape. The layer below roughly translates to "solution architecture" and addresses individual applications. By switching the focus from collections of systems to individual systems, his framework deviates from the ones described before.

2.3 System Complexity Revisited

In the previous chapter, we discussed complexity in the context of EAM and, among other things, established·

- Over the course of time, large IT landscapes have a natural *tendency to emerge into very complex systems*.
- Complexity impacts the digital ecosystem negatively in respect to transparency, agility, and redundancy. The *results are higher costs* and lower efficiency of system development and maintenance.
- A core *objective of EAM is to steer complexity* and keep the enterprise-wide digital ecosystem simple, lean, and ordered.

Now, what exactly defines complexity? Intuitively, complexity is understood as the result of a high number of system elements and a high number of relationships between these elements. In a similar vein, Beese and Haki (2016) name the following drivers of system complexity:

- Size: overall size of the system and its components
- Diversity: variety and disparity of components
- Integration: level of interconnectedness
- Dynamics: rate of change of overall system

Complexity Rises with the Number of System Elements and Their Dependencies
To illustrate the impact of complexity, we come back to the analogy of building architecture. Figure 2.8 shows brick-and-mortar examples of differently sized systems. Obviously, when architecting and building one of the displayed objects, the

| City | Building complex | Complex building | Simple building | Many simple buildings |

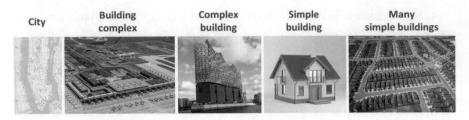

Fig. 2.8 Construction projects of different sizes and complexities. © From left: Shutterstock/ Porcupen, Shutterstock/Mario Hagen, Wikimedia Commons/CC01.0 Aschroet, Shutterstock/Studio Harmony, Shutterstock/Roschetzky

corresponding projects will differ significantly regarding complexity, coordination effort, capital requirements, and time horizon. However, they also bear significant similarities (e.g., all projects will need approval from government agencies, electricity, water supply and connecting streets, fire protection and security measures, as well as a suitable interior design). Now, imagine the project of architecting a "building complex"—like a large airport—and compare this to the project of architecting a development area with 500 houses ("many simple buildings"). If both projects would cover about the same area, for example, 0.5 square kilometers, which project would be harder to architect?

500 Standard Family Houses Are Easier to Develop than One Large Airport
The usual answer would be the "building complex." In the case of "many simple buildings," both architecting a simple building and the standard infrastructure are done all the time and rather trivial. By increasing the number of houses, the complexity does *not* rise significantly, because the system elements (the individual houses) are not connected with each other; there is no direct dependency between them. Though they might share the same infrastructure, for example, electricity and water supply, house #1 does not care about other architecture features of house #500. In IT-architecture terminology, it could be said that the houses are *loosely coupled*. In contrast to that, the system elements of the airport are strongly coupled and depend on each other. For example, the smoke detection system and evacuation plan need to consider the whole building; the size of the entry hall needs to be coordinated with the size of the terminals, gates, transfer tunnels, and so on.

Thus, apart from the number of system elements, *the number and type of dependencies* between the elements increase the system complexity significantly. Many dependency types and classification schemes were described in the context of system interoperability, loose coupling, Service-Oriented Architecture, and Enterprise Architecture. Murer et al. (2011, p. 5), for example, distinguish between functional dependencies, semantic dependencies, temporal dependencies, technical dependencies, and operational dependencies.

Simple Metamodels Induce Homogenous Systems and Low Complexity
On a closer look, complexity depends not only on the number of system elements and their dependencies but also on the *heterogeneity* of the elements and their

relationships. If we have 300 applications with similar non-functional characteristics and identical interface types between them, the overall system complexity is rather low. If we have 300 applications with completely heterogenous non-functional requirements and with 300 different integration mechanisms, complexity is rather high. In this vein, Johnson (2001, p. 19) characterizes a system with complex behavior as "a system with multiple agents dynamically interacting in multiple ways, *following local rules and oblivious to any higher-level instructions.*" In business informatics terminology, if a system has a simple metamodel, then the system is simple as well.

Note that this contradicts the intuitive understanding of enterprise IT's complexity (the more system elements, the more complexity). Having, for example, a very large number of client computers inside an enterprise alone does *not* induce complexity, if these follow the same model, for instance, having identical operating systems, configurations, security mechanisms, and one joint help desk. However, complexity does rise strongly if these client computers stem from various service providers with different help desks and processes of incident management, if they follow various models, different operating systems, different application configurations, and different security mechanisms.

The Internet Is Not Complex
The impact of standardization on complexity is also exemplified with the most famous digital system these days: the Internet. It has billions of elements—for example, servers, web sites, and interfaces—and dependencies between those, like hyperlinks and transmitted data. But *in relation to its huge size, the Internet is amazingly simple and not complex at all.* The reasons for the simplicity of the Internet and the World Wide Web (WWW) are:

- *Simple metamodel:* Though on the "model level" it has a gigantic size, the core idea and the construction principle of the WWW are extremely simple: a set of web sites related with each other only via hyperlinks, where HTML is used to specify a web site's content and Uniform Resource Identifiers (URI) to interlink web sites.
- *A small amount of strictly enforced standards:* The layers below the WWW are thoroughly designed into a straightforward, simple architecture, i.e., the decoupled layers of the Internet protocol suite.
- *Lean but thorough governance:* Bodies like the IETF govern core standards to enable interoperability. Beyond this standardization, there is no central governance.

Thus, based on an extremely simple and thorough "metamodel," a large, efficient system was created that provides its users a large amount of creative freedom. *The implication for EAM here is to provide thorough, "hard" standards that resemble a simple enterprise-wide metamodel on a high level, instead of trying to steer the characteristics of every subelement.* For example, the enterprise-wide standard could prescribe which interface type (API) business applications must use; but it would leave the implementation of the application itself—for example, the programming language—to the local builders. In a similar vein, Rao et al. (2018) wrote that "architecting is performed on the things that matter, rather than attempting a comprehensive representation of every aspect of the enterprise."

2.4 Core Principles for Architecting Socio-Technical Systems

Preliminary Assumptions
Before delving into the individual principles and parameters that shape the Enterprise Architecture, let us recapitulate the boundaries and conditions that frame the work of an enterprise architect. When engaging in the architecture of the enterprise-wide digital ecosystem, the following should be assumed:

- *The optimization of the overall system is the goal:* We assume that the organization aims at optimizing the overall enterprise-wide digital ecosystem system and is not satisfied by piecemeal, local optimizations that neglect or even hinder the optimization of the big picture.
- *Business functions are defined foremost in the business organization:* As an architect, stereotypically, you provide a model and a roadmap for realizing the *requirements of your customer.* You act as a trusted advisor, and thus you must be knowledgeable about the business domain of your customer. For example, you must be able to advise for or against certain requirements or point out which digital possibilities exist to fulfill a requirement. However, the architect is neither a business domain owner nor the central business strategist of an enterprise. In other words, we assume that the essence of the required business functions is defined in the business organization. Based on this input, enterprise architects *deliver the high-level design of the required digital ecosystem.* However, within this design process, there typically are various iterations, in which the business adapts the requirements in the light of proposed solutions.
- *Enterprise Architecture is a creative design process.* There is no repeatable cooking recipe for creating a good song or poem. You can learn about rhythms, measures of verses, iambs, and dactyls; however, in the end, it is a unique creative process. Likewise, there is no detailed recipe for architecting the perfect enterprise-wide digital ecosystem. However, it is the task of Enterprise Architecture Management to provide a frame for this creative work and to provide guidelines and principles to steer the creative work toward a coherent "big picture" of the enterprise-wide digital ecosystem, which fits to the strategic and operational business requirements.

2.4.1   Business and Digital Systems Follow the Same Structures

After having worked a couple of years in the digitalization of large business organizations, the distinction between architecting IT systems and organizational systems can become blurry. That is because—unsurprisingly—the IT system is supposed to implement the organizational processes with digital means. Thus, at least to a certain degree, it must be shaped similarly (here we abstract from the fact that process digitalization often induces business changes that go beyond pure automation). On an abstract level, social business organizations and digital business systems always do the same, simple thing: *An actor with certain roles, rights, and duties uses a tool to perform a business function on an input object, with the goal to produce an output for a customer.* The only difference between a manual business process and a digital business process is that in the latter case, the actor is a program running on a computer. And with todays' high level of business digitalization, digital and manual labor is often closely interwoven.

The idea of business-driven development of digital systems was always the core of business informatics, rooted in IT-oriented business administration and enterprise modeling [cp. Scheer (1984, 2000)]. However, this approach was also embraced by the software engineering community:

- Around the year 2000, the paradigm of Service-Oriented Architecture (SOA) was coined. According to SOA, software systems are formed of loosely coupled, coarse-grained "services" offered on a network, whose *forms follow that of business functions*. For example, the boundaries of the technical service "check credit worthiness" are determined by the business function of the same name.
- Evans (2004) rediscovered "domain-driven design" as basis for structuring software systems and related it to software engineering concepts.
- In the last years, Conway (1968) was quoted in more or less every software engineering conference: "Organizations which design systems are constrained to produce designs which are copies of the communication structures of these organizations."

Designing the structures of a digital ecosystem along the structures of the business system has various advantages:

- *Simplicity:* The digital system must be easy to understand for both business and IT. More specifically, the structure of the enterprise-wide digital ecosystem should make it easy for the business to understand which parts of the digital ecosystem it owns and which digital service exactly supports which business capability. Likewise, it should be easy for an IT engineer to understand the business context of a digital system.
- *Functional alignment:* If the digital implementation is also structurally close to the supported business system, the chances increase that the digital system implements what the business requires.

- *Clear accountability and ownership:* After all, the business provides the money for the IT, and the business needs to understand the effects of its investments. Generally, digitalization can only be successful if roles and responsibilities on the business and the IT side are clear and both sides work closely together on all levels of the organizational hierarchy (this sounds easier than it is in practice).
- *Independence of technology lifecycles:* Technology lifecycles are often shorter than business lifecycles. For example, the core booking engine of a cargo airline as well as the policy management system of a life insurance company might easily be 30 years old. In this time—astonishingly enough—the core processes of these systems changed only a little. So, instead of refactoring the system every 10 years according to structures inferred by changing technology paradigms, it is more efficient to structure them along the more constant business processes and functions. For example, in large enterprises, you will find legacy COBOL applications with modules that 30 years ago were designed along business functions. Today, this structure makes it easier to migrate COBOL legacy code into new programming languages, where the modules are likewise structured along business functions.

In the following, we will briefly describe core principles for structuring large business systems and large digital systems.

2.4.2 Hierarchical Layers in Social and Digital Systems

To reduce complexity and enable efficient control, large socio-technical systems are structured into hierarchies. Take, for example, a global aviation group with 100,000 employees and major business areas for (1) passenger airline; (2) cargo airlines; (3) maintenance, repair, and overhaul; (4) IT; and (5) other services. Now, imagine 1 CEO alone would have to orchestrate these 100,000 people talking to each one individually. Obviously, this would be hard to realize. So instead of 100,000, she could only talk to 5 people, for example, the leads of the 5 business units representing the above-named areas. These 5 "directs" again lead 5 to 10 people, and so on, until the 100,000 people are managed via 5 horizontal layers.

The digital ecosystem is structured into hierarchies as well, i.e., to form applications, (micro-)services inside applications, (Java-)classes inside Micro Services, and modules inside the classes. With a good architecture, the structure of the business capabilities is echoed in the structure of the digital ecosystem. Thus, usually, there is a close relationship between a department and its flagship application. For example, the claims handling department of a car insurance typically has one major application: the claim management system. Correspondingly, Fig. 2.9 illustrates "department" and "application" on the same level.

The resemblance of IT elements to organizational elements is not restricted to the function dimension; also, the elements of the data, process, and organization dimension have digital counterparts on various levels of granularity. A business process,

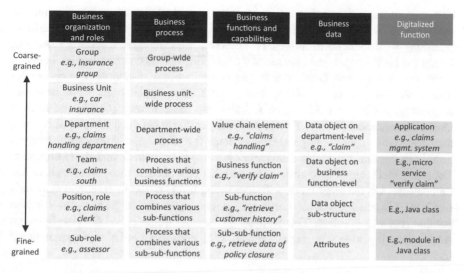

Business organization and roles	Business process	Business functions and capabilities	Business data	Digitalized function
Coarse-grained Group *e.g., insurance group*	Group-wide process			
Business Unit *e.g., car insurance*	Business unit-wide process			
Department *e.g., claims handling department*	Department-wide process	Value chain element *e.g., "claims handling"*	Data object on department-level *e.g., "claim"*	Application *e.g., claims mgmt. system*
Team *e.g., claims south*	Process that combines various business functions	Business function *e.g., "verify claim"*	Data object on business function-level	E.g., micro service "verify claim"
Position, role *e.g., claims clerk*	Process that combines various sub-functions	Sub-function *e.g., "retrieve customer history"*	Data object sub-structure	E.g., Java class
Fine-grained Sub-role *e.g., assessor*	Process that combines various sub-sub-functions	Sub-sub-function *e.g., retrieve data of policy closure*	Attributes	E.g., module in Java class

Fig. 2.9 Organizational and digital elements exist in different granularities

for example, can specify the sequence of organizational tasks on various levels and can have a direct instantiation in the IT world, for instance, in the form of a cross-application service orchestration. On a more fine-grained level, the processes in the digital world are called algorithms.

2.5   Parameters of the Enterprise-Wide Digital Ecosystem

Above, we described two core principles for architecting socio-technical systems: first, that the digital ecosystem should follow the structures of the business ecosystem and second, that to reduce the complexity of a very large system, such systems are usually decomposed into subsystems via hierarchies. Going beyond these basic constants, this section describes more flexible, often-varying parameters for architecting social and digital ecosystems.

Introduction: Changing Paradigms in the History of Enterprise IT

Every couple of years, the CEO of the BEI insurance group ordered some strategy consultants to optimize the IT organization. While this provoked some unease among the employees, the chief architect's credo remained the same over the years: "don't worry; the only thing that can happen is that we will be *more centralized or more decentralized*."

Generally, in the history of digital enterprise systems, the pendulum of centralization-decentralization keeps swinging back and forth. Thus, around the 1960s, the large business applications were decentralized and isolated from each other. To overcome the operative separation of business units in the value chain of a company, a more integrated approach was needed. This was realized with the introduction of *ERP (Enterprise Resource Planning) systems*, where the business functions of different domains were bundled inside one integrated system. However, inside the ERP system, the amount of system elements and dependencies between them was getting too large, which called for a more *decentralized, decoupled approach*. Thus, next to ERP systems, other large applications were installed, addressing, for instance, Customer Relationship Management (CRM) and Supply Chain Management (SCM). To enable interoperability between these applications, they were connected via large central systems for "Enterprise Application Integration." On the one hand, this *integration* became a bottleneck and quite complex, since the applications used different standards that needed to be translated in the middleware. On the other hand, with increasing usage of the Internet and standards like XML (Extensible Markup Language), a more dynamic integration of web-based components was possible. This resulted in the next trend, called Service-Oriented Architecture [cp. also Scheer et al. (2004)]. Further examples of changing paradigms include:

- *Centralization and decentralization of workplace computers:* In the last decades, here the pendulum swung from (1) large, central mainframe computers that hosted the complete compute power (also for the decentral "terminals" used by the workforce), to (2) decentral "fat clients," and back to (3) "thin clients," where the compute power is centralized again (this time in the cloud).
- *In- and outsourcing of infrastructure:* Anybody who worked for some time in a large corporation will have witnessed painful migrations where the central, company-owned data center was outsourced to a specialized service provider or, after (a) being disillusioned regarding the capabilities of the external provider and (b) realizing that operating the infrastructure has more business-specific elements than previously thought, witnessed the remigration, i.e., insourcing the data center back into the company. Obviously today, the infrastructure again is getting outsourced: into the cloud.
- *Centralization and business orientation of the IT organization:* In the year 2010, IT organizations were usually centralized and structured around the large IT functions (e.g., "plan landscape," "build systems," "run systems"). Today, in the age of hyper-digitalization, the IT departments are rather decentralized and structured along the local business departments. In Chap. 3 we will have a closer look at this topic.

Eight Essential Parameters for Structuring the Enterprise-Wide Digital Ecosystem

As the examples in the previous section illustrated, the structure of the enterprise-wide digital ecosystem is strongly influenced by a few core parameters (e.g., "degree of centralization" and "degree of outsourcing"). The values of these parameters change over time and vary from enterprise to enterprise. Complementing the parameters named above, Fig. 2.10 summarizes the core parameters for structuring the enterprise-wide digital ecosystem. Generally, these parameters are disjoint and can

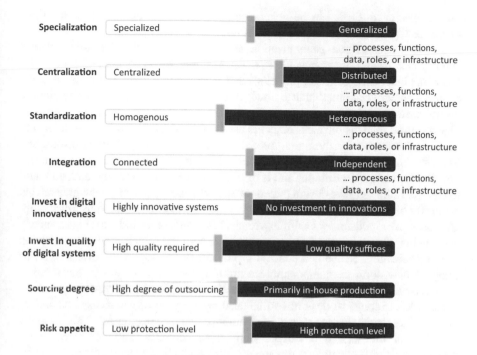

Fig. 2.10 Core parameters for structuring the enterprise-wide digital ecosystem

have different values on a scale from "high" to "low." However, to varying degrees, they are correlated with each other. For example, a higher degree of centralization usually induces a higher degree of standardization, system homogeneity, integration, and specialization. A tangible example of this is the introduction of a central software platform and the advantages coming with it (we will come back to this in Chap. 5). The following sections describe each of these parameters.

2.5.1 Specialization, Generalization, and Reuse

Following Taylorism, business units, departments, and employees are organized into groups that specialize in defined tasks. Comparable to this, information systems follow the principle of modularization, where applications and application components are shaped to fulfill only the one function they specialize in.

An example for specialization in the business world is the insurance claims clerk, who handles claims only for the *car* insurance. However, during a task generalization, her job could be "enlarged," and now she handles claims from three different insurance types: (a) car insurance, (b) life insurance, and (c) liability insurance. The same can happen on the IT site: the micro service "verify claim" inside the application "claims management system" can be implemented to address claims only from the car insurance. Or it can be generalized to address the claims of all the three insurance types (a), (b), and (c) named before.

Above we described generalization and specialization for *functions* ("verify claim") and *roles* ("insurance clerk"). An example for *data* generalization is a business object used across applications and business units. Take, for instance, the business object "customer" that is used in the BEI insurance group. Concretely, a central customer management application offers various APIs, where this business object is used in. This business object is used not only for the business unit "health insurance" but also for the units "property insurance" and "industrial insurance." Since the business object needs to implement the requirements of 3 business units, now it comprises 300 attributes and is overly complex, hard to understand, and hard to change. Following the design pattern of specialization, instead of one generalized business object, three specialized business objects would be used: "customer property insurance," "customer health insurance," and "customer industrial insurance."

Note that the principle of *reuse* is correlated with the principle of generalization and centralization. Reuse is a concept prominent in the context of digital systems design, where software components are not only used in one context but invoked from various processes in various contexts. For example, the above-named service "verify claim" could be designed to be used not only by one business unit but by three business units (car insurance, life insurance, liability insurance). This normally induces that the service is offered only once, centrally, and not three times, decentrally. It also means that the service implementation is generalized to handle claims of the other insurance types, instead of only supporting function "verify claims for the car insurance."

2.5.2 Centralization vs. Decentralization

Centralization means that functions are allocated in one central location instead of being instantiated multiple times in various, peripheral locations. The parameters of centralization, standardization, and specialization are correlated: If inside one large enterprise you have one central service, this normally induces standardization and homogeneity, since all decentral consumers are now using the same service. However, this central service could also be specialized in the sense that it offers different variants of the service to different consumer groups.

Other effects correlated with centralization are *economies of scale and economies of scope*: If a service is used more often, by more consumers, you can hire a critical mass of professionals that specialize on that service. For example, in a decentral scenario, ten business units could offer the service of application integration, each with one general software engineer working on this subject with 40% of her time. In the centralized scenario, instead of four full-time equivalents (FTE), it would suffice to engage only three FTEs with this task, i.e., three integration architects doing this task with 100% of their time. Since the three persons specialize on the task, the

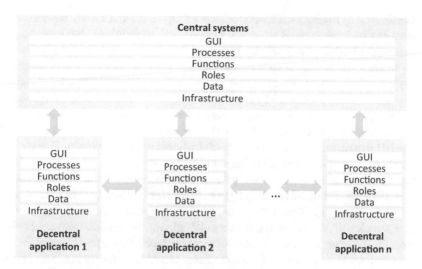

Fig. 2.11 Central and decentral elements of the digital ecosystem

quality of the service increases as well as the efficiency of providing this service. Naturally, there is a downside; disadvantages of centralization include:

- Central service providers can become *bottlenecks* that are not able to scale fast enough to fulfill the demand of the decentral service consumers.
- Central service providers can become a *single point of failure*, with the risk that the whole organization cannot consume this service once it fails.
- The service offered by the central service provider does not *fit to the local requirements* of the decentral service consumers.

Examples of Centralization in the Digital Ecosystem

Figure 2.11 shows some typical elements of the digital ecosystem that are offered centrally and decentrally; these comprise:

Centralization of GUIs: The user interfaces of applications can be offered both centrally and decentrally. Say, for example, three different passenger airlines are part of an international airline group. Since the airlines were formerly independent, competing legal entities, each of them had their own "decentral" web site for customers. Now the business decides to offer only *one central platform* to the customer instead of the three decentral ones. This helps the customers, who mainly care for the service and the price but do not differentiate between the three brands. It also decreases IT redundancies and increases IT efficiency.

Centralization of processes: We already saw in Fig. 2.9 that business processes can appear on different levels of granularity. Some processes are implemented locally, in decentral applications. Other processes are central in the sense that they invoke various of such local applications. For example, the business unit-wide insurance process "Create New Insurance Policy" could use services offered by applications from the domains of policy management and customer management.

Centralization of functions: Closely related to processes and GUIs, business functions can be implemented as central or decentral applications. For example, in a decentral scenario, each of the ten large business units could have its own application for human resources management. In the central scenario, the ten business units would use the same, centralized application. Besides the digital implementation of a business function in the form of a business application, also the organizational functions can be centralized or decentralized. In the decentral scenario, each business unit has its own HR department; in the central scenario, one HR department is responsible for all business units. Obviously, at least in the latter case, also the HR application should be centralized.

Centralization of data: Also, in the case of enterprise-wide data, the pendulum of centralization-decentralization swings back and forth. Already some decades ago, so-called Enterprise Resource Planning (ERP) systems provided large, central data stores with the objective to integrate all enterprise-wide-relevant business data. On the other hand, in a digital ecosystem shaped by the paradigm of Service-Oriented Architecture (SOA), data is stored decentrally: Every business application or even every micro service (inside an application) has its own, independent data store. Complementary to these decentral data sources, today in large enterprises, also central, application-independent operational and analytic databases exist, for example, data lakes or operational data stores. These are fed by the decentral applications and provide services to other decentral applications.

Centralization of roles and rights: In practice and in the science of enterprise information systems, the dimension of rights and roles does not receive as much attention as, for example, the dimensions of function and processes; but it is equally important for enterprise digitalization. As described, for example, by Scheer (2000), elements of the organizational dimension appear in various granularities on the different hierarchy levels. The column "business organization" in Fig. 2.9 displays examples of such units and roles. In the practice of large digital ecosystems, roles and rights are often managed both centrally and decentrally: on the one hand, in central user identity directories and repositories for the rights and roles of users and on the other hand, inside large decentral business applications, which bring their own system for managing rights and roles. Architectural topics here are, for example, how these central and decentral repositories relate to each other, where the primary place for managing identities and rights is allocated and how the various repositories are synchronized.

Centralization of infrastructure: Naturally, IT infrastructure can be allocated centrally or decentrally as well. For instance, in so-called fat clients, the operating system and the applications are running on the computer of each user. In this highly decentral scenario, the user usually has more liberties to configure her computer. However, with this possibility for individualization, the maintenance costs rise. In the centralized scenario, on the other hand, thin clients are used. Here, the operating system and the application software are located on central servers from which program updates and system administration are carried out. This generally improves system reliability and lowers maintenance costs.

2.5.3   Standardization vs. Individualization

Standardization is a core process of Enterprise Architecture Management, and the degree of standardization and homogeneity are fundamental parameter of the digital ecosystem. We understand standardization as the homogenization of system elements by means of a common specification—i.e., a standard—that the system elements must comply with. Referring to business informatics concepts, a standard can be seen as a metamodel that specifies the characteristics of all models. In contrast to bilateral, local, informal ad hoc agreements, a standard implies a multi-lateral, global, precisely defined, and mature consensus about system characteristics. However, standards can differ in scope:

- *Enterprise-specific* standards specify, for example, which kind of products, vendors, syntax and semantics, and infrastructure technologies are used inside an enterprise.
- *Industry-specific* standards, among other things, describe the semantics of messages exchanged in B2B scenarios between companies inside one industry. Taking the example of the airline industry, here the International Air Transport Association (IATA) defines the Airline Industry Data Model (AIDM).
- *Industry-independent* standards define, for example, how to protect data (GDPR) or technical matters like the syntax of messages (XML, JSON).

Standardization is generally positively correlated with homogeneity inside a system, reuse of system elements, cross- and intra-enterprise interoperability, repeatability, and system (element) quality. From a managerial perspective, standardization inside an enterprise reduces learning and change costs. Following a quality standard for products reduces purchasing risks and thereby purchasing efforts [compare, e.g., Schneider (2021)].

Standardization, Homogeneity, and Redundancy
Standardization induces *homogenous systems* since all system elements following the standard have the same characteristics (except when each of the system elements follows a different standard; in this theoretical case, the degree of homogeneity inside this system would not increase). In the context of EAM, standardization is primarily used to reduce the system's heterogeneity inside an enterprise. Here, the opposite of standardization is *individualization*, where the system elements of the same type have different characteristics; the result is a system with *heterogenous* system elements. For example, inside a large enterprise, ten applications for Customer Relationship Management (CRM) could stem from ten different vendors.

As indicated before (cp. Fig. 1.7), the right degree of standardization and homogeneity depends on many factors. For example, standardization can get a negative connotation when applied to *core business* applications, making these uniform to the business applications of competing enterprises. In this vein, a rule of thumb is that standardized commercial off-the shelf software should be used primarily for the *non-differentiating processes* of a company. For the core processes, used by the company to differentiate itself from competitors, bespoke software should be used instead.

Like in the CRM example named above, heterogeneity can lead to *redundancy*: Instead of having solutions from ten different CRM vendors and ten times the corresponding application management processes instantiated inside our enterprise, should we rather have only one large CRM platform from one vendor? This certainly would decrease costs and lead to more specialization and professionalization. On the other hand, maybe we would we like to have a certain degree of *technical redundancy* to improve the stability of the systems in case one component fails. Maybe we also would like to have some "commercial redundancy," i.e., source CRM systems from three different vendors to reduce the risk of a vendor lock-in.

Examples of Standardization in the Digital Ecosystem
In the context of EAM, examples of standardization comprise:

Standardization of GUIs: For example, the GUIs of functionally similar applications can be standardized to provide a similar look and feel to the users. Obviously, this is only necessary if there is no centralized GUI or a set of GUIs in one central application (assuming that inside this application the look and feel of GUIs are harmonized).

Standardization of processes: For example, the HR processes for hiring employees could be standardized, so that every of the 15 HR units in a group with 100,000 employees uses the same process. *The standardization of processes across business units is an important prerequisite for a harmonization of the application landscape*: If the business units a, b, and c have completely different processes, for example, Customer Relationship Management (CRM), it will be difficult to convince them to use the same CRM application.

Standardization of functions, capabilities, and applications: Like processes, also the business functions can be standardized inside an enterprise. Note that in the process dimension, a white-box approach is pursued, where the sequence of several functions is specified. In the function dimension, on the other hand, a black-box approach is pursued; here primarily, the *interface* of the function, its goals, its input, and its output are described. For example, a main concept of Service-Oriented Architecture is to standardize the service contracts expressed in the APIs of the services. Thus, a service can be offered by different decentral applications but always deliver the same service. Note, that in the context of EAM the terms "business function" and "business capability" are often used synonymously. On a technical level, functions are implemented as IT applications. Here is an example for application standardization: Currently, the ten business units of a large insurance industry use five different products (A, B, C, D, E) for managing the worktimes and times of absence of their employees. To leverage economies of scale and scope, the EAM department defines the product C as the "standard," implying that from now on, every business unit uses only application C. As mentioned above, the "technical" application standardization is closely related to the business-level standardization: if the business processes and functions differ strongly among the ten business units, it will be difficult to find one product that covers all their requirements.

Standardization of data: In the context of digital systems, the standardization of data and documents inside protocols is probably the most intuitive form of standardization. This comprises technical, industry-independent standards, like the protocol stack of the Internet. There are also industry-specific bodies that standardize, for example, the messages exchanged in the airline industry or the insurance industry. Moreover, there are also enterprise-internal standards for data and documents. For instance, document forms used in internal support processes—like HR or purchasing—often are standardized. Also, for exchanging messages between application interfaces, the syntax and semantics of the exchanged business objects can be standardized. For example, the attributes of the object "customer" can be standardized, so this object can be reused by various APIs and applications inside the enterprise.

Standardization of roles and rights: On the one hand, there are technical cross-industry standards that provide the syntax for describing rights and roles (e.g., XACML) or for describing claims (e.g., W3C Verifiable Credentials). On the other hand, inside enterprises, the concept of role-based access control (RBAC) "standardizes" the rights that persons endowed with certain roles have (for instance, the role "Underwriter" in an industry insurance can be endowed with the rights "Assess risk," "Confirm risk assessment," and "Contract closure"). Now the set of rights of everybody having this role is clear and homogenous throughout the enterprise. In practice, departments specialized on identity and access management or security architecture should address this topic. However, roles and rights are an essential part of the enterprise-wide digital ecosystem, and the quality of this topic also needs to be monitored by EAM.

Standardization of IT infrastructure elements: By definition, IT infrastructure elements are independent from functional business requirements and thus can be reused in various business areas. Therefore, IT infrastructure is usually the first and largest part of enterprise-wide IT standardization activities. To this aim, a technology standard catalog is defined that specifies which product from which vendor to use for which infrastructure service. Such services include, for example, databases, servers, and firewall products.

Challenges of the Standardization Process

In the context of EAM, the process of standardization is challenging: First, a set of standards optimal for the overall enterprise must be found. Second, these standards must be accepted by a critical mass of the business units in the enterprise. This can be difficult, because usually there are some units for whom another standard would fit better to their local requirements. Thus, a process for finding consensus, establishing transparency, and formal standards declaration must be established. Within this process, all stakeholders are informed about the contents of the standards, as well as about the enterprise-wide *benefits and implications* of the standard. The critical question is how the individual units react to standards on the enterprise-wide digital ecosystem. Say, for example, the enterprise architects declare JSON as the new standard for inter-application communication, replacing the former standard XML. Now the following archetypical situations can occur:

1. *Short-term migration of existing solution to new standard:* Most of the owners of the existing applications appreciate the new standard and will implement the standard in the next 12 months. They understand the standard is beneficial from various perspectives; and they would have made the same decision on their own, locally, sooner or later as well. Now they are thankful to receive guidance, technical support, and cross-department coordination from the central architecture department.

2. *Long-term migration of existing solution to new standard:* In case of high invests in systems that follow the old standard, in practice, units will not be forced to switch immediately to the new standard. Instead, they keep the old system but are obliged to switch to the new standard once their current system reaches its end of life.

3. *Implementation of new system following the standard:* A new system is currently built; the project lead was informed about the new standard. He agrees that this standard is future-proof and makes sense from a technological perspective. He also can show his project sponsor that the costs of using the new standard are reasonable.

4. *Unknowing disregard of new standard*: The project lead of a new system was not informed about the new standard and does not have access to the repository where architectural knowledge is stored. Thus, he implements the former standard instead of the new one.

5. *Willful disregard of new standard:* The project manager for a new system knows the obligation for the new standard but ignores it. He does so because the standard implies local disadvantages. For example, the commercial off-the-shelf application the project selected currently only supports the former standard (XML). Enabling the product with the new standard (JSON) would jeopardize the project closure in time and budget. In this decision, the project manager is supported by the business owner of the unit that ordered the new system. This manager needs to produce some success stories within this year. Thus, he prioritizes the local, short-term benefits for his unit over the global, long-term benefits for the enterprise-wide digital ecosystem. Accordingly, the project "flies under the radar," and the enterprise architects are informed of the new system only when this goes live.

Technical Debts

In case a project implements an only locally optimal, short-term beneficial solution that does not comply with enterprise-wide standards, a so-called technical debt can be assigned to the solution. The technical debt represents the opportunity costs induced by the short-term, local decision and the fact that the opportunity for a long-term viable, globally optimal solution is missed. A technical debt is the obligation for the solution owner to adapt the solution toward the enterprise-wide optimal solution. For example, the project could be responsible for assuring a budget that in the next 2 years, the solution will be adapted to follow enterprise standards. The opposite mechanism is that a project receives a *compensation*, if it succumbs to local disadvantages for the sake of the greater good, i.e., a standard that is beneficial from a "global" enterprise-wide perspective, but suboptimal locally [cp. Beimborn

(2021)]. Unfortunately, in practice, the mechanism of "technical debts" is difficult to realize because it requires a firm, enterprise-wide budgeting process. To make this more tangible, once a project is over, the "technical debts" assigned to the created solution in practice often get ignored. Why? Because the budget for enhancing digital solutions usually lays at the local business owners. These only have a limited interest in paying for an enhancement, which is beneficial for the enterprise-wide digital ecosystem but does not realize immediate additional benefits for the local business owners.

2.5.4   Integration vs. Autonomy

The beginning of business information systems in the 1960s was characterized by isolated application systems, which inhibited an efficient information flow between individual workplaces and departments. The reduction of such barriers by an optimal form and degree of integration was and is a major topic of enterprise digitalization.

Integration means to combine two or more elements so that they form a unified whole. Recapitulating the terminology displayed in Fig. 2.1, we see that the terms integration and system are closely related: a system is a set of elements that form a unified whole because the elements have qualitatively and quantitatively stronger dependencies among each other than to elements outside the system. One could also say that a system consists of elements that are integrated with each other.

Connecting Integration, Merging Integration, and Centralization
With the definition from above, two flavors of integration become apparent:

- First, focusing on the aspect of the "unified whole," integration means that the elements of an integrated system content-wise complement each other and there are no redundancies in the system.
- Second, focusing on the "combining" part and taking a rather technical perspective, integration means to connect elements and to establish dependencies between them.

In a similar vein, Rosemann (1996) distinguished between connecting and merging integration: A *connecting integration* is the creation of a system out of hitherto unconnected systems. In the connecting integration, these subsystems are explicitly related to each other, but not altered themselves. In the *merging integration*, on the other hand, elements of the subsystems may be altered; for example, in case that two subsystems contain the same element, redundant elements can be deleted.

Note that *centralization* implies a merging integration. Say, for example, that we migrate customer data from the local, decentral applications into a central, enterprise-wide Customer Relationship Management system. In this case, the data should not only be lifted and shifted physically into the central system, but the data from the various decentral locations should also logically be adapted to form a "unified whole."

Different Degrees of Connectivity and Dependency: Integration vs. Autonomy
As mentioned above, the degree of system integration is a core parameter for EAM
(cp. Fig. 1.8). With an increasing degree of integration, the quantity and quality of
semantical, syntactical, and technical connections and *dependencies* between system
elements increase. In other words, with more integration, the system elements
become more *dependent* from each other, instead of becoming more "loosely
coupled" and autonomous.

A practical example illustrates the relation between integration and autonomy:
Imagine a large aviation group that comprises four large, mostly independent airlines
allocated in four different countries. These airlines developed independently from
each other and are traditionally closely connected to the nation they are allocated
in. Now, on the one hand, the business asks for group-wide synergies and harmonized processes among all airlines in the group. On the other hand, if the economic
situation should require it, any airline can be sold away from the group ("carve out").
In addition, for political reasons, each airline has its own CIO. Thus, even though
each business unit has the same business model (passenger airline), in practice, it can
very well be that each airline in the group uses disjoint, redundant core applications,
different standards for describing business objects (e.g., passenger information), and
even different metrics for business intelligence to gather Key Performance Indicators
(which makes the quarterly group-wide business analysis challenging). In other
words, due to the de facto *business independence* of the four airlines, also the digital
ecosystems of the airlines are not highly integrated, but rather loosely coupled.

Horizontal vs. Vertical Integration
Another often-used distinction is that between *horizontal and vertical integration*:
Horizontal integration refers to the integration of elements on the same (vertical)
layer of the enterprise hierarchy, like the interlinkage of the operational value chain
functions "assess insured object," "create insurance policy," and "send policy to
customer." Orthogonal to that, vertical integration spans different levels of the
enterprise hierarchy. Here data from the lower, operational levels is condensed and
transported to the higher levels, e.g., the integration of a decision support system
with data from operational processes of the value chain.

Collaborative Views for a Connecting, Horizontal System Integration
Figure 2.12 illustrates a core concept of the Architecture of Interoperable Information Systems [cp. Ziemann (2010)]. Horizontally, three collaborative views enable
the systematic connection of the digital ecosystems:

Private view on internal system elements: Most processes, functions, roles, and data
    elements are used only inside an enterprise and must not leave the company
    boundaries. They represent valuable business knowledge and must be kept secret.
    These elements are captured in the "private view."
Public view on system interfaces: Now, if enterprises engage in a digital collabora-
    tion to *interoperate* with each other, these "private views" must relate to each
    other. Naturally, here the internal elements can only partially be visible to the
    other enterprise. Besides privacy protection, further reasons for this *information*

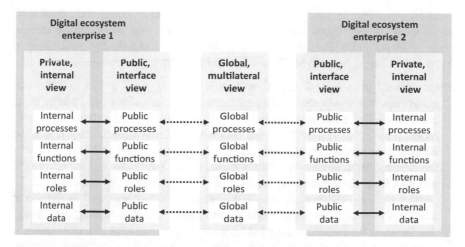

Fig. 2.12 Collaborative views enable a horizontal, connecting integration

hiding are the logical decoupling between the digital ecosystems and the reduction of the overall systems complexity. Thus, instead of exposing the complete private view, the enterprises use a dedicated interface layer called "public view." Via the specification of this view, the systems know how to interact with each other. Note that the interfaces of the two interacting systems must be complementary, for instance, comprising the complementary functions "send insurance policy" and "receive insurance policy." Technically, a public view today is implemented usually via so-called API gateways. Such a gateway serves as a proxy between the internal processes and the outside world. Often, the API gateway also *translates between formats* used inside the system and external formats. Now it is possible to establish a connection between digital ecosystem 1 and digital ecosystem 2 using the bilaterally agreed elements of the interface view.

Global, multi-lateral view on collaboration elements: However, if the interaction is supposed to be implemented not only between two enterprises but by many enterprises, it makes sense to have a multi-lateral, "global" specification of the elements comprised in the interfaces. Technically, a "global view" comprises two or more public views and connects those to form a multi-lateral view. Examples of such "global views" are industry standards that describe how the enterprises inside an industry can digitally interoperate. To this purpose, for example, the International Air Transport Association (IATA) published the Airline Industry Data Model (AIDM).

Dimensions of Intra- and Inter-enterprise Business Process Integration
Though some frameworks for intra- and inter-organizational business processes also offer dimensions for describing security aspects, transactions, and the semantics used in a collaboration, most frameworks support four core dimensions: *process,*

function, organization, and data. These four dimensions in practice are most relevant for integrating digital business systems. They are also supported by classic, widespread standards like BPMN, WSDL, JSON, or XACML. Figure 2.12 illustrates these dimensions; we briefly describe them here:

Integration of processes: If digital processes are integrated across systems and enterprises, the computers in the collaborating organizations can execute these processes fully or partially automated. Say, for example, an external insurance broker (ecosystem 1) wants to trigger the creation of a new insurance policy at the BEI insurance (ecosystem 2). This process comprises at least two functions: after the first message is sent, the BEI insurance has 3 days to ask for additional material from the broker; the sending of the response is the second step. To prepare such a collaboration, at least the internal processes as well as the public interfaces offered to the partner system must be specified, including the correlation between the internal and the public view. Maybe this type of collaboration is even specified by an industry-specific standard, which describes the interaction between the two parties in the form of a "global process."

Integration of roles and rights: In the organization dimension, roles and rights relevant for the collaboration are described and related to their internal counterparts. This ensures that the collaboration partners have a common understanding of the adjacent roles and their rights. In the example from above, the insurance broker would transmit a user ID (e.g., "Jane Doe"), her venue (the insurance broker company), and her role ("broker for car insurance"). Inside the BEI insurance, this information would be correlated to the right for executing certain functions, like "trigger process for creating a new policy." Note that even inside one enterprise, roles and rights are often defined and managed in two places: (1) in an *enterprise-wide, central system for identity and access management* and (2) decentrally, in large applications with complex permission structures. The topic of specifying "global" cross-organizational identities, roles, and rights is addressed by standards like W3C Verifiable Credentials and W3C Decentralized Identifiers.

Integration of functions: The function dimension describes how business functions of collaboration partners relate to each other. Here we address on the one hand that the interfaces shared between the collaboration partners fit to each other. On the other hand, it is described how the publicly visible function relates to one or more internal functions. For example, an insurance could offer the service "Retrieve Policy Information" to several of its insurance brokers. When this service is invoked, inside the insurance, this call could be routed to the specific internal system that might differ depending on the broker. Apart from the routing, also the syntactics of the service call might differ between the externally visible interface and the internal applications, and then also a syntax transformation is required. Instead of using bilaterally agreed service definitions, we could also use the specification of a "global function," for instance, the API specification of an insurance industry standard that specifies the syntax of B2B-interfaces. If used inside one enterprise, such service specifications are also called *Integrated*

Service Model (ISM). These are enterprise-internal standards that define the syntax of essential business functions for the complete enterprise.

Integration of data: In the *data dimension*, document types used in the collaboration are defined and related to internally used document types. In the example above, it would make sense to have a cross-enterprise definition of the attributes in a "car insurance policy." This could be a bilateral specification, where, for example, the insurance broker suggests a format and the BEI insurance agrees to use that. Or it could be multi-lateral defined, industry-wide standard that specifies typical data formats. If used inside one enterprise, such data specifications are also called *integrated data model (IDM)*. These enterprise-internal standards define the syntax of essential business objects for the complete enterprise. Note that here we focus on data integration in the context of business process integration, i.e., a "connecting, horizontal integration." Other forms of data integration include vertical, merging data integration and horizontal, merging integration. An example for the first case is an analytic data warehouse that integrates data from various operational systems. An example for the second case is an operational data store that integrates data from various operational systems.

2.5.5 Further Parameters

Besides specialization, centralization, standardization, and integration, further essential parameters for the enterprise-wide digital ecosystem include:

Invest in Digital Innovativeness
According to Porter (1985, p. 177), technology strategy must address three fields:

1. Which technologies must be developed
2. The extent to which technology is obtained or offered externally
3. To what extent technical excellence ("leadership") must be pursued

In the context of EAM, the third point translates to information technology and thus addresses the question "how much should a company invest in digital innovations?". For example, around the year 2010, in the fictional BEI insurance, the stance toward digital services was "we use mature, stable software; we do not need the newest innovations." Did this change in the year 2020, when the importance of digitalization was perceived even greater than 10 years ago? In most large enterprises, you will still find decade-old legacy applications, being responsible for core business processes and representing huge investments.

Now where should an enterprise engage in IT innovation activities? At the customer-facing systems, e.g., by developing an enterprise-wide customer portal? At the provider side, by automating the supply chain? At the core production processes of the company or maybe even at the supporting business processes? What about the digitalization functions and tools, like software development and cyber security; they should probably be state of the art? A detailed discussion of enterprise digitalization goes beyond the scope of this book. However, in general, the allocation and degree of digital innovativeness depend on the business model of an enterprise and the position of the digital system inside the enterprise.

Thus, a relatively new enterprise with a completely digital business model like "provider of a major internet search engine" will use state-of-the-art technology in all core business processes and have research departments to extend the state of the art. This enterprise will also have a relatively homogenous landscape, since it does not have to operate IT systems from the last six different decades, like a traditional insurance company. A large insurance company (or any other large enterprise that is several decades old) will have a more complex, heterogenous stance toward the innovation of its digital technology. Several approaches have been described to classify the need for innovation of the digital ecosystem:

- *COBIT* describes the *technology adoption strategy* as a major design factor for the enterprise governance. According to this, an enterprise can choose between three technology adoption strategies: (1) *first mover*, where the enterprise generally adopts new technology as early as possible to gain a first-mover advantage; (2) *follower*, where the enterprise waits for new technologies to be mainstream and well-tested; and (3) *slow adopter*, where the enterprise is "very late" with the adoption of new technologies [cp. ISACA (2018)].
- In a similar vein, already Porter (1985) stated that it depends on the business strategy, in which parts of the enterprise *technical leadership* and in which parts *technical followership* should be pursued.
- Being more fine-grained, Gartner described *Pace Layering* as an approach for clustering the enterprise-wide digital ecosystem. This approach clusters digital systems according to their need for innovation and the corresponding change-frequency into three classes: (1) systems of innovation, (2) systems of differentiation, and (3) systems of record [cp. Mangi et al. (2017)].

Invest in Quality of Digital Services

A rule of thumb is that the *digital systems for the core business processes* of a company must be of high quality; after all, these systems are directly responsible for the revenue of the enterprise. The *supporting business processes*, like human resources management, usually receive less digitalization budget than the core business processes. Thus, the web site for job applicants usually will be functionally (e.g., look and feel of the GUI) and non-functionally (e.g., stability and availability of the web site) of worse quality than the highly polished and highly reliable customer portal.

Note that the quality of a digital system and its age are only loosely correlated. To be clear, generally, advances in technology lead to improved quality. Thus, to a certain degree, the quality of digital services and the amount of money you invest to keep them "modern" are correlated. However, for example, in banks and insurance, you will find very reliable, high-performance "work horses" for core business processes that have been implemented 40 years ago on large mainframe computers.

Despite being far behind the state of the art, these systems have a very high quality, at least from a business perspective.

In-House Production vs. Sourcing of IT Services
As mentioned before, another classical strategy parameter addresses whether digital services should be developed in-house or rather be sourced from third parties. Here, COBIT (ISACA, 2018) distinguishes four IT procurement models:

1. Outsourcing—IT is provided by third party.
2. Cloud—the enterprise uses the cloud wherever possible.
3. Insourced—IT is developed and operated in-house.
4. Hybrid—a mixture of the three previous models.

In our experience, today, large enterprises always use cloud services of third-party providers "wherever possible." However, they also have at least a small portion of in-house development. The third model, where IT is not only developed but also operated in-house, is very rare. In other words, *most large enterprises use the "hybrid" model*. Also addressing the topic of in-house vs. sourced IT, a widespread EAM principle states "reuse before buy before make," meaning:

- If a digital function is needed inside an enterprise, we first try to reuse an existing in-house service.
- Only, if the required service does not exist in-house, we buy it on the market.
- Only if we cannot acquire it under reasonable conditions on the market, we produce the digital product inside our enterprise.

Now, this principle is useful as a coarse-grained rule of thumb; it serves as a reference for starting a more fine-grained discussion when it comes to the procurement of digital capabilities. Such a more detailed discussion must address:

- Is this a differentiating, core business capability that distinguishes our enterprise from the competitors? A common rule of thumb is to use *standardized* commercial off-the-shelf (COTS) product from third parties for all non-differentiating business processes, as well as for IT infrastructure. Self-developed, *bespoke* systems, on the other hand, are only used for distinguishing core processes.
- If we acquire the product off-the-shelf, will we be able to stick to the standard provided by the vendor? Or do the business processes of our company require a heavily customized, bespoke solution? The latter causes high change and maintenance costs.
- If we procure the service from a third party, is it *easy to integrate* into our digital landscape, and does it support the standards we already use?

Further exemplary *reasons to keep IT services inside the company* include: Keep a critical mass of digital talents inside the company, keep enterprise secrets in the company, remain independent from pricing strategies of vendors, reduce frictions and transaction costs between in-house and external service providers, and be more flexible regarding the service functionalities (e.g., there might be lengthy discussions with an external provider, if the change of a service functionality is covered by the current service-level agreement or not). Exemplary *reasons to source IT services* from outside are: Reduce the internal complexity of the IT service provider, free internal resource to concentrate on core processes, use economies of scale and scope of the service provider, and use a pay-per-use model from the service provider in case such elasticity is needed.

Risk Appetite and Protection Level
A precondition for architecting the digital ecosystem is the assessment of the sensitivity of the digital services and data comprised in it. For instance, if our enterprise does not store valuable data and is not responsible for a critical infrastructure, we need to architect for a comparatively low protection level. If, on the other hand, we are responsible for the digital ecosystem of an online bank, of a health insurance, or of a military basis, we need to architect for a high protection level. Based on the assessment, classic security measures must be planned, like firewalls, encryption mechanisms, and identity and access management (IAM). On the one hand, the protection level must address the risk that somebody compromises the *integrity* and *confidentiality* of our data and our services. On the other hand, it must address the risk of (non-)*availability* of the digital services. Here, the classic security measures help as well, like a firewall against denial-of-service attacks. Besides planning for protection measures, we need to adjust the non-functional requirements of our digital ecosystem, for instance, regarding availability, system redundancy, maturity of services, and the service location (e.g., which what kind of data and service will be allocated in which cloud).

In the same vein, COBIT (ISACA, 2018) describes the governance design factor *risk profile of an enterprise*. This refers to the IT-related risks to which the enterprise is currently exposed and indicates which areas of risk are exceeding the risk appetite. Among others, COBIT names the following examples for risks: (bad) IT investment decision-making and portfolio definition, hardware incidents, noncompliance, and malicious attacks. Another "design factor" named by COBIT in this context is *threat landscape* under which the company operates; COBIT here lists the two classes: "high" or "normal" threat level. We will come back to the topic of risk management in the following chapter.

Chapter 3
Strategic and Tactical Context of EAM

This chapter addresses the strategic and tactical context of the EAM capability in an enterprise. To provide a basis for the following sections, first essential terms in the context of enterprise strategy and tactics are defined. Afterward, core parameters of the business strategy and the business operations of an enterprise are sketched out. These include classic strategy parameters, like cost focus, quality focus, or the market coverage of an enterprise. More operational parameters include the degree of business process integration, process standardization, and innovation within an enterprise. When these overarching enterprise parameters are clarified, we describe the parameters of the EAM capability itself. These include, for example, the scope of the EAM capability, its allocation, its stance toward standardization, and its planning horizon. In the following synthesis, we correlate the parameters for the enterprise strategy, the operative enterprise, and the EAM capability. The last section describes the operative context of EAM, i.e., the structure and the capabilities of the IT organization. Here, we first discuss the general shape of the IT organization (e.g., centralized vs. decentralized) and fundamental tasks of the IT organization (e.g., managing IT applications and infrastructure). Finally, we describe the individual capabilities of the IT organization that are most relevant for EAM.

3.1 Introduction and Basic Terms

3.1.1 EAM Must Be Tailored to the Enterprise Context

Why do we bother understanding the enterprises business strategy or the tactical context of EAM? Is there even a correlation between the EAM capability and the business strategy? Or are these separate worlds? You will find enterprises where it feels like that; but in such cases, the EAM capability will encounter significant problems, for instance, a lack of acceptance in both business and IT and a lack of

© The Author(s), under exclusive license to Springer Nature Switzerland AG 2022   61
J. Ziemann, *Fundamentals of Enterprise Architecture Management*, The Enterprise Engineering Series, https://doi.org/10.1007/978-3-030-96734-5_3

vision when it comes to developing strategic target pictures. Instead, EAM should be the "conveyer belt" that connects the business strategy and the digital ecosystem. In these days, the digital ecosystem clearly is of strategic business importance for most enterprises. Since EAM means the steering of the enterprise-wide digital ecosystem, it must be tailored to the strategic and tactical requirements of each enterprise. Note that even inside one enterprise, EAM parameters need to be adjusted to the specifics of the different business units and application types. A one-size-fits-all approach, where the same EAM measures are applied to all areas of the enterprise, often will not work.

Should Every Company Have a "Bezos Mandate"?

To make the relationship between the business strategy of an enterprise and Enterprise Architecture Management more tangible, let us look at the so-called Bezos mandate: Since a couple of years, this anecdote has been circulating through the tech media landscape [cp., e.g., Mason (2017)]. According to this anecdote, in 2002, the Amazon founder issued a mandate on integration architecture—normally not a hot topic being on every CEO's mind. Allegedly, this mandate was part of Amazon's success, because it ingrained a clear paradigm for developing digital interfaces in the organization and thus laid the basis for an agile digital ecosystem, including both internal and external digital services. The mandate is said to comprise six commandments:

1. "All teams will henceforth expose their data and functionality through service interfaces.
2. Teams must communicate with each other through these interfaces.
3. There will be no other form of interprocess communication allowed: no direct linking, no direct reads of another team's data store, no shared-memory model, no backdoors whatsoever. The only communication allowed is via service interface calls over the network.
4. It doesn't matter what technology they use. HTTP, Corba, Pubsub, custom protocols—doesn't matter. Bezos doesn't care.
5. All service interfaces, without exception, must be designed from the ground up to be externalizable. That is to say, the team must plan and design to be able to expose the interface to developers in the outside world. No exceptions.
6. Anyone who doesn't do this will be fired."

Now, this seems to be a very good reference for an integration architecture principle: It is easy to understand, technology agnostic (and hence stable over time), and ambitious (e.g., services must also work externally) and leaves no doubt about the level of bindingness. However, could any EAM capability in any company issue such a hard, clear-cut Enterprise Architecture principle? Rather not. To enforce such a principle, the enterprise must meet at least the following conditions:

- A *homogenous business model* that demands *highly digitalized*, often changing processes and business partners.
- *One central manager* has the power to mandate this expensive to implement paradigm in all parts of the enterprise.

- The business has the demand for a *highly flexible and agile ecosystem* where services are potentially used both internally and *externally*.
- The ecosystem is just being built, consistently using the technology of the current era, and the enterprise does not have to bother with hundreds of *decade-old core legacy systems*.
- An *enterprise culture* that appreciates harsh top-down mandates.

On the other hand, you will not be able to issue such a principle for the complete enterprise, if, for example, you work in a large aviation group with the following characteristics:

- A group with completely heterogenous business models in a historically loosely coupled, federated structure where many managers are involved in the architecture of the digital ecosystems.
- The business models inside the group comprise IT only in a supporting role, most digital services are used only company-internal, and system-to-system dependencies rarely change.
- A highly heterogenous digital landscape with many legacy IT systems that are up to 40 years old and still business critical.
- A rather "agile," people-oriented bottom-up culture.

In other words, the shape of the Enterprise Architecture and the shape of the EAM capability depend on core parameters of the enterprise, including the business model, the enterprise structure, the business need for agility, the age, and the complexity of the IT landscape, as well as on the enterprise culture. Among other things, in this chapter, we will have a more detailed view on such parameters.

3.1.2   Basic Terms

Strategy

The word strategy has its roots in the ancient Greek terms *Stratos* (legion) and *Agos* (leader). In the context of enterprises and enterprise digitalization, it is understood in two ways:

1. *Strategy is the specification of an essential long-term goal and a plan how to reach this*, including the comprised actions. In this vein, Chandler (1962) stated that strategy can be defined as the determination of the basic long-term goals and objectives of an enterprise, the adoption of courses of action, and the allocation of resources for carrying out the goals. Note that the description of the as-is situation and the motivation for change can be subsumed in this conception since the as-is situation implicitly is part of the goal description. For instance, a strategy of the BEI insurance group could be: "our profits in the retail market are too low and the German market is saturated (as-is situation); thus, we plan to increase profits in two years by 10% (goal); we will achieve this by offering the product internationally (the way how to reach the goal)."

2. *Strategy is a set of rules,* whose compliance increases the probability of reaching or maintaining a desired target state [cp., e.g., Müller-Stewens and Gillenkirch (2018)]. An example from the business world would be "we always manufacture high-quality products and offer our customers a highly individual service (and thus maintain our competitive advantage)."

Strategy vs. Tactics

While tactics refers to reaching short-term goals with medium impact, strategy is about reaching long-term goals with an essential impact. Compared to tactics, strategy addresses a broader scope of a system from a higher vantage point. Thus, strategy and tactics are two sides of the same coin: how to improve a system, in the short term and in the long term. They are not antagonists but need to be congruent with each other.

IT Strategy vs. Business Strategy

The concept of strategy can be applied to all kind of systems. For example, a strategy can address the business side of the enterprise, as mentioned in the examples above. It can also address the long-term development of the overall IT organization of an enterprise or only parts of the digital ecosystem. Examples of goals addressed by IT strategies are:

- There is one central IT service provider for all business units of the enterprise. It is responsible for all business applications and information management.
- The IT infrastructure is operated externally by a third-party service provider.
- There is exactly one central Customer Relationship Management application for the entire group.
- Seamless interoperability of all business applications will be achieved via joint standards and central integration hubs.

Figure 3.1 illustrates that IT strategy is part of the enterprise strategy. The essential nature and the impact of strategies imply that the business side of the enterprise generally must be involved in any new IT strategy [cp. also Bente et al. (2012, p. 43)]. In practice, IT strategies vary in their business impact. For example, the business might not care if the IT organization uses a central integration hub or not. However, the business does care for the results, for instance, that applications can efficiently exchange data with each other and that new applications can efficiently be integrated into the digital ecosystem. If IT strategies lack business support, problems will arise: Probably, the concept will not receive enough funding to implement it with the right scope and quality. Maybe it will get implemented as "piecemeal," and there will not be enough momentum to achieve the benefits that were envisioned. And, if the IT strategy is implemented without sufficient business agreement, there will be constant discussions and pushbacks, also from the IT within the various business units, that question the usefulness of the concept.

Internal and External Factors Influencing Strategy

Figure 3.1 summarized the relationships between terms described above, including the factors that influence the strategy. Regarding external factors, strategy must be

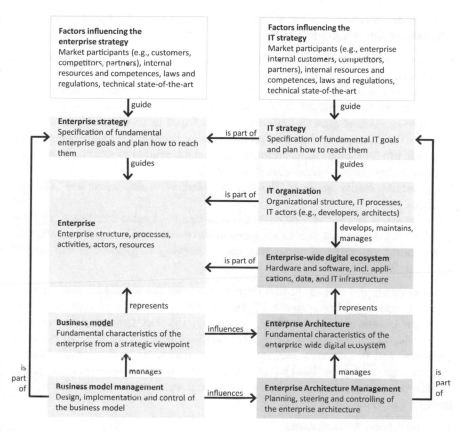

Fig. 3.1   Core concepts in the context of business strategy and EAM

based on the technical state of the art, laws and regulations, and the market participant that surround the industry and a specific enterprise, like customers, competitors, and partners. Regarding the internal factors, the available core competences and resources must be considered [cp. Prahalad and Hamel (1990)]. The factors influencing the overall IT strategy are similar to the ones influencing the overall enterprise strategy. However, in the case of an IT organization situated inside an enterprise, the customer is mainly the enterprise (though in large enterprises the internal IT organization might also provide services to other companies). From the perspective of enterprise strategy, the enterprise-wide IT digital ecosystem can be seen as an internal resource that confines the possibilities of the strategy. From the perspective of IT strategy, the enterprise-wide IT digital ecosystem and its development are the object of the strategy. We will describe these relationships further below in this chapter.

Business Model

A business model is a strongly abstracted representation of an enterprise with the purpose to describe the strategy of the enterprise, in particular, its relations with the environment and the value-adding mechanisms. This understanding is based on the following definitions:

- A business model "describes the rationale of how an organization creates, delivers, and captures value" (Osterwalder & Pigneur, 2010).
- A business model is "an abstract representation of an organization, be it conceptual, textual, and/or graphical, of all core interrelated architectural, co-operational, and financial arrangements designed and developed by an organization presently and in the future, as well all core products and/or services the organization offers, or will offer, based on these arrangements that are needed to achieve its strategic goals and objectives" (Al-Debei & Avison, 2010).
- A business model describes "the way an enterprise makes its money" (Scheer, 2016).
- In a business model, "in addition to the *architecture* of value creation, strategic as well as customer and market components are considered in order to realize the overriding objective of generating and preserving a *competitive advantage*" (Wirtz, 2018).

Osterwalder and Pigneur (2010) list nine elements that should be described in a business model: (1) key partners, (2) key activities, (3) key resources, (4) added value for customers/unique selling proposition, (5) cost structure, (6) customer relationships and customer retention, (7) customer access channels, (8) customer segments, and (9) revenue streams. Note that compared to the classic strategy concepts, the concept of "business model" is relatively new. However, it has gained in importance and today is considered by both academics and practitioners as relevant [cp. Wirtz (2018)].

Business Model Management

Figure 3.1 illustrates the proximity of the concepts "business model" and "Enterprise Architecture": both represent the fundamentals of an enterprise from a high-level, strategic perspective—the business model with the objective to manage the fundamental business strategy and the Enterprise Architecture with the objective to manage the fundamental characteristics of the enterprise-wide digital ecosystem. This proximity is also illustrated when Wirtz (2018) calls a business model the "architecture of value creation." Interestingly, he also describes the concept of "business model management," which he defines as follows: "business model management is an instrument for the governance of a company and comprises all target-oriented activities concerning the *design, implementation, modification and adaptation as well as the control of a business model*, in order to realize the principal objective of generating and securing competitive advantages."

Architecture vs. Strategy: Form Follows Function

Strategy and architecture both address the fundamental system characteristics. To illustrate this, an informal definition states that "architecture is about things difficult to change once implemented." Likewise, strategy has a high impact on a system, and the effects of an implemented strategy are hard to change as well.

Fig. 3.2 Not only in nature "architecture" and strategy are closely related. © From left: FOTOGRIN/Shutterstock, Gregory Wilson/Public Domain CC 3.0

Architecture can also be part of a strategy description: As mentioned above, strategy consists of knowing where you stand (baseline), a target picture, and a plan of how to get there. In the case of a business strategy, the baseline and the target picture can be described as the current and the future *business model*; for example, "today we focus on the European market, in three years we will have expanded globally." Similarly, an IT strategy can be expressed as a baseline *Enterprise Architecture model*, the model of the Enterprise Architecture in 3 years and the way of how to achieve this transformation.

Figure 3.2 illustrates the proximity of the concepts of architecture and strategy. The architecture of a turtle permits only slow movements but includes a heavy-weight shell that serves as defense mechanism. Corresponding to the "architecture" of its body, the survival strategy of the turtle is not to outrun assailants or to attack them, but to hide under its shell until the attacker is gone. The architecture of the cheetah on the other hand allows for high velocity but does not include significant shielding. So, with the architecture of a cheetah, it would be a bad strategy to stop moving when attacked and to wait until an assailant has vanished. Here, a better strategy is to outrun attackers as well as prey. Comparable to natural ecosystems, also for digital enterprise ecosystems goes: (1) there is a close relationship between architecture and strategy; (2) even in a defined environment, it is hard to derive the optimal strategy and architecture; and (3) instead of the one perfect solution, there might be various viable architectures and related strategies.

On the business side, the correlation of strategy and structure is a classic topic. Thus, Chandler (1962) argued that *structure follows strategy*, while later authors argued that *strategy follows structure* (Hall & Saias, 1980). Naturally, both are true, since strategy is supposed to guide the way for the enterprise based on the potential of the current enterprise structure. Note that Enterprise Architecture roughly translates to *structure* of the enterprise-wide digital ecosystem. Just like business strategy and business structure are two sides of the same coin, IT strategy and Enterprise Architecture are two sides of the same coin. In other words, managing the Enterprise Architecture (EAM) is part of the IT strategy.

3.2   Parameters of Business Strategy and Operations

Chapter 2 already described major parameters for configuring socio-technical systems. While these parameters focused on architecting the enterprise-wide digital ecosystem, in the following, we briefly examine the overarching strategic and operational parameters of an enterprise.

Porter's Generic Strategies: Cost or Quality, Complete or Niche Market
Figure 3.3a illustrates two classic strategy parameters that have been introduced by Porter (1985): On the one hand, a company must choose if it addresses the complete, industry-wide market or if it focuses and addresses only a certain part of the market. In EAM terminology, one could speak of the degree of specialization and generalization of the offered products. Are you going to develop a generalized "one-size-fits-all" product, which can be sold globally, industry-wide? Or will you specialize on certain requirements to satisfy a selected, local group? On the other hand, a company must choose between producing a solid, low-cost product and producing an outstanding high-quality product. The types reflect an orientation, but also quality leaders must take care of costs, and cost leaders must take care of quality and differentiation [cp. Porter (1985)].

Porter also described the *correlation between the generic strategies and technology strategy*. He stated that it depends on the business model where technical excellence and "leadership" or technical "followership" should be pursued: If the company pursues the strategy of *cost leadership*, it will seek technical leadership only in techniques for cost-effective production or cost-effective, directly value-adding activities. Technology that is related to the product quality, on the other hand, the enterprise will adopt from the market leaders to save research and development costs. For example, a car insurance that addresses the mass market will invest highly in process digitalization, to automate each of the simple, standardized processes as much as possible. Via this technology, the insurance can gain a competitive advantage in the industry. If the company pursues the strategy of *quality leadership and differentiation*, it will seek technical leadership in techniques for high-quality, unique products and services. It will also focus on indirect support activities and, if necessary, learn from market leaders to perfect the product.

Highly Individualized vs. Standardized Retail Products
Figure 3.3b illustrates that business models can differ in their degree of product customization and market scope, thus revisiting the fictional BEI insurance group shown in Fig. 1.4. The insurance industry serves to illustrate two extremes of product customization:

A property insurance or a car insurance is an example of a *retail business model*, where the same, *standard product* is sold without customization to millions of customers. A typical scenario is that the customer finds the products via the Internet, fills out some forms via the web site of the insurance company, and afterward digitally signs the insurance policy. The digital ecosystem of such a company is optimized for highly automated mass production and business process digitalization.

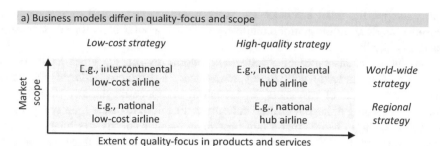

a) Business models differ in quality-focus and scope

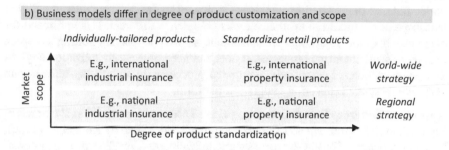

b) Business models differ in degree of product customization and scope

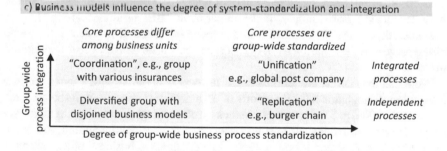

c) Business models influence the degree of system-standardization and -integration

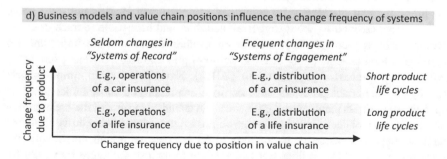

d) Business models and value chain positions influence the change frequency of systems

Fig. 3.3 Business model parameters as basis for the Enterprise Architecture

For example, the retail insurance company invests large amount of money in a bespoke application integration architecture to have a solid basis for cross-system process digitalization.

An industrial insurance or a reinsurance company, on the other hand, is an example of an industry with *highly customized, individually tailored products*. Instead of millions of customers, an industrial insurance maybe has 10,000 customers, consisting of large industrial enterprises that need to insure their companies. A typical scenario here is that a large car manufacturer already has long-standing relationships to the BEI industrial insurance. When the car manufacturer opens a new plant, it contacts the insurance. Now, over a process that takes several months, specialists from the BEI and the car manufacturer design and negotiate an insurance policy tailored to the specific situation. Compared to the car insurance, the digital landscape of the industrial insurance looks completely different: It is optimized for data, insights, and knowledge management as well as for supporting complex manual or semi-automatic processes. It does not need process digitalization engines that pump millions of completely automated processes through the systems nor an elaborate, bespoke application integration platform.

Ross et al.: Different Enterprise Areas Have Different Operational Parameters
Figure 3.3c shows four types of "operating models" identified by Ross et al. (2006), based on a matrix of business process standardization and business process integration. They understand the term *business process standardization* as "defining exactly how a process will be executed regardless of who is performing the process or where it is completed." For example, if the department "BEI Insurance group, human resources department in London" hires somebody, they follow exactly the same hiring process as the department "BEI Insurance group, human resources department in Paris."

Note that they define the term *business process integration* with a focus on *data* integration: "Integration links the efforts of organizational units through shared data" (Ross et al., 2006, p. 27). However, business process integration today has a broader scope: It refers to having all business processes dimensions integrated with each other across organizational boundaries, like departments, business units, or enterprises. To make this more tangible, if you start a business process in department A, the processes will seamlessly be continued in department B. It is not only about exchanging data but also about triggering activities and being able to trace to cross-cutting business process. Thus, besides data, other dimensions are important, for example, a joint understanding of cross-cutting rights and roles, business functions, and business processes [cp. Ziemann (2010)]. Nevertheless, this simple matrix conveys an important point: as an enterprise architect, you must understand the operational business parameters for the area—in technical terms, for the collection of systems—you architect. Even inside one company, you cannot necessarily apply the same strategic and operative parameters to all business units and domains of the company. For example, it does not make sense to impose the same standards for applications and IT infrastructure on all business units in a highly heterogenous, diversified corporation. In this setting, it neither makes sense to create a portfolio of complementary business applications across these business units.

Change Frequency and Rate of Innovation
Above, we already established that the change frequency and innovation frequency are important parameters for the digital ecosystem. Coming back to this point from a strategic, business perspective, Fig. 3.3d) shows an example of different areas of one enterprise, where each area has its own speed: If the lifecycle of a product is short, the IT systems that support this product will change often. Following this business agility, the digital ecosystem also needs to be designed for agility and frequent changes. As also expressed by Gartner's Pace Layering approach, the change velocity of digital system depends on their position in the value chain: Frontend systems change more frequently than backend systems. For example, the customer-facing portal of an insurance will change more often than the backend system for storing and managing insurance claims.

Gartner's Elements of Business Strategy Influencing IT Strategy
Gartner (Mack & Frey, 2002) described elements of the business strategy that the influence IT strategy, which partially overlap with the ones we described in the previous chapter:

- *Geographic:* In which nations is the enterprise allocated, and where should the IT be allocated?
- *Power structures:* This category, called "governance" by Gartner, addresses if the enterprise structure is centralized or decentralized and which other power structures exist. The (EAM) governance structure must consider the power structures inside the business.
- *Long-term thinking:* Does the enterprise plan far ahead into the future or does it only react to immediate events? In the latter case, it will be difficult to develop broadly scoped target pictures of the digital landscape.
- *Business agility*: Gartner dubbed this category "legacy IT" but describes it as the willingness or the need of the enterprise to change its business model and its business processes.
- *Integration with suppliers and customers:* If the company outsourced many services and relies heavily on B2B-partners, this induces the need for elaborate digital integration capabilities. Similarly, highly digitalized products and customer interaction require corresponding IT capabilities.
- *Funding:* As Gartner points out, in the end, the extent of any IT strategy is determined by the available funding. This impacts EAM, since the creation of strategic IT roadmaps is an EAM process. The possibility that such a roadmap will be funded increases the motivation of the involved stakeholders significantly.

COBIT's Parameters for Designing the IT Governance
COBIT describes a set of parameters for designing and optimizing an enterprise's IT governance system [cp. ISACA (2018)]. Since Enterprise Architecture Management represents an important part of this governance system, these so-called factors are also valuable for configuring the EAM capability. Above we already described some of the parameters that COBIT mentions here: risk profile, IT sourcing model, and

technology adoption model. In addition to that, COBIT describes the following parameters:

- *Enterprise strategy*: As introduced above, companies can pursue different strategies. COBIT names four strategy archetypes: focus on growth and revenue, focus on innovation and differentiation, focus on cost leadership, and focus on "stable and client-oriented service."
- *Current IT issues*: Here, current IT-related problems of the enterprise are listed. Examples from COBIT include frustration with IT due to perceived low business value, too many incidents, compliance issues, redundant activities, and an overly complex IT operating model.
- *Compliance requirements:* Depending on the industry and the geopolitical condition, the compliance requirements of an enterprise are classified either as high, medium, or low.
- *Role of IT:* This factor expresses the role of IT in the enterprise. If the company has a digital business model, i.e., a high percentage of core digital processes and products, the role of IT will be crucial. If the enterprise has a brick-and-mortar business model, the role of IT will be only supportive. COBIT distinguishes four roles: (1) *strategic*, where IT is crucial for running and innovating the companies' processes and services; (2) *turnaround*, where IT is a driver for innovation but not critical at all times for the operations; (3) *factory*, where IT needs to be continually available for operations but is not a driver for innovation; and (4) *support*, where IT is neither crucial for innovations nor for the business operations.
- *IT implementation methods*: Here COBIT names four classes:

  1. *Agile*—the enterprise uses agile software development.
  2. *DevOps*—the enterprise uses DevOps for building, deploying, and running systems.
  3. *Traditional*—the enterprise uses primarily waterfall methods and separates software development from operations.
  4. *Hybrid*—the enterprise uses a mix of traditional and modern methods.

Today, you will find few large enterprises that do *not* engage in agile and DevOps. However, at least until now, most enterprise did not switch completely and thus again fall in the "hybrid" category.

- *Company size*: COBIT defines two simple categories for the design of a company's governance system: "large-" and "small- and medium-sized enterprises."

3.3   Parameters of Enterprise Architecture Management

3.3.1   Changing Focus of EAM: EAM, Quo Vadis?

Current Influences by Cloud, Digitalization, the Agile Movement, and DevOps
Since the beginning of EAM around the year 2000, many articles have been written on how EAM should be improved or calibrated; since circa 2010, a lot of authors

have conveyed how "the new EAM" should become more "agile," "collaborative," and "adaptive," for instance, Bente et al. (2012), Korhonen et al. (2016), or Open Group (2020a). To get a first idea on EAM parameters, it is helpful to look at the development of EAM in practice: Not surprisingly, the state of California was one of the early adopters of EAM and published the first version of the Californian Enterprise Architecture Framework in 2003. In CEAF (2020a, p. 4), they described how EAM has developed since then in the state of California. Core points include:

- From enterprise-wide target pictures and roadmaps to area-specific target pictures and roadmaps.
- From infrastructure and technology standardization to portfolio rationalization and digital innovation opportunities.
- From domain and platform expertise toward cross-functional hybrid skill and "institutional learning".
- From overseeing project toward participation in projects ("consulting engagements").

The first reason for these developments can be seen in the proliferation of the *cloud*. On the one hand, the cloud turns many infrastructure and platform services into commodities; thus, decisions which infrastructure service to take become easier. Also, if the company infrastructure is provided by potentially many different cloud providers—instead of having to rely only on the one central enterprise data center—it is technically easier for individual enterprise areas to have their own, local portfolio of infrastructure services. Naturally, besides a rising enterprise-wide complexity, the downside here are the costs induced by lost economies of scale and scope that an enterprise-wide sourcing of a selected cloud services would enable. However, these costs will be lower than in pre-cloud times.

The second reason is the hyper-digitalization of the last years, which made IT everybody's business: Instead of obtaining technical innovations from one central department, the IT went closer to the local units, who need to digitalize their processes and products.

The third reason, for the developments described by CEAF, is closely connected to the previous two points: *agile* software development and *DevOps*. Both methods foster decentralization (empower the autonomous, local, pizza-sized team) and generalization (everybody is responsible for everything). Here also the abovementioned point of "institutional learning" fits in, which can be interpreted as collaborative, bottom-up knowledge management and organizational learning methods.

The Need for EAM Increases, but EAM Might Be More Decentralized
Does this mean that enterprise- or domain-wide architecture management is not needed anymore? Not at all. If you ask somebody working in the IT of a large enterprise with a significantly sized digital ecosystem, most probably, you will hear of a lacking global coordination and too much chaos, in the digital landscape as well as in the selection of current projects. And due to the increasing business digitalization, the enterprise-wide digital ecosystem becomes larger. At the same time, the

requirements for enterprise-wide, coherent 360-degree views, end-to-end business process digitalization as well as fast changes rise. This *increases the need for complexity management and architectural coordination*. This trend is also indicated by the amount of job advertisements for general enterprise architects or specialized technical domain architects (e.g., architects for enterprise-wide design of the identity and access management landscape), which in our observation increased significantly in the last years.

However, the mentioned technical and methodical macro trends induce a *stronger decentralized structure* of the enterprise-wide architecture capabilities and hence a *stronger focus on collaboration* inside the architecture community. Take, for example, our fictional use case of the BEI insurance group: In the year 2010, the group had one central EAM department that interacted directly with the solution architects of all business units. In addition, as small team for integration architecture was part of the EAM department. In 2020, the central EAM department still existed. However, each large business unit, e.g., for health insurance, car insurance, and industrial insurance, in addition had their own, business unit-specific architecture department. Moreover, large architecture domains, like integration architecture and middleware, have been carved out of the EAM department into independent services factories, where business owners, architects, developers, and operative administrators jointly produced the service of their domain. Other than for integration architecture, these were, for example, the domains of cloud, data analytics, and security. How did the central EAM department foster transparency and coherency among the output of these many specialized architects? On the one hand, with classic EAM artifacts, for instance, with overarching big pictures, principles, and reference architectures. On the other hand, with a stronger focus on community work, tools for joint knowledge management (Wiki), and collaboration tools for threaded conversations across department boundaries.

3.3.2 EAM Stereotypes: Who Am I and How Many?

Metaphors for the Role of the EAM Capability
In the endeavor of pinpointing the tasks of an enterprise architect in one picture, practitioners and scientist came up with several colorful metaphors. The brick-and-mortar analogy probably closest to Enterprise Architecture Management is the one of the *city planner* and the *landscape architect* (cp. Fig. 1.1). Further, EAM metaphors found in practice are:

- *Law enforcement*—ensuring that projects stick to architectural guidelines.
- *Forrester*—developing a (digital) ecosystem, in the sense of a managed evolution.
- *Technology preacher*—advocating and communicating architectural concepts.
- *Harbor pilot*—navigating projects through architectural knowledge and processes.

In a similar vein, Greefhorst and Proper (2011) distinguished between these roles:

- *Regulative*—a role that defines architectural guidance and supervises the compliance of architectural work.
- *Instructive*—a role that coaches and instructs stakeholder on how to apply architectural guidance.
- *Informative*—a role that merely informs stakeholders but does not regulate or coach.

Depending on the enterprise and the position of the EAM capability, architectural roles might lean toward either one of those stereotypes. However, in the practice of large companies, enterprise architects usually fulfill all three roles to varying degrees. Getting closer to a *collection of EAM activities*, Op't Land et al. (2009) provided the following list of EAM roles:

- Change agent (promoting innovations)
- Communicator (conveying architecture to stakeholders)
- Leader (leading in creating visions)
- Manager (of the EAM team)
- Modeler (depicting architectures)

In the next chapter, we will describe the individual tasks of an Enterprise Architect in detail.

Anti-patterns the EAM Capability Should Avoid

Complementary to the metaphors described above, EAM anti-patterns have been created. Note that these are exaggerated, extreme stereotypes—but in milder forms, such anti-patterns can be found in practice:

- *Fire fighter*, i.e., a situation where the architectural knowledge of the EAM capability is only used to undo damage and help in incidents or problem-related task forces.
- *Lost in the ivory tower with broken conveyer belts*: To be clear, there is nothing wrong with high-level strategies and corresponding IT target pictures. On the contrary, a coherent strategic picture for an effective and efficient digital ecosystem is extremely valuable—proven by the salaries of strategy consultants who also produce such artifacts. However, it gets problematic, if the architects creating these high-level concepts have a poor understanding of the operational situation "on the ground" as a basis for creating a strategy. It is also a problem, if the strategy does make sense, but never gets conveyed to the organization, put into the project portfolio, implemented in projects, and evaluated afterward.
- *Bureau for the protection of historic sites*: A core EAM task is to keep complexity and costs low by ensuring that not too many new, redundant product types are bought. However, if this is overdone and not enough new standards are coming in, the innovativeness of the digital ecosystem will suffer. Thus, instead of sticking too long with legacy standards, EAM needs to foster innovations to the right degree and support systematic end-of-life management to replace outdated systems and standards.

- *Technology chaser*: On the other hand, architects should not jump on every new, "hot" technology trend, just because a technology works in some famous digital company. At least when it comes to larger investments and architectural decisions with a large impact on the IT landscape, the technology must be well-understood, and it must fit to the business requirements and the digital ecosystem of the enterprise.

3.3.3   Collections of EAM Parameters

Compared to the amount of literature on Enterprise Architecture modeling frameworks, literature on configuring the Enterprise Architecture Management capability via a thorough system of parameters is scarce. As mentioned above, such parameters are highly relevant in the practice of an EAM department: EAM has only been around since ca. two decades. In this time, EAM departments often had to explain the position and effectiveness of this new capability; and, in synchronization with IT trends like centralization and decentralization, managers had to adjust the position of the EAM department inside the enterprise. In the following, we sketch out exemplary approaches that provide collections of EAM parameters.

Foundational EAM Parameters
Aier et al. (2012) described five basic parameters for designing the EAM capability, independent of contemporary trends like "agile" or "collaborative EAM":

- *Scope* refers to the architecture domains covered (e.g., business architecture, application architecture, cloud architecture).
- *Level of detail* refers to the depth of architectural work, e.g., if the whole enterprise is addressed in a high-level roadmap, if also enterprise segments are addressed, or if also individual systems are addressed.
- *Requirements management:* Here they distinguish two extremes: In the stakeholder-driven, reactive "outside-in" approach, EAM only addresses those aspects explicitly asked for by stakeholders. In the seemingly more proactive, "inside-out" approach, an EAM approach is first defined, and afterward, usage scenarios for EAM are sought. In practice, this distinction is difficult. Naturally, EAM needs to be stakeholder driven. The question is rather: by which stakeholders? The most important one should be the CIO, who has an interest in an effective and efficient enterprise-wide digital ecosystem. On the other hand, in the turbulent reality of large enterprises, often ad hoc, short-term requirements from local stakeholders must be balanced with the centrally mandated, rather long-term EAM tasks for developing the enterprise-wide digital ecosystem.
- *Impact*: Here they distinguish between a "passive" and an "active" EAM approach. In the passive approach, EAM mainly collects information and established transparency. In the active approach, EAM, for example, defines and enforces architecture principles as well as roadmaps and target pictures.

- *Allocation* refers to the organizational position of the EAM capability. For example, it could be allocated directly below the CIO. However, today, in most large enterprises, EAM follows a federated approach, where EAM is spread over various decentral departments complemented by one central EAM department.

EAM Parameters in the Context of Agile Architecture

In the quest of defining the rather vague term "Agile Enterprise Architecture," Kotusev (2020) proposed six dimensions in EAM capabilities. Slightly adapted, these comprise:

- *Strategic planning.* This refers to the degree that the EAM capability engages in strategic planning, for example, in the specification of long-term target pictures and roadmaps. In this dimension, Kotusev describes four sub-categories:

  (a) The time and effort the capability devotes to strategic planning
  (b) The organizational scope covered by strategic planning, e.g., only the core business or the complete enterprise
  (c) The horizon of strategic planning, e.g., 1 year, 2 years, or 5 years
  (d) The level of detail of the target picture, e.g., only a coarse-grained idea or a detail-level concept

- *"Initiative delivery."* This refers to the process of developing individual IT solutions, thereby touching the core of agile software development. Here two dimensions are relevant: first, how iterative the process is, e.g., a strictly sequential, waterfall process without iterations or a highly iterative process typical for agile methods, and second, the volume of EA artifacts developed in the process, referring to both the quantity of the artifacts and their detail level.
- *Finance allocation and budgeting process.* This point is related to the planning horizon and describes in which periods budget needs to be planned in the enterprise. Is the company investing only ad hoc, responding to immediate outside events? Or are the investments rather carefully planned long ahead? Is there a yearly budgeting process, or is there a continuous budgeting process, that allows for new investments all through the year? Note that in addition to these points provided by Kotusev, it is not only relevant *when* but also from *where* the budget comes: Is there one central IT budget that the CIO can distribute at his will? Or are there decentral IT budgets at each local business segment? In the latter case, it will be difficult for EAM to steer investments in a direction that sustainably optimizes the *enterprise-wide* digital ecosystem.
- *Rigidity of architectural governance.* Here, two aspects are named:

  1. The *formality of decision-making processes*: Are architecture decisions reached via formal processes and architecture panels or through informal, bilateral agreements?
  2. The *enforcement of decisions*: Are the architecture decisions, including, for example, guidelines and standards, enforced and exceptions granted only scarcely? Or are architectural decision merely vague references, hardly relevant for projects?

- *"Architecture function."* This refers to the *size and permeation of the architecture capability*. Note that when addressing the EAM size, not only the architects directly in the EAM department count but also the architects distributed across the enterprise, i.e., domain architects, segment architects, and solution architects. According to Kotusev, this size varies between 1% and 2% up to 6–8% of the IT headcount. Obviously related to that is the extent to which architects participate in projects: Are only architectural critical projects endowed with architects, or does every project of a significant size have an architect? In practice, every project with a mentionable complexity will have an architect (though maybe bequeathed with a different role name). However, that does not mean that the central EAM department is connected to this architect or is aware of the architectural activities of it.
- *"Standardization"* here refers to the *granularity of architectural guidance* and the "depth" of the architecture activities: According to Kotusev, some enterprises develop comprehensive standards capturing every technology, pattern, and guideline, while other companies focus on a few core standards, like vendors and major products. Clearly, for a central EAM department with limited resources, it makes sense to focus on selected architecture aspects or on a defined depth, instead of trying to provide fine-grained architectural guidance for all possible aspects of the digital ecosystem. A second question is which aspects in which level of detail are covered by the decentral architects—including, for example, architects responsible for certain business domains or technologies. However, in the end, "standardization" addresses the classic EAM topic of "how much freedom is provided to development projects" versus "how constraint are the projects by the need to use defined standards."

EAM Parameters in the Context of Collaborative EAM

Preceding the above-described parameters from Kotusv, Bente et al. (2012, p. 14) described four parameters in the context of "collaborative" EAM:

- *"Perspective."* This category again refers to the *depth of architectural work*. Does the architecture work focus on the enterprise level, where target pictures of enterprise-wide concerns and corresponding high-level roadmaps are created? Does it focus on large business domains on the segment level or on the solution level? Related to this is the question to which degree enterprise architects are involved in projects that address individual systems.
- *"Governance."* With this point, Bente et al. refer to the *degree of creative freedom in the decentral capabilities*, i.e., the local departments and projects for solution development. Obviously, this depends (a) on the quantity and quality of architectural guidance produced by a central EAM capability and (b) on the rigidity in which compliance to the guidance is enforced.
- *"Strategy."* With this criterion, they address two aspects: First is the depth of architectural work, i.e., the quantity in which the EAM capability addresses the level of enterprise-wide target pictures and roadmaps. The second aspect refers to the time horizon of these roadmaps, i.e., if long-term plans are made or "there is

no long-term planning at all." The risk of having plans too far in the future and of engaging too much in strategy while neglecting the operational level is that the EAM capability loses contact to reality and gets lost in the ivory tower.

- *"Transformation."* This criterion refers to the *change frequency of the digital ecosystem.* If the IT landscape changes too often, it can become a chaotic "permanent construction site," where the multitude of changes does not form a coherent picture anymore. If the changes initiated by the enterprise architects are too few and too slow for the business requirements, the local business departments might enter the driver seat and plan changes of the digital ecosystem without the architects.

3.3.4 Additional Individual EAM Parameters

Culture in the Enterprise and the IT Organization

Clearly, the formal, "hard" EAM parameters must be tailored to a specific enterprise. Such factors are, for instance, the scope of EAM, the shape of the formal EAM processes, and the allocation of the EAM department. However, the informal, "soft" EAM parameters and their fitting to the organization are highly relevant for the success of EAM as well [cp. also Lange et al. (2016)]. The most prominent example of such a "soft" factor is culture.

In the context of sociology, culture is defined as "the way of life of particular people, especially as shown in their ordinary behavior and habits, their attitudes toward each other, and their moral and religious beliefs." In the context of the workplace, culture is defined as "the ideas and ways of working that are typical for an organization, and that affect how it does business and how its employees behave" (Cambridge, 2021a). Above, we described the example of a manager threatening to fire everybody who does not follow the integration architecture guidelines of the enterprise. It is safe to assume that the viability of such behavior depends on the culture of the enterprise. Generally, enterprise architects must be highly aware of the enterprise culture, because they must steer a significant part of the enterprise and in this endeavor must interact with a broad range of stakeholders and interests, from high-ranking managers and project leads, who protect their local interests, to software engineers, who appreciate support but do not want to be restricted in their creativity. And if a strategic EAM target picture does not fit to the enterprise culture, Peter Drucker's famous proverb comes into play: "culture eats strategy for breakfast."

Accordingly, the subject of culture in the context of EAM has been addressed by various authors. Aier (2014), for example, proposed two dimensions for distinguishing different types of culture: (1) the degree to which an enterprise is open for change or rather prefers stability and (2) the degree to which an enterprise is seeking exchange with external influences or rather sticks to internal resources.

Buckl (2011, p. 276) on the other hand differentiated four types of culture in the context of EAM:

- *Open culture*, where the company is open for transparency and change induced by the EAM capability
- *"Political" culture,* where local stakeholders fear negative repercussions through enterprise-wide transparency and enterprise-wide optimization induced by EAM
- *Culture of negative feedback*, where management strictly enforces its mandates via control and the threat of punishment
- *Culture of positive feedback*, where management control is not as fine-grained and is realized primarily through positive incentives to motivate employees

The last two points address the classic business administration topic of leadership style. Here, already Wöhe (1996, p. 133) distinguished between patriarchalic, charismatic, autocratic, bureaucratic, and cooperative leadership styles. For a more detailed discussion of culture in the context of EAM, refer to Rao et al. (2018).

Different Forms of Power Distribution
Clearly, the EAM department and its processes must be aligned to the processes and mechanisms by which the business departments finance their IT. Imagine the following situation: You are an enterprise architect positioned in the enterprise headquarter and responsible for the group-wide harmonization of IT solutions. However, the business units fund their local IT decentrally, i.e., there is no central, group-wide IT budget. In this case, it will be difficult for you to convince the local IT department to follow the group-wide standards: In case the local business owners prefer a deviating solution, this most probably will be implemented, due to the power of the local funding. As discussed before, in this context, major parameters for the distribution of power are centralization vs. decentralization (is the budget concentrated or distributed?) and integration vs. autonomy (do the parts of the enterprise have to work closely together, or can they be technically isolated from each other?). In a similar vein, Broadbent and Kitzis (2005, p. 114) distinguished six different "governance styles": business monarchy, IT monarchy, feudal style, federal style, duopoly, and anarchy. The reasoning behind these types again boils down to a matrix of two dimensions:

1. Are architectural decisions regarding the digital ecosystem taken in the business, in IT, or in both?
2. Is the company structure centralized or decentralized?

Different Altitudes: Strategic and Operational, Core and Supporting Processes
It is an old discussion, in how far EAM should address the strategic development of the enterprise-wide digital ecosystem or engage with a "hands-on" mentality in the machine room of IT, delving deep into the details of individual solutions and technologies. In this vein, already Niemann (2006, p. 23) pointed out that EAM

has an operational and a strategic dimension. Of course, as illustrated in Fig. 4.8, EAM needs to address all levels and dimensions of the enterprise-wide digital ecosystem.

How does the practice look like? In our experience, in large, decentralized enterprises, the central EAM department focuses on supporting projects for large digital solutions, leading selected architecture domains (e.g., enterprise-wide integration architecture), leading architecture compliance checks, managing the IT asset inventory, and maintaining architectural guidance (e.g., principles and reference architectures) and standards. The creation of strategic enterprise-wide target pictures and roadmaps is also part of the EAM department's task, but, compared to the other activities, a rather seldom one.

So, one question is on which of the vertical levels (Fig. 4.8) the central EAM department should focus on. A related question is if the central EAM department should focus on the core EAM processes (envision, specify, implement, evaluate architecture) or rather on the supporting processes (cp. Fig. 4.9). In large, decentralized enterprises, where the *decentral* business and technical architects create the target picture for their segments and domains, the central EAM department might very well prioritize the supporting EAM processes and leave the majority of the core processes to the adjacent architecture departments.

Different Weight Classes: Lean and Agile EAM
Similar to "agile EAM," "lean EAM" is propagated since a couple of years. Thus, Bente et al. (2012, p. 175) proposed to apply the principles from lean management to EAM, including, for example, the principle of "eliminate waste." Now, when does it make sense to have a lean EAM capability? The answer is of course: Always. Like for all management disciplines, also for EAM goes that it should be as lean as possible and as extensive as necessary. The more constructive question is how "lean" exactly EAM should be and which extent it should have. Unfortunately, there is no easy answer to that. Instead, we must look at the specific enterprise, its strategic and operative parameters (including the complexity of the digital ecosystem), tailor the parameters of the EAM capability, and define which processes, roles, artifacts, and tools are needed. Note that the parameters we described above implicitly addressed lean EAM already, i.e., in the parameters addressing the *size and permeation of the architecture capability*. More concretely, the following parameters influence the extent of EAM:

- *Strong decentralization*: If the architecture work is primarily done in decentral business units and cross-cutting service factories that address technical architecture domains, the central EAM team can be smaller.
- *Bottom-up standards development:* If enterprise-wide standards are developed decentrally, fewer central EAM work is needed.
- *Low enterprise-wide standardization*: If the enterprise engages rather in a laissez-faire approach, fewer processes and artifacts for enterprise-wide standardization are needed.

- *Short planning horizons*: If the enterprise mainly reacts to real-time events and does not plan far ahead, fewer strategic roadmaps are needed.

The last point illustrates that "lean" is related to agility and emergent systems in fast-changing environments, where long-term plans do not make sense. Regarding such emergent environments, Rao et al. (2018) stated that the "Enterprise Architecture in such enterprises serves as a knowledgebase for option exposure and exploration rather than as a compass for transformation planning. Architecting is performed on the things that matter, rather than attempting a comprehensive representation of every aspect of the enterprise." Note that the last sentence should apply not only to highly dynamic enterprises but to every enterprise.

Another question is if by "lean EAM" we only refer to the central EAM department or also to the decentral architecture activities which significantly influence the enterprise-wide digital ecosystem. This is relevant because today EAM usually is an interplay of central and decentralized architecture capabilities. For example, the central EAM capability could focus on the supporting EAM processes (cp. Fig. 4.9), on standardization, and on the demand-driven creation of *enterprise-wide* target pictures. Other guidance, like *domain-wide target pictures* and corresponding IT roadmaps, would be the responsibility of the decentral architects.

Different Standardization Directions: Top-Down vs. Bottom-Up
In the context of EAM, "top-down" and "bottom-up" have at least two meanings: In the first meaning, top-down refers to business-driven EAM approach, and bottom-up to a technology-driven EAM approach [e.g., Ahlemann et al. (2011, p. 67)]. The second meaning, described, for example, by Rao et al. (2018), is practically more relevant: Here, top-down means that guidance on enterprise-wide architecture is pushed from the central EAM department to all other, decentral architecture capabilities. Bottom-up on the other hand means that the enterprise-wide architecture is a collection of the products developed by all decentral architecture capabilities. The reality in large enterprise is a mix between both, which Rao et al. called "middle-out" approach. The central EAM capability must, for example, ensure the right degree of standardization vs. redundancy and provide a "big picture" as well as constraints to the decentral architecture departments. The other side of the coin is that the architects in decentral business units and technical domain architects are experts for their domains and thus also have a say in the enterprise-wide standards for such domains. To make this more tangible, imagine the five big business units of the BEI insurance had their own architects for business analytics. Unfortunately, these five architects would each like to use a different product from a different vendor for the service "data lakes" in their business unit. In consequence, the central EAM selects two from the five products and declared those as acceptable standards in the group. This allows for a certain redundancy while at the same time enabling economies of scale and scope.

3.3.5   Synthesis of EAM Parameters

Based on the previous sections, Tables 3.1 and 3.2 summarize the strategic and tactical parameters that influence EAM. The overview again highlights that the organizational ecosystem and the digital ecosystem are shaped by similar parameters. This proximity must be used when aligning the parameters of the EAM capability with the parameters of the enterprise, the digital ecosystem, and the IT organization. For example:

- When the enterprise and the IT organization are structured in a highly decentral way, then the EAM capability should have a decentral structure as well. For instance, there could be dedicated EAM departments for each business unit.
- If business processes and products are highly standardized throughout the enterprise, then EAM must have a strong focus on standardizing the corresponding elements of the digital ecosystem. For example, if inside an aviation group, the processes in three airlines (e.g., Austrian, Swiss, German) are the same, then it is easy to install the same IT products in each airline.
- If the priority of the enterprise is to have highly integrated, fast enterprise-wide processes, then a central EAM department must enforce rigid standards for the enterprise-wide integration of data and applications, for instance, an integrated data model, standardized APIs, and standardized communication platforms.

Table 3.1 Overview of Business Parameters Influencing EAM

Strategic business parameters	• *Cost* or *quality* focus • *Extend*, e.g., complete market or niche market • *Digitalization*, e.g., digital or traditional business model • *Risk* and *compliance*, e.g., extent of regulations and security requirements • *Culture*, e.g., authoritative or collaborative culture • *Strategic agility*, e.g., fast changing or rather constant business model
Operational business parameters	• *Location, distribution, size, complexity* and *age* of the enterprise and its product portfolio and processes • *Centralization, standardization* and *integration* degree of enterprise-wide business processes, functions, data, roles and rights • *Digitalization*, e.g., extend and importance of digital business processes, and *technological innovativeness* • Requirements regarding *risk, security, stability*, and *availability* • *Operational agility*, i.e., change frequency of products and processes • *Major issues* that need immediate attention, e.g., instable systems

Table 3.2 Overview of IT Parameters Influencing EAM

Parameters of the enterprise architecture and the digital ecosystem	• *Location, distribution, size, complexity* and *age* of the digital ecosystem • *Centralization, standardization*, and *integration* degree inside the digital ecosystem; *heterogeneity,* e.g., "best-of-breed" versus single-product focus • *Specialization*, e.g., degree of off-the-shelf products vs. customized products • *Sourcing policy*, e.g., rate of "buy" vs. "make" products • *Agility* and *change frequency* of the digital ecosystem • *Cost or quality* focus regarding digital systems, as well as requirements regarding *risk, security, stability*, and *availability*
Parameters of the IT organization	• *Role* of the IT (e.g., strategic or supporting) • *Culture* in the IT organization, e.g., authoritative or collaborative culture • *Location, distribution, size, complexity* and *maturity* of the IT organization • *Centralization, standardization*, and *integration* degree of the IT capabilities, *IT structure*, e.g., business function-oriented or IT-function-oriented, *IT-budget distribution*, e.g., via central IT or decentral business units • *Long-term planning* or rather ad-hoc reactive IT-organization • *Primary development paradigm*, e.g., rather waterfall or agile • *Vendor policy*, e.g., "best-of-breed" sourcing versus single-vendor focus • *IT service sourcing-level*, e.g., mainly outsourced or mainly in-house IT functions
Parameters of the EAM capability	• *Location, distribution, size* and *maturity* of EAM capability • Quality of *complementary capabilities* (e.g., purchasing, portfolio management) • *EAM breadth, depth*, and *horizon* (e.g., focus on long-term planning) • *Centralization, standardization*, and *integration* of EAM capabilities • *Top-down* or bottom-up architectural work • *Rigidity* and *formality* of architectural guidance and compliance checks • *Prioritized architecture goals*, e.g., focusing on agility, innovation, quality, costs, stability or security in the enterprise architecture • *EAM service portfolio*, e.g., focusing on EAM core or supporting processes

3.4   Structure and Capabilities of the IT Organization

The sections before addressed the alignment of the parameters of the enterprise, the digital ecosystem, the IT organization, and the EAM capability. When such basic parameters and requirements are clarified, the question arises: Which functions and processes does the EAM capability exactly fulfil, and which functions are realized by adjacent departments in the IT organization? Addressing this point, the coming sections describe the IT organization, its possible structures, and the capabilities adjacent to EAM.

No Matter How You Distribute Them, You Always Need the Same IT Functions
As described above, the shape of EAM inside an enterprise also depends on the shape of the IT organization in the enterprise. Now, the paradigms for structuring the IT in organizations change over the years; most notably, the pendulum swings back and forth between centralization vs. decentralization and outsourcing vs. insourcing. However, despite changing fashions for structuring the IT organization, the functions needed inside this organization roughly remain the same:

- *System management:* Digital systems need to be planned, built, and run (operated and maintained).
- *IT landscape, individual applications, and infrastructure elements:* The abovementioned management functions need to be applied to the overall digital ecosystem, the individual applications, and the infrastructure elements that provide services to the applications.
- *Business unit-specific IT functions:* The above-described functions must be provided to fulfill the requirements of each individual business unit.

To make this more tangible, imagine an insurance with 10,000 employees, including 2000 employees working in IT. This IT is clustered into three large units:

- *IT strategy and governance:* In this unit, the overall IT organization and the complete digital ecosystem are managed to ensure an effective and efficient delivery of IT services. On a very high level, also this area can be structured into the lifecycle phases of planning, building, and running the complete IT. However, in contrast to an application, for the overall IT, the "run" phase does not merely translate to operations and maintenance; here, the focus is rather on evaluating the performance of the landscape to start initiating another plan-build-run lifecycle. Below, we will describe the various capabilities of this area (e.g., demand management, IT strategy, IT portfolio management, purchasing, license management, IT controlling, IT process management, and EAM).
- *IT application services:* This unit takes care of the complete application lifecycle. At the start of the lifecycle, new business applications are planned and developed. If the business demands a new application, this unit receives the corresponding requirements and builds a suitable application. Traditionally, this means programming a new application; today, it increasingly means to customize and integrate a cloud-based SaaS application. *Application management* is the runtime

counterpart of the application development capability. Here, for example, the application owner keeps track of the functional and non-functional performance of her application and keeps a backlog of items to be implemented.

- *IT infrastructure services:* This unit takes care of the complete infrastructure lifecycle. Applications need some infrastructure to run on, like servers, databases, and networks. Corresponding to the "plan" and "build" phases, here this unit *provides* the infrastructure needed by the applications. Traditionally, this means, for example, that a server is provided in the data center of the enterprise. Today, this infrastructure could also be sourced more flexibly as a cloud-based PaaS or IaaS service from a third party. If the IT functions are structured along the plan-built-run lifecycle, IT infrastructure operations belong to the *run* part. This function, also called *infrastructure management*, is the runtime counterpart of infrastructure provisioning. Now the systems are "live," staged in the production environment, and end users can work with them. The goal of infrastructure management is to ensure that the systems remain productive, for example, by handling incidents. Therefore, it keeps track of the infrastructure performance and initiates changes if needed.

3.4.1 Centralized or Decentralized Allocation of IT Functions

Figures 3.4, 3.5, and 3.6 illustrate typical ways of shaping the IT organization to address the functions described above; we will describe those stereotypes briefly in the following.

The first is a *highly centralized* scenario where all business units share the same central IT functions. All business units share one unit for IT strategy and governance, including, for example, demand management, project portfolio management, and IT governance. They also share the units for applications and infrastructure services.

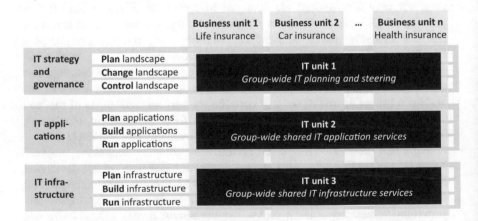

Fig. 3.4 Centralized IT functions are shared by business units

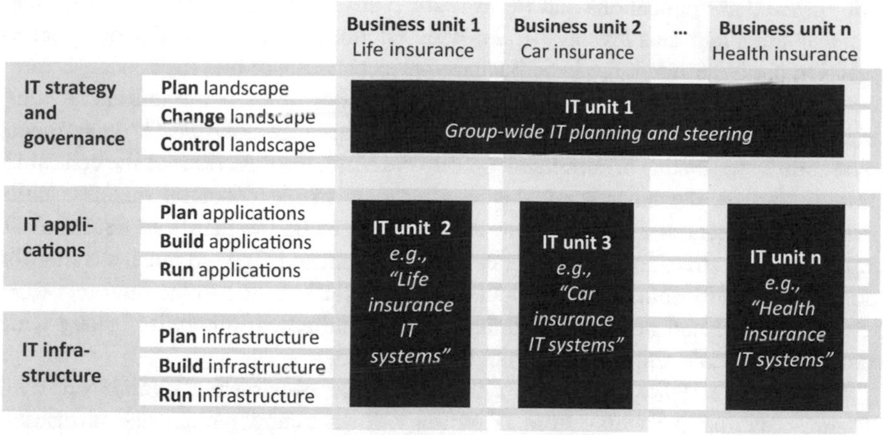

		Business unit 1 Life insurance	Business unit 2 Car insurance	...	Business unit n Health insurance	
IT strategy and governance	**Plan** landscape		IT unit 1			
	Change landscape		*Group-wide IT planning and steering*			
	Control landscape					
IT appli- cations	**Plan** applications	IT unit 2 *e.g.,* *"Life* *insurance* *IT* *systems"*	IT unit 3 *e.g.,* *"Car* *insurance* *IT systems"*		IT unit n *e.g.,* *"Health* *insurance* *IT systems"*	
	Build applications					
	Run applications					
IT infra- structure	**Plan** infrastructure					
	Build infrastructure					
	Run infrastructure					

Fig. 3.5 Decentral IT units steered by a central IT governance

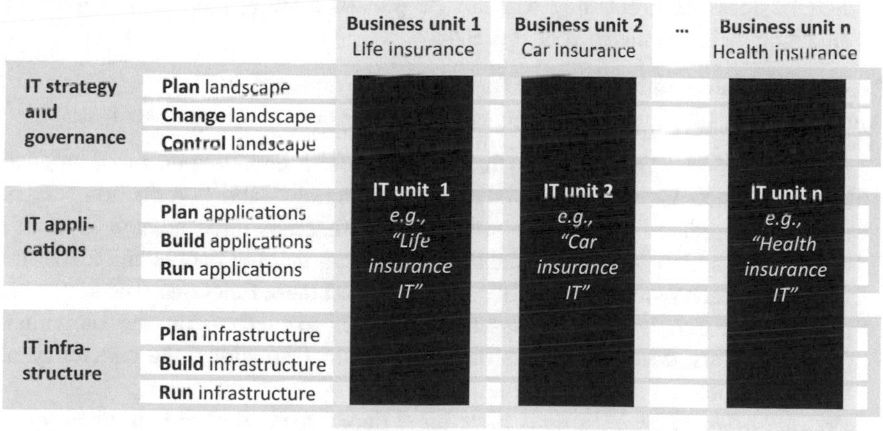

		Business unit 1 Life insurance	Business unit 2 Car insurance	...	Business unit n Health insurance	
IT strategy and governance	**Plan** landscape					
	Change landscape					
	Control landscape					
IT appli- cations	**Plan** applications	IT unit 1 *e.g.,* *"Life* *insurance* *IT"*	IT unit 2 *e.g.,* *"Car* *insurance* *IT"*		IT unit n *e.g.,* *"Health* *insurance* *IT"*	
	Build applications					
	Run applications					
IT infra- structure	**Plan** infrastructure					
	Build infrastructure					
	Run infrastructure					

Fig. 3.6 Completely decentral, decoupled IT units

The benefits of this model are high economies of scale and scope. There are few frictions inside the IT functions since the chains of command remain in one unit (the central IT unit) and are easy to understand. On the downside, we have the risk of a lower sensitivity to requirements of the decentral business units. This usually leads to a feeling of "the central IT does not provide what the business units need," and elaborate demand-supply organizations must be installed to compensate this.

The second is a *federated approach*: one central unit for IT strategy steers the decentral units for individual applications and infrastructure elements allocated at the business units. Thus, economies of scale and scope occur primarily in the IT strategy unit. However, if the EAM department allocated in this central unit performs well, it will ensure that applications and infrastructure are harmonized across the different business units and thus leverage group-wide economies of scale and scope here as well. On the other hand, the local business units can ensure that their local requirements are realized at their local IT department responsible for the individual solutions. Unfortunately, in practice, frictions occur, because now the IT departments must follow two chains of command: on the one hand, the directions of the central IT strategy and on the other hand, the requirements of the decentral business units owning the decentral IT department. And it tends to be the nature of decentral IT departments to strive for independence from the central IT governance, striving for more power and resources for the local leaders. Frictions due to the dual reporting between central and decentral IT units must be addressed; otherwise, group-wide economies of scale and scope will not be leveraged.

The third is a *highly decentralized* scenario. Here, each business unit has its own IT unit, covering everything from IT strategy down to applications and infrastructure. No group-wide economies of scale and scope can be leveraged, but the digitalization departments are close to the business requirements. The employees in the IT organization will be deeply knowledgeable about the requirements specific to their business unit; but they will not be part of a large, more professional IT organization as in the scenario of Fig. 3.4.

Product-Oriented and Function-Oriented IT Organizations

Already Scheer (2000, p. 8) distinguished two types of enterprise structures:

- *Function-oriented organizations* have large central departments for individual business functions, like "sales," "product planning," and "production." Each individual product runs through these generic functions. The advantage of this approach is a high "resource efficiency," meaning that the people and machines working in each function are highly specialized on these functions. The downside of this approach is that the resources are *not* specialized on the individual products. Thus, due to the focus on the individual functions, the coherency of the overall product is jeopardized.
- *Product-oriented organizations* have large departments for the individual products, and each organization has its own sub-departments for the core functions (sales, product planning, and production). The advantage of this approach is a high product efficiency, meaning that the people and machines working in the departments are highly specialized on the quality of the individual product types. The downside here is that the resources are *not* specialized on the individual functions. The risk is that due to the focus on the product, the individual functions do not reach a sufficient level of professionalization and efficiency.

While Scheer described this regarding the business structure of an enterprise (arguing for coherent business processes and value streams), the same mechanisms apply to the structure of IT organizations:

Around the year 2010, IT functions were rather centralized to leverage economies of scale, like shown in Fig. 3.4. This led to a high level of specialization and professionalization of the individual digitalization functions, like planning, developing, and operating IT systems. Typically, the infrastructure was centralized in one large data center, either company-owned or outsourced. This functional orientation came with a price: The coherence and the quality of an individual digital product X suffered, because the individual production functions were not tailored to product X but generalized to fulfill the requirements of many different products (Y, Z, etc.).

Motivated by the digital business disruptions to efficiently create high-quality IT products in an agile manner, *in the last decade, enterprise IT has been rather product-oriented*, resulting in decoupled development pipelines for each product or each segment. The pendulum swung to highly integrated digitalization pipelines close to the local business units, and IT functions were rather decentralized (cp. Figs. 3.5 and 3.6). On the one hand, this supported a close connection between the requirements of the local business units and their implementation. But with the *DevOps movement*, not only the chain of requirement-to-build but also the chain of build-to-run was focused. To enable fast deployments and to ensure that runtime requirements were regarded stronger in the development phase, the developers (build) and the IT operators (run) were stronger connected with each other or even part of the same "pizza-sized" team.

Figure 3.7 details the previous coarse-grained pictures and shows the individual IT products delivered in every segment of the enterprise. Agile organizational models like the Spotify model or the SAFe model (SAFE, 2020) are product oriented. Here, the coherency and completeness of the individual teams are the priority, while cross-cutting functions and enterprise-wide economies of scale are less important. In the example of Fig. 3.7, in a *product-oriented enterprise*, the business area of "policy management" does not only provide the requirements but also owns the IT resources for architecting, specifying, implementing, and operating the digital ecosystem of the area. In a *function-oriented enterprise*, the technical function of "implementation" would be bundled inside one large department for "application development" that fulfils this function not only for one business area but for all business areas (sales and marketing, policy management, claims management, etc.) and possibly also for the rather technical areas (e.g., process digitalization and integration platform).

Agile Speedboats and Slow Tankers
Yet another way of clustering the IT is the *bimodal IT* model, also known as two-speed IT. The term bimodal IT was established by Gartner in the context of digital business transformation and distinguishes two "modes" of IT: Mode 1 comprises IT that needs to be predictable and stable and is well-established. Here, innovation does happen, but in an iterative, evolutionary way. Mode 2 addresses fundamentally new functions that need to be "explored"; here, innovation has a rather revolutionary character [cp. Gartner (2021a)].

A similar approach, also from Gartner, is *Pace Layering*. The idea here is simply to cluster applications according to the "pace" in which they change. And it does make a difference—especially for EAM processes—if a digitalized function must

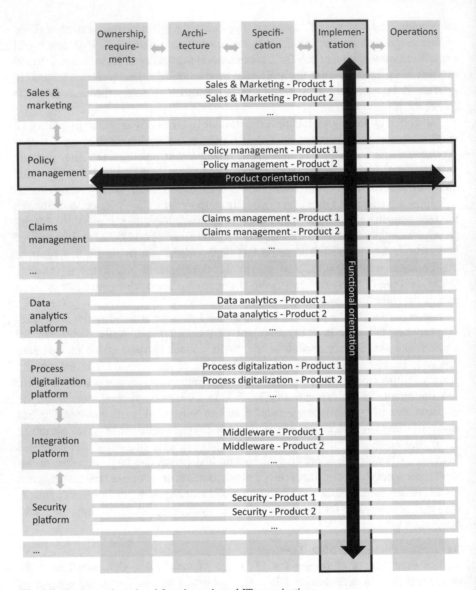

Fig. 3.7 Product-oriented and function-oriented IT organizations

change very often, sometimes, or very seldomly. Gartner labeled these three modes as follows:

- *Systems of innovation* are designed to support new innovative business models and experimental technologies. Today, examples for this would be the introduction of a prototype for artificial intelligence, which is built outside the ecosystem of the existing IT to produce fast a "minimum viable product." Hence, here, the leading architecture principle is *speed before stability*. An enterprise architect who tries to impose principles of long-term stability and reuse to this kind of systems is fighting a losing battle.

- *Systems of differentiation* provide a unique functionality and ensure the competitive advantage of the company. They are constantly changing to support the uniqueness of the company. To enable the fast connection of these systems with other system, they need to be highly interoperable. An example for this would be the customer-facing portal of a large airline.
- *Systems of record* implement basic and standardized business processes, for example, via standard software systems. The evolution of these systems takes place slowly and with rather few release cycles. The leading architecture principle here is *stability before speed*. An example for an application in this category is the contract management of a life insurance, which needs to endure many decades and needs to be highly reliable [cp. Mangi et al. (2017)].

Going beyond that, an endless number of permutations and adaptions of these basic patterns exist in real-life enterprises, providing strategy consultants all couple of years the opportunity to implement a new IT organization design.

3.4.2   Managing Individual Elements and Portfolios

Before getting to concrete structures of the enterprise IT, it is helpful to understand a core capability in the context of EAM: managing portfolios of IT elements. The word capability here implies that these functions can be allocated in one dedicated department, but they can also be less prominently allocated as a subfunction in another unit. For example, the capability "application portfolio management" could have a corresponding organizational unit of the same name, but it could also be only one task in an organizational unit called "Application Services Steering."

Portfolios in the Context of EAM

A portfolio is the complete, optimized collection of assets owned by a person or an organization. These assets could be the services a company offers, the shares owned by one person, or the digital technologies owned by one enterprise. An optimized portfolio is often associated with the adjectives "balanced" and "diversified." And in the context of business strategy, a portfolio is often displayed in a matrix, e.g., the *BCG growth-share matrix*. This matrix has two dimensions to cluster the products of a company: relative market share and market growth rate. Based on the two dimensions, four clusters are formed: cash cows, dogs, question marks, and stars. Depending on the cluster they are in, products must be further developed, maintained in the current state, or discontinued. In the context of EAM, a typical portfolio matrix displays the major enterprise applications along two dimensions: "technical fit" and "functional fit."

Another way of displaying portfolios in the context of EAM are maps, foremost application maps, and business capability maps. These maps show redundancies in the application portfolio and point toward possibilities for leveraging synergies by consolidating applications. For example, an application map could illustrate that

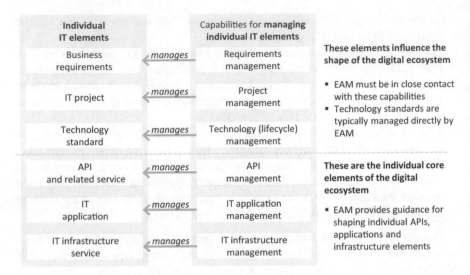

Fig. 3.8 (Lifecycle) management of individual IT elements

today, the three business units A, B, and C use the three different applications "aCRM," "bCRM," and "cCRM" for Customer Relationship Management. Based on this finding, a target picture could be defined, where the three business units use only one shared application. We will come back to these artifacts in Sect. 4.3.2.

Managing Individual Elements of the Digital Ecosystem
The goal of EAM is to manage the enterprise-wide digital ecosystem and the systems comprised in it. Now, in the context of EAM, already various capabilities exist that address the management of individual digital systems as well as the artifacts for planning and developing digital systems. So, before delving into the complete picture of enterprise IT capabilities, we must understand the capabilities that address *individual* IT elements and capabilities that address *portfolios* of IT elements. Since both influence the shape of the digital ecosystem, both are relevant for EAM.

Figure 3.8 displays individual elements of the digital ecosystem and the corresponding management functions. Taking the example of the CRM system of a car insurance, these capabilities would look as follows:

Requirements management: The business owner of the CRM application manages the requirements of this application. Among other things, she keeps a list of requirements that should be implemented within the next 6 months.

Project management: For larger changes, the application manager hires a project manager. For example, now a project is set up for installing a new function to analyze customer data for finding out which customers should be part of the next sales campaign.

Technology management: To find out which technologies for data analytics are available in the insurance, the project lead searches through the technology standards catalog. This catalog is managed by the enterprise architects and describes—independent of concrete service implementations inside the insurance—which technologies are available in the insurance. Here, the project lead finds a cloud service for data analytics from a well-known vendor. The service is already sourced in the insurance and would be available for the CRM system as well. Inside the EAM department, the *data analytics architect* manages the lifecycle of this technology. She is in close contact with the vendor of the data analytics service and knows the market, where similar services are provided by other vendors. For example, if she would find out that the current vendor is not investing in the modernization of the service or feels that the service is not "fit for future" for other reasons, she would switch to another vendor.

API management: The CRM system offers many services to other applications via well-defined interfaces. Each of these APIs is managed to ensure that they remain of good quality; thus, they *do not* end up as an assembly of unintelligible attributes, and they *do not* foster confusion, misunderstandings, and inconsistencies. In the insurance company, the IT application owner or its application architect is also responsible for managing the APIs of their application. In the case of the new data analytics function, two existing APIs of the CRM application must be modified, and three new APIs must be created. To this aim, the CRM solution architect coordinates with the central integration architects on the design of the interfaces and the next steps toward their implementation.

IT application management: The IT counterpart to the requirements manager is responsible for the management of the IT application. He ensures that the application runs stable within the given service-level agreements and coordinates the implementation of pending requirements. In the sense of *lifecycle* management, the application manager realizes that in 2 years, the technology of the current CRM system will reach its end of life; thus, the application manager already plans the complete renewal of the application.

Infrastructure management: Just like business applications, infrastructure elements have lifecycles and service-level agreements that need to be monitored and managed. Our CRM system, for example, is implemented on infrastructure services that include a relational database and a web server. In the infrastructure department, a dedicated owner of the relational database below the CRM system manages this system. She is responsible for operational tasks, like coordinating maintenance downtimes with the business application owners. But she also is responsible for the lifecycle management of this particular infrastructure implementation. For example, she is observing the end-of-life date of the database and, in case this is near, plans for the migration to a successor product.

Managing Portfolios of IT Elements
Complementary to the management of individual functions, Fig. 3.9 illustrates that each of these elements can and should also be managed in portfolios. Above, our focus was the management of one individual element—but we also need to consider the overall group of elements and dependencies between them, to steer the complete

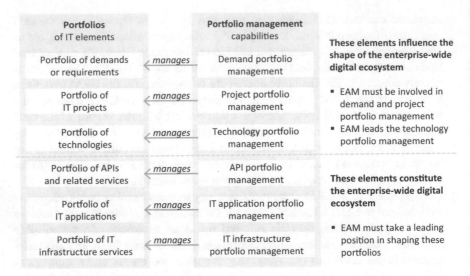

Fig. 3.9 Capabilities for managing portfolios of IT elements

ecosystem in the right direction. Expanding the example from above, now we look beyond one application, at the sum of digital systems inside the car insurance:

Demand portfolio management: Starting at the top, the business counterpart of the CIO has an overview of all requirements IT could implement in the coming year. Inside this central *demand portfolio management*, each strategic requirement is correlated with its business benefits and a rough cost estimation.

Project portfolio management: When the requirements are prioritized from the business perspective, they are taken to the *project portfolio management*. Here again a prioritization takes place, now based on more details like the urgencies of implementation, detailed implementation costs, and resource availability. Note that for smaller changes, each application has a fixed local budget. But the large, strategic changes need to be discussed centrally on the level of the enterprise-wide requirements and project portfolio. In our example company, now the CEO must make a tough decision: various high-ranking business managers urgently need extended digital functions for their departments, but the budget does not suffice for all demands. Finally, she decides that the largest chunk of the budget will flow to the creation of a completely new customer portal with a high degree of process digitalization, while some other demands must be postponed to the next year.

Technology portfolio management: The portfolio of available technology standards strongly influences the shape of the technology implementations in the digital ecosystem. Note that these standards address all digital technologies, covering both business applications and IT infrastructure. For instance, on the application level, the question is asked: How many *standards* for CRM should we have in the target picture? Are we strongly pursuing economies of scale via standardization and choosing to have only one CRM system for all business units? Or do we allow for more heterogeneity and redundancy, for example, to increase competition among the products and to better address heterogenous requirements? The same question is asked on the infrastructure level: Do we only allow for one data lake product inside the enterprise, or should we rather have three different products from three vendors? This kind of technology portfolio management is a core task of EAM.

API portfolio management: As stated above, an API is the interface of a service provided by an application (service provider) to other applications (service consumer). The API portfolio is constituted by the sum of all APIs in the enterprise. Coming back to the example of the CRM system, typical questions here would be: Do we already have a service in the insurance that provides core customer information, like name, address, and date of birth? Does it make sense to have more of such services, e.g., one for the car insurance and one for the health insurance? Or do we want to have just one service that addresses the requirements of all business units? Do we cluster our APIs into disjoint domains? API portfolio management is usually allocated in the central integration architecture.

Application portfolio management: In the technology portfolio described above, we already decided *what types of applications* are used in the enterprise, for example, that the insurance only sources three types of CRM applications, from three different vendors. However, the scope, number, and allocation of the individual application instances were not decided. Should the business units of car insurance, health insurance, and property insurance use the same application instance? Or, albeit using the same product from the same vendor, should each unit have its independent application? A classic optimization scenario here is to leverage synergies by consolidating the three disjoint CRM systems into one joint application, used by all three business units.

Infrastructure portfolio management: Like the application portfolio, the portfolio of infrastructure implementations needs to be constantly optimized. Thus, the idea here is the same as above, though now instead of application instances, here we optimize the portfolio of infrastructure instances. A typical question in this context is: Do we really need three web servers in this business domain, or can the three small applications of this domain there share one web server? Do we want to focus on cost savings through synergies and joint infrastructure? Or do we foster the independence and stability of the applications by endowing each with its own web server?

Note that the question of pros and cons of central vs. decentral implementations also arises in the context of portfolio management. With too much centralization, the portfolio becomes too large to be steered by one party. For example, it is difficult for 1 central department to judge how 1000 applications out of 50 business domains should develop. Thus, if the overall pool reaches a certain size, it should be divided into various smaller portfolios that can be managed decentrally.

3.4.3 Standards for IT Capabilities: COBIT and ITIL

Now, other than managing individual and portfolios of IT elements, which IT functions does an enterprise need? Standards addressing this question are foremost COBIT and ITIL; both are being used since decades in countless enterprises. Figure 3.10 shows the view of *COBIT* on capabilities needed for IT governance and management; we highlighted the functions most relevant for EAM. Again, COBIT focuses on IT governance and management functions, not on the operational processes for developing and managing applications and IT infrastructure. Nevertheless, the core areas of COBIT also follow the lifecycle phases of plan, build, and run or, in the words of COBIT, "align, plan, and organize"; "build, acquire, and implement"; and "deliver, service, and support."

ISACA ©2018

Evaluate, direct and monitor

| Governance framework management | Ensure benefits delivery | Risk optimization | Resource optimization | Stakeholder management |

Align, plan and organize   *Monitor, evaluate and assess*

IT framework management	Strategy management	**Enterprise Architecture Management**	Innovation management	Portfolio management
Relationship management	Service agreement management	Vendor management	Quality management	Risk management	Peformance and confor-mance mgmt
Budget and cost management	Human resource management	Security management	Data management		Managed systems of internal control

Build, acquire and implement

| Program management | Requirements definition management | Solution identification and building | Availability and capacity management | Organizatio-nal change management | IT change management |
| Knowledge management | Asset management | Configuration management | Project management | IT change acceptance and transition | Compliance with external requirements |

Deliver, service and support   Managed assurance

| Operations management | Service request and incident mgmt | Problem management | Continuity management | Security services management | Business process control mgmt |

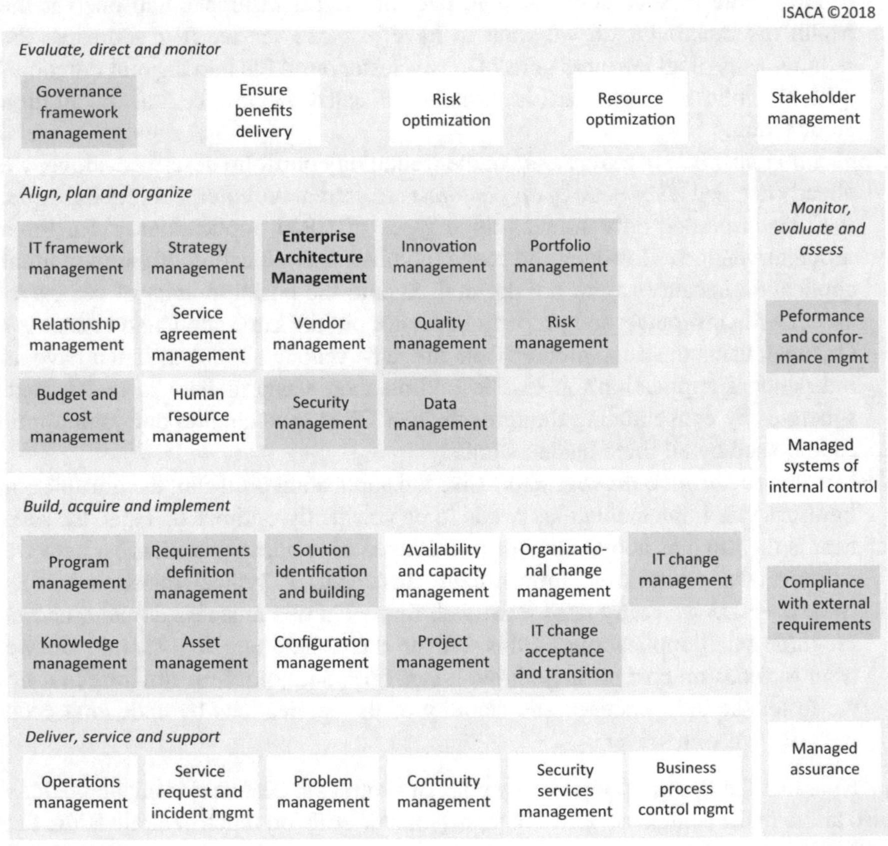

Fig. 3.10 IT management and governance capabilities according to COBIT (This is a slightly adapted version of a graphic from ISACA (2018): COBIT 2019 Framework: Governance and Management Objectives, ISACA ©2018. All rights reserved. Used with permission)

ITIL on the other hand originally did not focus on IT strategy and governance but on processes for IT infrastructure management. However, recently, ITIL has become more comprehensive and now also addresses general IT management processes. ITIL today clusters processes in three areas: (1) general management, (2) service management, and (3) technical management. Inside the area of general management, ITIL (2019) describes processes similar to those of COBIT, for example, architecture management, strategy management, and portfolio management.

The Meaning of IT Governance
The term governance stems from the Latin word *gubernare*, which means to direct, rule, or guide. And, as described above, EAM is about the long-term steering and global optimization of an enterprise's digital ecosystem, including the definition of target pictures and the controlling of standards compliancy. In other words, *Enterprise Architecture Management and IT governance are closely related*. However, in practice, governance usually is connoted primarily with reactive controlling and compliance checks; EAM, in addition, has the proactive aspect of creating new digital landscapes. And while IT governance focuses on steering the *IT organization*, EAM focuses on the steering of the *enterprise-wide digital ecosystem*. Beyond that, the term "IT governance" is defined differently in literature, for example:

- According to Asprion and Knolmayer (2021), IT governance is about leading and organizing the IT departments and their tasks, competencies, and responsibilities. They distinguish an *internally oriented perspective*, which focuses on the performance of the governed system. The other side of the coin is the *externally oriented* perspective, which focuses on the compliance of a system with laws and regulations.
- *Gartner* defines IT governance generically as "the processes that ensure the effective and efficient use of IT in enabling an organization to achieve its goals." They distinguish between *IT demand governance and IT supply-side governance*. IT demand governance controls the IT from a business perspective, i.e., from the perspective of the CEO. IT supply-side governance on the other hand refers to the steering from inside the IT organization, i.e., from the perspective of the CIO [cp. Gartner (2021a)].
- *COBIT* is the leading standard for IT governance. They distinguish between "governance" and "management," where "governance" is about the highest level of steering and controlling, executed by the board of directors. "Management," on the other hand, is about reaching the objectives provided by the "governance" via more operational planning, steering, and controlling processes. In this dichotomy, "management" is the responsibility of the CEO. Note that the governance processes are depicted only in the "evaluate, direct, and monitor" area of Fig. 3.10, while COBIT refers to all other processes in the figure as "management" processes [cp. ISACA (2018)].

3.5   Capabilities in the Vicinity of EAM

Figure 3.11 shows the enterprise IT functions most relevant for EAM. As discussed above, these capabilities can be allocated either centrally or decentrally in an enterprise or a group of enterprises. The capabilities highlighted in gray are, depending on the enterprise, sometimes also explicitly part of the Enterprise Architecture Management capability.

Three of the overarching areas were already described above: 1. IT strategy, 2. application development and management, and 3. infrastructure development and management. In addition to these, Fig. 3.11 depicts another area: *cross-cutting IT concerns*. The concerns are called cross-cutting because they are used across different business applications. For example, API management and identity and access management are required by all business applications to communicate and provide access to each other. In many enterprises, such cross-cutting functions are closely steered by EAM or are directly allocated inside the EAM department. The reason is that these functions have a large impact on the enterprise-wide digital ecosystem—since they are cross-cutting, they address many or all applications of the enterprise. Thus, it is no surprise that the early EAM departments often emerged from the area

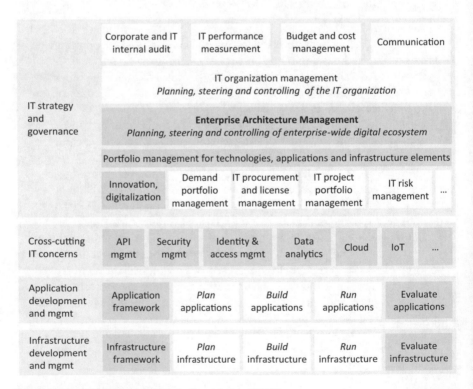

Fig. 3.11 Essential IT capabilities in the vicinity of EAM

of cross-cutting IT concerns. Further examples of cross-cutting IT concerns are security management, data analytics, cloud, and the Internet of Things (IoT).

Note that these cross-cutting concerns could also be classified as infrastructure. However, due to the reasons given above, in practice, often the three areas applications, cross-cutting concerns, and infrastructure are distinguished [cp. also Hafner and Winter (2008, p. 5)]. In the following, we briefly describe the individual capabilities depicted in Fig. 3.11.

3.5.1   IT Strategy and Governance Capabilities

In this area, the capabilities for steering the overall IT organization and the overall IT landscape are bundled. In real-life enterprises, this IT department sometimes is called "planning and steering" (of the overall IT). This is the department of the CIO, where EAM is allocated and typically also the above-described portfolio management capabilities. Other than those, the following capabilities are highly relevant for EAM:

Capability for Corporate and IT-Internal Audit
These classic governance capabilities perform audits to verify that external and internal regulations and quality standards are met in the company, with either a general business focus or an IT focus. As mentioned above, EAM can also be seen as a governance function, but in that sense focuses more on the "internal" governance perspective for improving the performance of the digital ecosystem, while the audit department focuses on the external view to ensure that the enterprise is compliant with external laws and regulations. In daily life, the interactions between the audit and the EAM department are seldom. However, the audit department can be an important ally of EAM, since both departments share the objective of having a high-quality enterprise system compliant with different forms of guidelines and regulations. Compared to the EAM department, the audit department usually has a closer relationship to the CEO. Thus, if needed, the audit department can support the EAM department to enforce company-wide guidelines.

Capability for Communication
In large enterprises, the IT unit has its own, dedicated communication department. On the one hand, this capability fosters communication inside the IT; on the other hand, it creates transparency of IT services inside the overall enterprise. Since the goal of EAM is to steer the enterprise-wide digital ecosystem, it is crucial to communicate EAM guidelines, target pictures, and innovative IT solutions at least to the IT organization. To this aim, EAM should work closely together with the communications department. An example is the publishing of EAM success stories in the intranet or the Internet, e.g., "EAM published a new IOT reference architecture for our enterprise; this streamlines the production of IOT solutions inside the group and reduces the time-to-market by 30%."

Capability for Risk Management

As introduced above, enterprise architects must understand the protection needs and the risks associated with individual systems as well as with collections of systems. For example, if the installment of a new CRM suite is analyzed in the context of an architecture board presentation, the following risk could be formulated: "Since the vendor of the CRM solution is small and only has a few customers, there is an elevated risk that it will go bankrupt in the next 5 years." The digital ecosystem then needs to be architected to address the identified risk level.

So, not surprisingly, Forrester names risk management as a feature of EAM tools, and some vendors include functions for risk management in their EAM suites (Barnett et al., 2021). However, risk *management* is not a core EAM process, and it is seldomly named in literature as such (cp. Fig. 4.3). In COBIT, there is a dedicated process for risk management, disjoint from EAM. In practice, risk management is rather the responsibility of the security capability than of the EAM capability. However, since enterprise architects need to know the protection requirements and risks associated with the digital landscape, it does make sense to import such data from dedicated risk management tools into the IT asset inventory. Refer to Keller (2012, p. 230) for a more detailed description of risk management in the context of EAM.

Capability for IT Organization Management

As illustrated in Fig. 3.1, the enterprise IT can be divided into the IT landscape and the IT organization, i.e., the digital systems and the people providing and maintaining these systems. While EAM manages the digital ecosystem, the capability of IT organization management plans, steers, and controls the IT organization. It defines the structure of the IT departments and the processes, artifacts, and roles inside the IT organization. This capability is relevant for EAM in various ways:

The structure of the IT organization mirrors the structure of the digital ecosystem: The notorious quote of Conway (1968) states that the digitalized business processes of an enterprise are copies of the previously existing brick-and-mortar business processes. On a higher level, a comparable relationship exists between the structure of the IT organization and the IT landscape: the quality of the IT organization is mirrored in the quality of the enterprise-wide digital ecosystem. If the organizational structures and processes inside the IT are not *extremely clear and simple on all levels*, there will be endless discussions on who is responsible for which system or architectural area. In consequence, the IT landscape will not be clean-cut and simply structured but a complex plethora of overlapping and redundant systems.

EAM can lead to organizational changes: Take, for example, a large insurance company where the task of integration architecture initially was highly distributed: Three API management products from three different vendors were provisioned in three different API management departments. In addition, every large business application had one person specialized on application integration tasks. After the EAM department showed that a consolidation to one product from one vendor would be beneficial for the enterprise, the previously three products were consolidated into one product, which was now managed centrally by one department. To further increase specialization, this central department also took over some of the tasks previously allocated at the decentral business applications. Thus, the IT organization was adapted in parallel to the IT products.

EAM processes need to be well integrated in the IT organization: EAM must steer the overall digital ecosystem and thus needs many touchpoints in the IT organization that develops and maintains this ecosystem. For example, EAM needs to be integrated in the IT processes for demand management, IT procurement, and IT project management. Generally put, EAM artifacts, roles, and processes must be integrated in the process model of the overall IT organization.

Capability for Digitalization and Innovation
In the introductory chapter, we already described the close relationship between EAM and enterprise digitalization. It is obvious that a good architect must always look for innovative, state-of-the-art solutions to address the requirements of the customer, i.e., the business. It is also clear that EAM addresses the *quality* of the enterprise-wide digital ecosystem; that includes the optimal degree of novel technologies and digitalization. Nevertheless, in the context of the digital disruptions in the last years, many large enterprises established dedicated digitalization units (some of those were rather short-lived and dissolved after 1 or 2 years).

No matter where it is allocated, in a large enterprise, central digitalization innovation is challenging since traditionally *a large part of digital innovation in an enterprise happens decentrally.* For example, innovations in the field of data analytics, artificial intelligence, business process digitalization, application integration, network technology, or identity and access management are usually realized by the respective departments and local architects specialized in these areas. And from the business perspective, the owners and architects for the business departments innovate their business capabilities. For example, in a large insurance, the domain architects and department owners responsible for the capabilities Customer Relationship Management, underwriting, and claims handling each innovate and digitalize their business areas. Alas, sometimes the line-of-business departments and roles are stuck in their established patterns based on their present resources and thus prevent the move to the next technology level. Now, a good central EAM department would challenge and inspire the decentral architects toward out-of-the-box thinking to reach the needed level of innovativeness. On the other hand, in some enterprises, EAM focuses too much on complexity reduction—by limiting the range of available technology standards—while neglecting the creation of innovative target pictures.

In this case, a complementary central department for digital innovation makes sense. Such departments incorporate the explorer mode of the bimodal IT. Together with prominent business stakeholders, they identify and implement a selected number of light house projects, showcasing innovative business functions and the applications of new digital technologies. While being in the explorer mode, the processes of this department are not restricted by the standardization efforts that aim at keeping the zoo of available technologies manageable. However, if these showcases should do more than shine brightly for a couple of months, the projects cannot roam free completely but must get input from the EAM department and further subject matter experts who know the enterprise-specific digital ecosystem and its boundaries. Otherwise, the minimum viable product (MVP) created by the innovation capability might function in an isolated sandbox but fail in the context of daily-life enterprise abilities and the surrounding laws and regulations. Let us take the example of an MVP for a new data analytics function inside a large bank: The MVP worked fine in the sandbox, because here a set of reliable, high-quality data was produced for the test. However, it never made it to go-live, because it turned out that (a) the data needed as input in daily life did not have the sufficient quality and (b) the needed functions for storing and accessing data were not GDPR compliant.

Capability for IT Procurement
The capability of IT procurement is mostly responsible for the rather operational and commercial aspects of acquiring digital products. In other words, IT procurement acquires the digital capabilities defined by the business and the IT strategy, namely, Enterprise Architecture Management. EAM defines strategic and tactical IT target pictures, including logical capabilities and IT services. Moreover, in practice, EAM often also chooses concrete products from specific vendors. For example, a typical EAM task is a so-called beauty contest, where the three products a, b, and c from the vendors x, y, and z are evaluated along various dimensions (e.g., functional fit, technical fit, costs, and risks) and the best option is chosen. Here, procurement should be involved to provide input to this evaluation, to state if this vendor is generally feasible and what the reasonable price range is. When the product is decided final, procurement engages in negotiations with the vendor, specifies the contract, and concludes the commercial transaction. Another example of a touchpoint between EAM and procurement is a *strategic procurement board*. In this panel, larger, strategically relevant purchases are discussed with various stakeholders, including a representative of EAM. On the first sight, this looks like a redundancy to *strategic architecture boards*, which also addresses decisions regarding the development or acquisition of large digital products and services. Unfortunately, in the reality of large enterprises, not all relevant projects are routed via the right governance boards. It might very well happen that an important change is not known to EAM until it surfaces in the procurement board. However, there must be a frequent interchange between the procurement capability and the EAM capability to ensure that both parties are aware and synchronized regarding the acquisition of new digital services and products.

Capability for IT License Management
The capability of *license management* is complementary to IT procurement and manages all licenses and contracts of software that the enterprise rents or has bought. Major tasks here include:

- Keeping inventories of the digital assets used in the enterprise
- Keeping inventories of the respective licenses and contracts
- Evaluating the findings of the previous steps, to assess if too many or not enough software licenses were acquired and take corrective actions

Thus, license compliance is ensured, i.e., that no unlicensed products are used in the enterprise. In a more proactive role, license management takes actions toward an *enterprise-wide optimized license portfolio*. For example, the ten business units of a large insurance group all rented the same CRM software X from the vendor Y in a software as a service model. However, each business unit had contacted the vendor separately and obtained their own individual contract and conditions. To leverage enterprise-wide economies of scale, now license management started a small project together with EAM to consolidate the licenses into one group-wide contract. After the consolidation, the group obtained a much better price. Another advantage was increased flexibility though *license pooling*: From the now large, group-wide pool of available licenses, licenses could flexibly be allocated at that business unit that currently needs those. For instance, when inside business unit A needs fewer licenses than before, business unit B can use those and does not have to engage in new vendor negotiations.

Capability for IT Performance Measurement
COBIT describes the objective of Managed Performance and Conformance Monitoring as follows: "Collect, validate and evaluate enterprise and alignment goals and metrics. Monitor, that processes and practices are performing against agreed performance and conformance goals and metrics. Provide reporting that is systematic and timely" (ISACA, 2018, p. 273). To make this overarching capability more concrete, we can distinguish different objects of IT performance measurement:

- *Digital ecosystem vs. IT organization:* As mentioned before, EAM evaluates the *digital ecosystem*. Complementary to that, usually a department exists that in German-speaking countries is called "IT controlling": This department measures the performance of the overall *IT organization* and traces who receives and spends how much money for what purposes. It focuses on evaluating organizational activities, actors, and areas, but not on the quality of the digital ecosystem.
- *Financial vs. architectural information:* In EAM, the evaluation of financial information is just one aspect; besides that, aspects like technical fit and functional fit play an important role. The capability for general IT performance measurement focuses typically on financial values. For instance, this department could report the following to the CIO: "The project for the new CRM system got funded with 15% of the annual budget for changing the IT; by now, it delivered 50% of the promised functions, but already spent 90% of its budget." EAM, on the other hand, could have triggered the abovementioned project with the following statement: "The business applications in the domain sales and marketing urgently need to be moved to the cloud and improved regarding interoperability, usability, and available business functions." The COBIT capability dedicated to planning and tracking IT finances is called "Managed Costs and Budgets."
- *Strategic vs. operative:* Strategic IT performance measurement ensures the achievement of long-term goals. Ideally, it helps to detect deviations from the roadmap to the strategic target picture at an early stage. It supports IT management in the design and monitoring of KPIs that indicate the status and progress of strategic activities. Operative performance measurement on the other hand

addresses short-term goals with a smaller scope. Instead of tracking the advancement of a large, strategic project, here we could track the Key Performance Indicators of a small IT department or an application.

In practice, the relationship between the department for general IT performance measurement and the EAM department is often too distant (the one department is seen as a bunch of boring number crunchers; the other department is seen as a bunch of techies with hard-to-understand target pictures). However, EAM needs the numbers to assess the economic performance of domains and application landscapes for producing a comprehensive architectural assessment. And the general IT performance department can use the target pictures defined by EAM as well as the structures typically produced by EAM, like domain maps or business capability maps.

3.5.2   Further Capabilities

Capabilities for Cross-Cutting Concerns

Depending on the structure and size of the IT organization, capabilities of the area *cross-cutting IT concerns* can either be part of the EAM department, or they can be implemented as large-sized, independent departments. For example, a retail bank that relies on a seamless process digitalization across many applications recently formed a large central department for API management. Inside this department, they formed an elaborated pipeline for *individual APIs*, ranging from requirements management, design, and implementation to operations. In parallel, they created a similar process for the integration *platform*, which was built as a combination of an API gateway and an event streaming solution. The department also is responsible for the requirements, architecture, design, implementation, and operations of this platform. In this scenario, the enterprise-wide architecture of the middleware solution is mostly addressed in this department. In consequence, the central EAM department does not have to worry too much for API management and middleware architecture; however, since this is such an essential area, in the central EAM department of the bank, there is one enterprise architect who also addresses this subject. In contrast to her colleague from the API management department, she also has insight into adjacent architecture areas, like data management, process digitalization, and identity and access management, thus adding a complementary perspective to the API management architecture.

Capabilities for Application Development and Application Management

Above we described capabilities that address portfolios of digital systems as well as cross-cutting capabilities that support many applications. Now we come to a capability at the heart of the digitalization process: the development and management of individual business applications. An example of such an individual business application could be a Customer Relationship Management (CRM) application in a large aviation group. Figure 3.11 illustrates the capabilities we describe below. Again, although each capability here is described separately, they can be put together in various forms in the organizational chart. For example, in the spirit of agile DevOps, the capabilities for planning, building, and running marketing applications could be integrated in one department (cp. Fig. 3.7).

Plan application: The first phase of the plan-build-run lifecycle starts with gathering business *demands*. Based on this, an *architecture* and a *coarse-grained specification* of the application are developed. Further steps include the creation of a development *roadmap* that specifies what is developed at which time for what costs. Recapitulating the classic role and task of an architect, the "plan" phase is of most relevance to EAM in the lifecycle of an application. If the application has a certain size and strategic importance, the central EAM department will directly support in assessing the demands and in the architecture of the application.

Build application: Here a *fine-grained specification* of the application is created, and the software engineers *implement* the application. Further steps are the *test* of the application and, related to the tests, its staging through different deployment environments, for instance, the environments of development, integration, acceptance test, and production. The last step, the staging of the application in the production environment, is called "go-live."

Run application: Now the application is productive; the users work with it and expect the application to function properly. In this phase, the application owners *monitor* the behavior of the application and ensure that it fulfills the specified service-level agreements. Engaging in *requirements management*, they keep a backlog of changes and plan when those shall be implemented. In case of *incidents*, they coordinate with the business users, software engineers, and infrastructure developers how to solve problems and repair the application.

Application framework: The plan-build-run lifecycle discussed above takes place at the level of an individual application. Now we zoom out and look at the application portfolio of our enterprise. Would it make sense if each of the ca. 50 major business applications in our example enterprise uses its own tool stack and its own *methods for developing, testing, and staging applications*? Or would it be more reasonable to streamline these methods and provide an enterprise-wide framework for application development? Now we are back at the discussion of independent, decoupled development teams versus enterprise-wide integrated application development. In the last years, the advances in cloud technologies, DevOps, and Micro Services gave new input to this discussion. However, to foster specialization, efficiency, and security and to enable software engineers to switch between different application departments, most enterprises will standardize application development to a certain degree. The level of standardization can vary, for example:

- One option is offering and maintaining a central, tailor-made, integrated framework. This comprises a development environment and corresponding pipelines that seamlessly connect high-level design, coding, testing, and staging to the production environment. For example, around 2005, the EAM department of the BEI insurance created such a framework that was used by all application developers in the enterprise.

- A second option is defining a set of allowed programming languages and tools to be used by the application development and application management departments. For example, the EAM department of the BEI insurance around 2015 gave in to constant complaints from the developers, that the centrally maintained framework would be too rigid, and discontinued offering this integrated framework. Today, they only define the products and standards to be used in the IT development departments and leave it to the decentral departments to implement and connect the products.

Note that since the capability "application framework" addresses many applications, it also classifies as a *cross-cutting capability*. Thus, historically EAM often did offer this capability.

Evaluate applications: Evaluation in the sense of application monitoring is part of the "run application" phase described above. Going beyond that, a good solution owner will also frequently take a step back from daily operations and evaluate her application regarding, for example, costs, functions, adaptability, modernity, and security. However, sometimes the EAM department is needed to enable a comprehensive, 360-degree evaluation of individual applications as well as the enterprise-wide application portfolio. Chapter 5 describes these core EAM activities in detail.

The Meaning of IT Infrastructure
The term infrastructure stems from Latin, where *infra* means *below*. Thus, infrastructure is a relative term; what is "below" depends on the height of the vantage point you are looking from. Accordingly, different understandings of IT infrastructure and various levels of IT infrastructure exist. What these concepts have in common is that infrastructure consists of rather long-lived elements that enable a variety of use cases (Patig, 2021). The NIST defines Infrastructure as a Service (IaaS) as the provisioning of "processing, storage, networks, and other fundamental computing resources where the consumer is able to deploy and run arbitrary software, which can include operating systems and applications" (Mell & Grance, 2011). Note that popular EAM frameworks like TOGAF and CEAF distinguish between four main elements of the digital ecosystem and do not include the word "infrastructure" in this list: business, information, applications, and technology. However, with "technology," they refer to IT infrastructure (in the sense of IT infrastructure expressed in the NIST definition).

Capabilities in the Area of Infrastructure Development and Management
Though infrastructure in relation to business applications has a lower position in the service provisioning chain, both business applications and IT infrastructure systems are digital systems that need to be managed in similar ways. Thus, as illustrated in Fig. 3.11, the capabilities needed in IT infrastructure are similar to those in business applications. For instance, let us assume a project lead is responsible for installing a new CRM business application in a large aviation company. The application

software is provided by a third-party vendor, but it requires three web servers and three relational databases as infrastructure. Now, the following steps are executed:

Plan infrastructure: The project lead contacts a dedicated capability for infrastructure planning. These colleagues advise him which kind of web servers and database to pick in which configuration. They also convey to him that, due to a current bottleneck, the provisioning of the web servers could take 2 weeks.

Build infrastructure: Endowed with this information, the project lead orders the infrastructure at an internal web shop. Since he does not understand some of the attributes that are required in the web shop, he contacts the enterprise-internal department that is responsible for the "build" part of infrastructures. They help him to *refine the specification* he already got and to finalize the order in the web shop. During the project, they frequently help the project lead when it comes to building and *testing* the infrastructure in the *different environments*. They also master the formal processes needed to bring new elements in the production environment and know the dependencies to related infrastructure elements.

Run infrastructure: After the go-live of the CRM application, not only the business application itself but also its infrastructure elements need to be monitored, fixed in case of incidents, and continuously improved. For example, the web servers and the databases have frequent maintenance windows where updates are installed. Thus, complementary to the application owner, a person is dedicated for managing the infrastructure of the CRM application.

Infrastructure framework: Here again we zoom out, away from individual infrastructure elements for one application, and focus on the enterprise-wide portfolio of infrastructure elements. Like with the application framework, the enterprise needs to decide which methods and tools will be used to acquire, configure, provision, and test the infrastructure elements. In other words, how should the infrastructure plan-build-run processes look like in our enterprise? Clearly, the frameworks for infrastructure and application management should be integrated with each other. It is enterprise-specific, how strong this integration is, or if—in the sense of DevOps—there will be only one joint framework for managing applications and infrastructure. Again, a reference for the elements of such a framework is provided by the IT4IT standard of the Open Group (2017).

Evaluate infrastructure: Like the evaluation of individual applications and the application portfolio, individual infrastructure elements and the infrastructure portfolio must regularly be evaluated in the sense of a comprehensive 360-degree analysis; the details of such analysis are described in Chap. 5.

As mentioned above, EAM must be strongly involved in the plan-build-run lifecycle of individual *business applications*. The EAM relationship to the plan-build-run functions of the *infrastructure* systems usually is not as close, because here the decisions are more clear-cut (e.g., which database to use for what type of applications). However, the standardization of the infrastructure portfolio, the shaping of the infrastructure framework, and the regular evaluation of the enterprise infrastructure are highly important EAM tasks. Other than the infrastructure elements and the infrastructure portfolio, the infrastructure framework needs to be evaluated and continuously improved as well.

Chapter 4
EAM Implementation

In the previous chapter, we clarified the contextual parameters of Enterprise Architecture Management. Addressing the core of EAM implementation, this chapter now describes in detail EAM goals, processes, functions, artifacts, roles, and tools. Thus, after revisiting EAM goals, an EAM process framework is described that provides a comprehensive overview of EAM processes and functions. On the one hand, the framework comprises the EAM cube with core EAM processes. On the other hand, it encompasses supporting processes for enabling and steering the EAM capability. Each process type and its practical implementation are described in detail. Next, EAM artifacts are addressed. After a two-dimensional classification of artifacts, we describe how to create coherent collections of principles. Further artifacts described include, for example, maps of the digital ecosystem, target architectures, and roadmaps. In a similar vein, the tools as well as the EAM organization and roles required to fulfill the EAM processes and capabilities are described in depth.

Enterprise Architecture Management is the process of planning, steering, and controlling the Enterprise Architecture. Now, every process consists of the same core elements: (1) *functions* implemented in a certain sequence inside the process, (2) *actors and roles* that carry out the functions, (3) *artifacts* that are used and produced in the functions, and possibly also (4) *tools,* used for executing or supporting the functions. The fifth element here is the *process* itself, which consists of several concatenated functions. The functions, and hence also the processes, are guided by *goals*. As Fig. 4.1 illustrates, these elements are also the core elements for defining the implementation of EAM inside an enterprise and will be described in this chapter.

© The Author(s), under exclusive license to Springer Nature Switzerland AG 2022
J. Ziemann, *Fundamentals of Enterprise Architecture Management*, The Enterprise
Engineering Series, https://doi.org/10.1007/978-3-030-96734-5_4

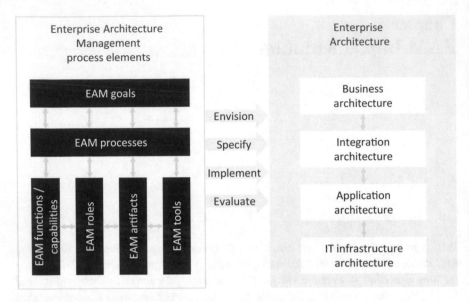

Fig. 4.1 EAM consists of processes, capabilities, roles, artifacts, and tools

4.1   EAM Goals Revisited

Chapter 1 provided a first summary of EAM goals. And, regarding the top-level goal of EAM, there is no need to overcomplicate things since the term "Enterprise Architecture Management" spells out its goals: managing the Enterprise Architecture. Based on the earlier definitions, this translates to steering the fundamental elements of the digital ecosystem toward a defined target picture, to obtain (and maintain) a coherent, "good" Enterprise Architecture. How can we break down "good" into operational subgoals? Here, terms like quality, fulfilment of business requirements, costs, and cost-quality ratio come to mind. As stated above, another simple way of decomposing the overall goal of a "good" digital ecosystem is that it functions efficiently—does things right—and effectively, i.e., does the right things. And, as discussed in Sect. 1.5, one subgoal to reach efficiency and effectivity certainly is to avoid an overly complex ecosystem by fostering a clearly structured, transparent IT landscape.

Exemplary EAM Goals from Literature
Since EAM is still a young discipline, literature so far has been incoherent at least regarding the subgoals of EAM. In the following, we have a brief view on three exemplary EAM goal systems: Tamm et al. (2011), for example, list four effects of EAM: organizational alignment, information availability, resource portfolio optimization, and resource complementarity. The enterprise benefits from these effects would be lower IT costs, higher strategic agility, and a more reliable operating platform. This list is correct in so far that it captures some important areas, but it

conveys only an incomplete picture of EAM goals. Niemann (2006) names three categories of EAM goals:

1. IT efficiency: Efficiency, i.e., "doing the things right," means that from a business perspective, IT is fulfilling the given tasks with an optimal cost-result ratio. According to Niemann, for achieving IT efficiency, the digital ecosystem should be redundancy-free, homogenous, integrated, and consistent. Further on, IT functions should be reused within the landscape.
2. IT effectiveness: This refers to "doing the right things" from a functional business perspective. It does not help if the digital ecosystem is very slim and cost-efficient but does not provide the functions required by the enterprise to stay competitive. Niemann names four subgoals contributing to IT effectiveness: goal conformity, strategy and means conformity, result orientation, and schedule orientation.
3. IT reliability: Here, the subgoals are "risk-free," "conformity," and "transparency."

Keller (2012) describes an EAM goal pyramid with *business-IT-alignment* at the top. As second-level goals, he describes quality (measured through customer satisfaction), costs (through purchasing and reduction of heterogeneity), time-to-market, compliance, and innovation. Business-IT-alignment is often named as a major EAM goal. That makes sense, because it would be bad if the digital ecosystem of an enterprise would not be "aligned" with the needs of the business. However, imagine you order the construction of a house and the architect conveys to you that the architecture is "aligned" with your requirements; this might sound a bit weak to you. Much rather, you would expect that the architecture *fulfils* your requirements. Nevertheless, what business-IT-alignment as overall EAM goal does express well is that creating a digital enterprise ecosystem is not a one-time project. Instead, the digital ecosystem needs to be adapted permanently to changing business requirements, market conditions, and technological possibilities.

The EAM Goal Pyramid
In the remainder of this book, we will use the EAM goal pyramid shown in Fig. 4.2, which incorporates elements of the abovementioned systems for clustering EAM goals. The pyramid comprises the following layers:

Overarching business goals. This layer contains the top-level business goals and provides a context for the digital ecosystem. Simply put, the overall goal of an enterprise is to achieve a sustainable competitive advantage over its competitors and sustainable earnings. To enable this, the enterprise needs *satisfied customers and enterprise employees*, and it must be *compliant with laws and regulations. Ecological sustainability* can be seen as a part of "compliance with laws and regulations"; however, today most large enterprises list ecological sustainability as an explicit goal. To achieve these goals, the enterprise must be able to adapt to changing customer requirements and other market conditions. Naturally, it needs *short-term agility* and efficiency regarding "time-to-market", e.g., to launch a new digital product before a competitor does. However, addressing a typical EAM concern, while acting fast, it must ensure not to damage its *long-term agility*. Another point

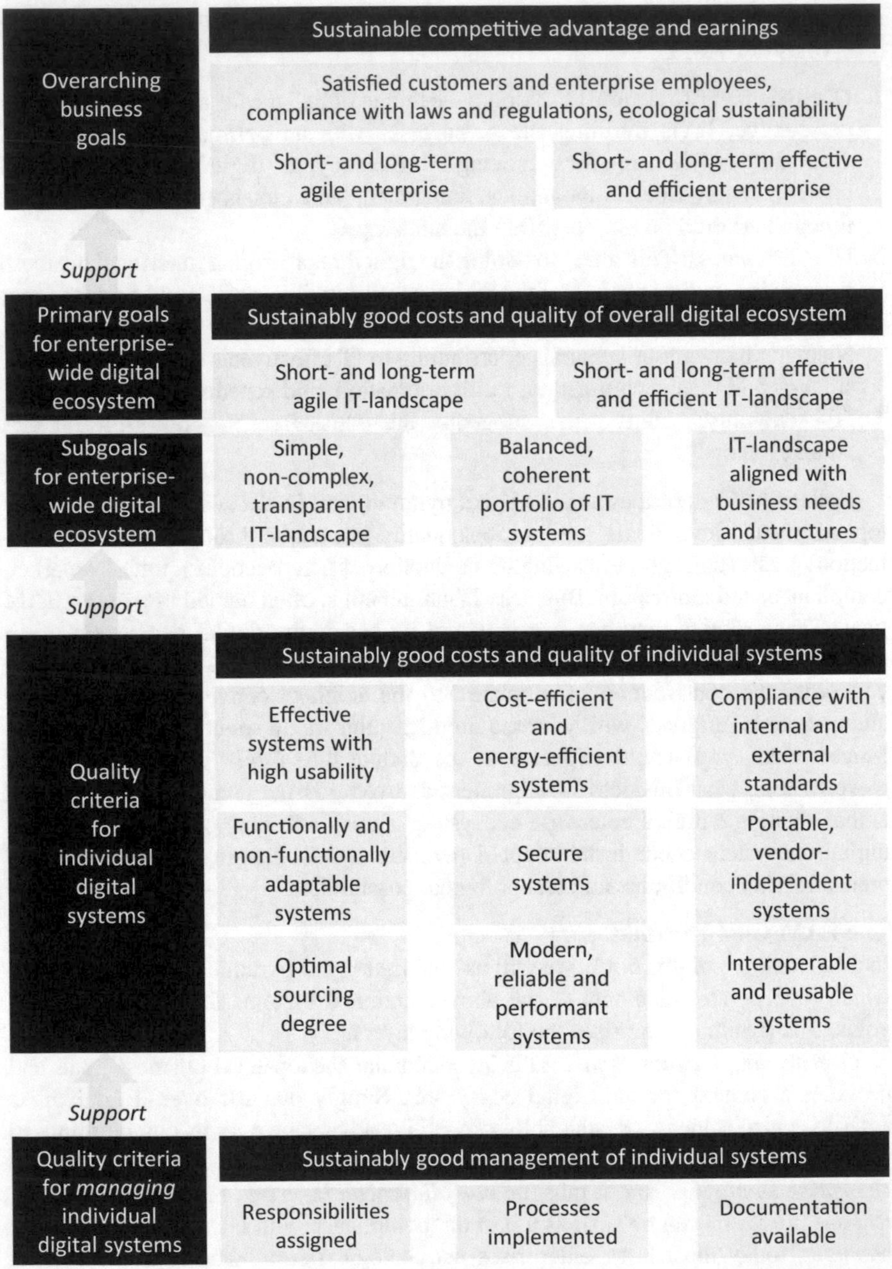

Overarching business goals	Sustainable competitive advantage and earnings	
	Satisfied customers and enterprise employees, compliance with laws and regulations, ecological sustainability	
	Short- and long-term agile enterprise	Short- and long-term effective and efficient enterprise

Support

Primary goals for enterprise-wide digital ecosystem	Sustainably good costs and quality of overall digital ecosystem		
	Short- and long-term agile IT-landscape		Short- and long-term effective and efficient IT-landscape
Subgoals for enterprise-wide digital ecosystem	Simple, non-complex, transparent IT-landscape	Balanced, coherent portfolio of IT systems	IT-landscape aligned with business needs and structures

Support

Quality criteria for individual digital systems	Sustainably good costs and quality of individual systems		
	Effective systems with high usability	Cost-efficient and energy-efficient systems	Compliance with internal and external standards
	Functionally and non-functionally adaptable systems	Secure systems	Portable, vendor-independent systems
	Optimal sourcing degree	Modern, reliable and performant systems	Interoperable and reusable systems

Support

Quality criteria for *managing* individual digital systems	Sustainably good management of individual systems		
	Responsibilities assigned	Processes implemented	Documentation available

Fig. 4.2 EAM goal pyramid

contributing to its competitive advantage is the *short- and long-term effectiveness and efficiency* of the enterprise. Note that agility enables efficiency, since it provides the enterprise with the ability to change its system, i.e., "to do the right business functions." Thus, we could also subsume agility below efficiency. However, since agility is only one part of efficiency, and agility has a prominent position among the EAM goals, we display it here as a distinct goal.

Primary goals for the overall digital ecosystem. From the viewpoint of the business, the requirements toward its digital ecosystem are also simple: Sustainably provide *high-quality services at low costs*. To be able to cope with changing business requirements, like the enterprise, the IT landscape needs to be *agile* and needs to stay agile, i.e., it must be able to change fast and at low costs. Also like the enterprise, the digital ecosystem needs to be *short- and long-term effective and efficient*.

Subgoals for the overall digital ecosystem. As discussed before, a *simple, non-complex, transparent IT landscape* is an essential precondition for an efficient, agile IT landscape. This goal is primarily enabled by standardized, homogenous ecosystem with a good degree of service reuse and the use of shared platforms. A *balanced, coherent portfolio of IT systems* goes in a similar direction: here a choice is made regarding the type of "things" that will be "done" in the ecosystem, i.e., this goal also contributes to effectiveness. The goal of an *IT landscape aligned with business needs and structures* purely focuses on effectiveness, ensuring that all business requirements are fulfilled.

Quality criteria for individual IT systems. Instead of addressing the complete IT landscape, this layer focuses on individual systems, like business applications or infrastructure platforms. Not surprisingly, the individual systems have goals like those of the overall digital ecosystem: effectiveness, efficiency, compliance, and adaptability. Additional goals often used in EAM to measure the quality of individual systems are that systems should be *secure, modern, reliable and performant, portable, vendor-independent, interoperable, and reusable* and have an *optimal sourcing degree*. Though these criteria are valid for individual systems, in an aggregated form, they can also be used as goals for the overall IT landscape. For example, it could be a goal that 70% of the business applications are *interoperable* with each other; that 80% of the systems are based on *modern*, "future-proof" technologies; or that 75% of business applications are *sourced* from third-party vendors as software as a service. In Chap. 5, we will discuss these metrics in more detail.

Quality criteria for managing individual IT systems. The goals above addressed the outcome of EAM, i.e., the direct qualities the digital ecosystem and its components should have when EAM was successfully applied. However, at least in the medium term, the quality of the digital ecosystem also depends on how well the systems are *managed*. This can be broken down into the goal that tasks, processes, roles, and artifacts for managing a system are defined and implemented in a good quality. For example, in IT asset catalogs, usually the business owner and the person responsible for operating the system are named. Another important flag is that documentation for the system is available. Note that this list could be extended, for example, with the quality of tools for changing the system; however, here we focus on the criteria typically used in the context of EAM.

4.2   EAM Process Framework

4.2.1   A Short Review of EAM Processes in Literature

Figure 4.3 provides an overview of EAM processes in the major standards and selected EAM literature. The steps are roughly sorted along the envision-specify-implement-evaluate process. Steps that do not fit in this category are highlighted in gray; usually these are one level higher or lower, i.e., they steer or enable the core process. In summary, it can be said that no standard today covers EAM processes comprehensively. The EAM processes described in publications of individual EAM practitioners and scientists do not form a comprehensive picture either and strongly deviate from each other. In the following, we briefly describe the approaches illustrated in Fig. 4.3:

Hafner and Winter (2008) suggested four EAM phases: *architecture planning*, *architecture development*, *architecture communication*, and *architecture lobbying*. Inside of each area, they distinguished several steps, like *update architecture principles* inside the first phase. Though the individual activities make sense, "communication" and "lobbying" are rather orthogonal to the EAM process and not just part of one phase.

Buckl (2011, p. 151) described a simple, generic EAM process, the first three steps being (1) *develop and describe*, (2) *communicate and act*, and (3) *analyze and evaluate*. These steps resemble the basic plan-do-check EAM process also proposed, for example, by Niemann (2006). The fourth step, *configure and adapt*, is about installing and steering the EAM capability.

Hanschke (2012, p. 143) describes four capabilities for the core cycle of EAM: *landscape documentation*, for the initial description of the as-is landscape; *landscape quality assurance*, to ensure that the models are complete, up to date, and compliant with modeling regulations; *landscape analysis*, to identify improvement potential; and *landscape development*, to define the target pictures. The fifth capability, *EAM method and tools*, supports the core activities with a framework and tools. The sixth capability roughly translates to *implementation governance*; it ensures that the defined target pictures are being implemented in the enterprise. The last point is achieved by integrating the target pictures and roadmaps in the portfolio processes of the enterprise and by tracing the advances of the roadmap implementation. Note that she sticks to the strategic level of EAM where collections of systems are addressed and does not address the architecture or quality assessment of individual systems.

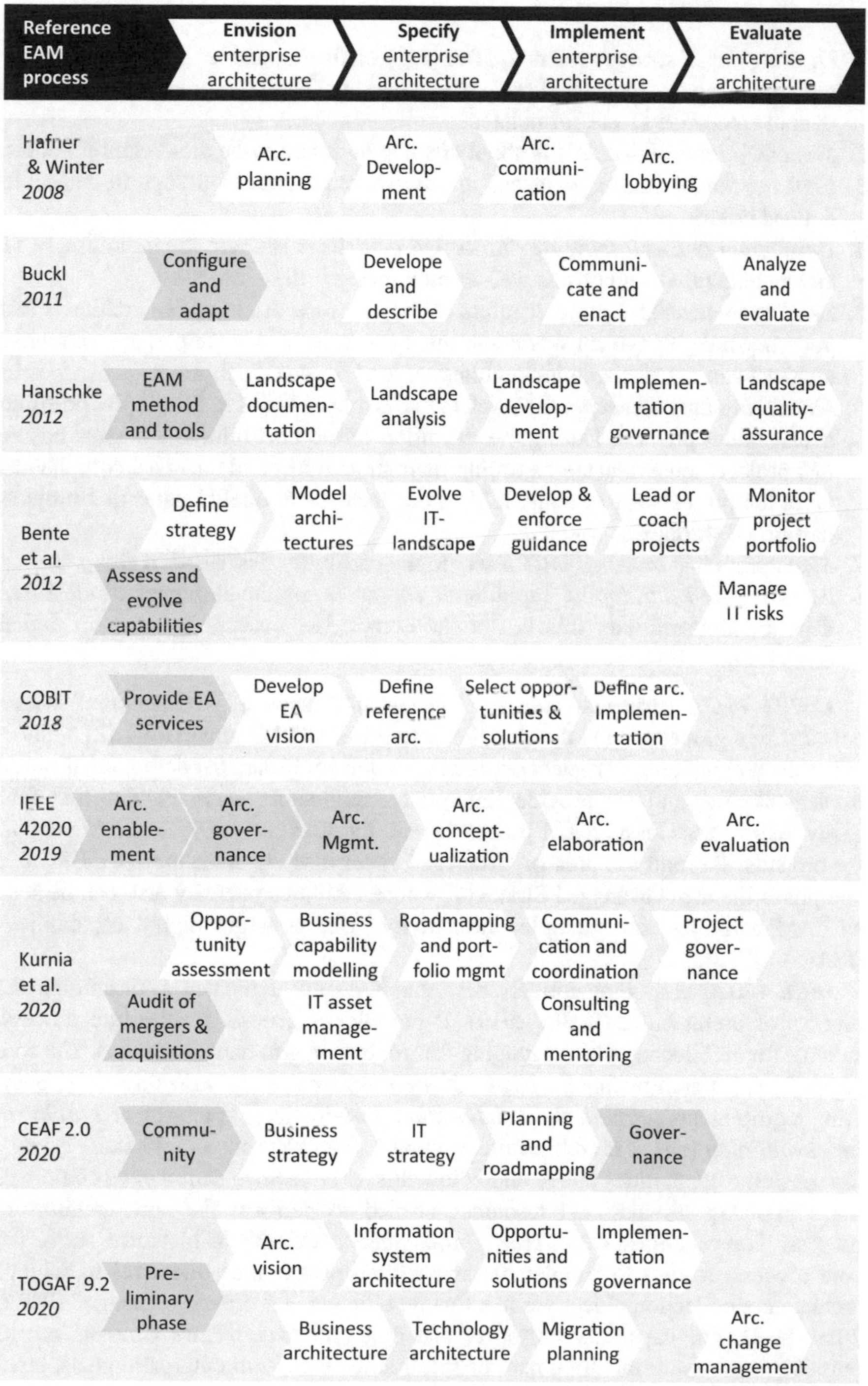

Reference EAM process	Envision enterprise architecture	Specify enterprise architecture	Implement enterprise architecture	Evaluate enterprise architecture
Hafner & Winter 2008	Arc. planning	Arc. Development	Arc. communication	Arc. lobbying
Buckl 2011	Configure and adapt	Develope and describe	Communicate and enact	Analyze and evaluate
Hanschke 2012	EAM method and tools / Landscape documentation	Landscape analysis	Landscape development / Implementation governance	Landscape quality-assurance
Bente et al. 2012	Define strategy / Assess and evolve capabilities	Model architectures / Evolve IT-landscape	Develop & enforce guidance / Lead or coach projects	Monitor project portfolio / Manage IT risks
COBIT 2018	Provide EA services / Develop EA vision	Define reference arc.	Select opportunities & solutions / Define arc. Implementation	
IEEE 42020 2019	Arc. enablement / Arc. governance / Arc. Mgmt.	Arc. conceptualization	Arc. elaboration	Arc. evaluation
Kurnia et al. 2020	Opportunity assessment / Audit of mergers & acquisitions	Business capability modelling / IT asset management	Roadmapping and portfolio mgmt / Communication and coordination / Consulting and mentoring	Project governance
CEAF 2.0 2020	Community	Business strategy	IT strategy / Planning and roadmapping / Governance	
TOGAF 9.2 2020	Preliminary phase / Arc. vision	Information system architecture / Business architecture / Technology architecture	Opportunities and solutions / Implementation governance / Migration planning	Arc. change management

Fig. 4.3 EAM processes and capabilities in literature

Bente et al. (2012, p. 39) name eight core activities of enterprise architecting:

1. *Defining the IT strategy* refers to IT strategy on the highest level, where, together with the business, high-level principles ("maxims") and requirements toward the overall enterprise IT are formulated.
2. *Modeling the architectures* is about creating as-is and to-be architecture models.
3. *Evolving the IT landscape* means to improve the digital landscape in respect to defined criteria.
4. *Developing and enforcing standards and guidelines* is about the definition of IT and architecture standards as well as monitoring if these are used.
5. *Leading or coaching projects* refers to project work of enterprise architects that goes beyond the typical advice-and-monitor role. For example, an enterprise architect can act as a solution architect or lead for a critical project.
6. *Monitoring the project portfolio* refers to the role of EAM in the project portfolio management process. During the definition of the portfolio, EAM must ensure that projects are evaluated regarding their strategic fit and standard compliance. Once the projects are running, EAM must implement quality gates that projects have to go through.
7. *Managing risks involved in IT* refers to the capability described in Chap. 3.
8. *Assessing and developing capabilities* addresses the development of the EAM department itself, i.e., this is not the core EAM process to develop digital ecosystem.

COBIT has a dedicated area for "Managed Enterprise Architecture," which contains five processes: (1) develop the Enterprise Architecture vision, (2) define a reference architecture, (3) select opportunities and solutions, (4) define architecture implementation, and (5) provide Enterprise Architecture services. The first four easily map to the classic EAM processes, and the fifth one refers to EAM support for projects. Beyond the area of "Managed Enterprise Architecture," COBIT also comprises the area "Managed Strategy," whose activities partially also can be seen as EAM activities, for example, the activity "Define target digital capabilities" (ISACA, 2018).

IEEE 42020 is a comparatively new standard only dedicated at describing the process of architecture (IEEE, 2019). It provides a generic architecture process, suitable for architecting objects ranging from enterprises to hardware items. The core capabilities for architecting a system are *architecture conceptualization* (e.g., gathering requirements), *architecture elaboration* (provide target picture), and *architecture evaluation* (check if architecture is suitable for its purpose). Interestingly, they also describe capabilities above and below this: *architecture enablement* comprises the supporting services and resources needed to perform the core architecture process. The capability *Architecture Management* logically is allocated above the core process. It aims to "implement architecture governance directives to achieve architecture collection objectives in a timely, efficient and effective manner" (IEEE, 2019, p. 8). The capability on top of that they call *Architecture Governance*; its purpose is to ensure the alignment of the architectures with enterprise goals, strategies, and related architectures.

Kurnia et al. (2020) identified eight major activity areas of EAM, based on 18 senior enterprise architects from different enterprises and industries:

- *Business capability modeling* in their understanding serves as an umbrella for "all activities of architects related to dealing with business capabilities," including the first creation of such models but also the "heatmapping" of individual capabilities (to indicate the state of capabilities and need for improvement).
- *Roadmapping and portfolio planning* encompasses all activities of architects related to defining future IT projects. The roadmaps show the planned IT investments in defined areas, their start and end dates, and the maturity levels inside the planned landscapes.
- *IT asset management* is a classic EAM task, where existing IT assets like applications and infrastructure are documented in a catalog. One the one hand, this serves as a high-level documentation needed for addressing individual systems, for example, in the case of incident handling. On the other hand, the information in the catalog is the basis for evaluating ("health-checking") and improving the landscape in the other EAM processes.
- *Opportunity assessment* encompasses the EAM activities for evaluating digitalization possibilities based on specific business needs.
- *Project governance* they define as the activities for reviewing and approving the implementation plans of IT projects. This includes foremost reviewing the target pictures produced by the projects, to ensure their standards compliance, discuss possible deviations, approve justified exceptions, and provide dispensations if needed.
- *Communication and coordination* are EAM activities needed in all lifecycle phases to ensure a productive dialog and trustful relationships with all stakeholders.
- *Consulting and mentoring* are activities needed in all lifecycle phases to support stakeholders with EAM expertise, comparable to "communication and coordination." However, it is especially important in the "EAM implementation" phase when the architectural target pictures must be conveyed to the architects and engineers of the projects implementing the changes.
- *Audit of mergers and acquisitions* is rather a special use case of applying EAM expertise than a general EAM process. The support of mergers and acquisitions is often named as an exemplary EAM activity, because here the stakeholders need an evaluation of the baseline and the merged target scenarios of the enterprise-wide digital ecosystem. However, in practice, this is only an exceedingly small part of EAM work compared to the daily operations.

CEAF (2020b) describes five EAM capabilities: community, business strategy, IT strategy, planning and roadmapping, and governance. Each capability comprises six sub-capabilities; we describe those only briefly here:

- The *community* capability comprises three sub-capabilities: collaboration, education, and innovation.
- In the *business* capability, the following sub-capabilities are described: coordinate business strategy, business transformation, digital business modeling,

customer experience lens to IT, digital opportunity demonstration, and digital strategy facilitation. Compared to the other frameworks, CEAF has a stronger focus on business architecture and uses more current concepts.

- In the capability of *IT strategy*, the following sub-capabilities deviate from the frameworks discussed above: assess vendors/partners, accelerate agile technologies, assess IT talent, and support IT workforce plan. The last two points stick out from the previous EAM frameworks, because they address the development of the IT organization and not the digital ecosystem.
- The fourth capability, *planning and roadmapping*, comprises sub-capabilities like those described by the other frameworks.
- That goes also for the fifth capability, *governance*. However, here it is noteworthy that CEAF explicitly lists a sub-category for "create and manage reference architecture" (reference architectures are only one of many artifacts).

TOGAF: When asked for a reference for Enterprise Architecture Management, most practitioners today point toward TOGAF (Open Group, 2020a). However, as the name suggests, TOGAF's core—the Architecture Development Method (ADM)—focuses on the *development* of the architectures of complex systems. The ADM is detailed, mature, and useful. However, it does not cover the processes used in the governance function of Enterprise Architecture Management in detail.

The ADM lifecycle starts with the *preliminary phase* where the EAM capability is configured. The next phase is the *vision*, where a high-level picture of the final system is sketched out. In the next phases, the *business, data, application, and infrastructure architecture* are defined. Based on this, physical solutions are selected. These are implemented in the real-life intricacies of large enterprise during the phases of *migration planning* and *implementation governance*. When the solution is running, the activity of *architecture change management* ensures that all changes to the system are compliant with the architecture vision.

4.2.2   The Essence of Architectural Work

Before delving into the details of EAM processes, let us recapitulate the archetype behind EAM: a classical *architect* that a *customer* hires to build a house at a *building site*. It might be the first and only time the customer builds a house, so the architect helps him to understand and articulate his requirements toward the house. In this endeavor, first the architect interviews the customer regarding his demands, his financial capabilities, and the envisioned time horizon. After this, the architect presents him a blueprint for the future house, a cost estimation, and a roadmap. The customer is satisfied with the proposal, since the architect obviously knows *the state of the art* of building technology and where to get high-quality *building materials* for reasonable prices. The customer also appreciates the creative design process behind the architecture blueprint. Thus, he accepts the proposal and asks her to also support in supervising the building of the house. Naturally, the architect also

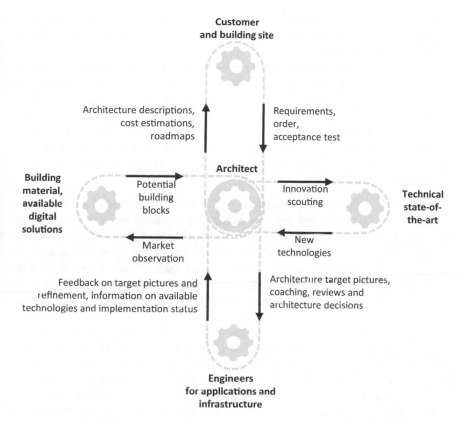

Fig. 4.4 The five forces of architecture

knows qualified *engineers* and construction workers that build the house. After a structural analysis from the engineers, the architect adapts the blueprint to make the house statically safe. During the construction period, the architect often visits the construction site to ensure that the implementation follows the blueprint. After all, the architect must ensure that the customers' requirements are implemented in the best way possible. Naturally, she is not as often on the construction site as the project lead, who controls the daily workings. When the house is finished, the architect visits it with the customer, who formally accepts the building.

Just like the architect of a house, the architect of a digital solution is part of five interacting architecture forces: customer, architect, engineers, builders, and technical state of the art and building material (cp. Fig. 4.4). This picture highlights two architectural core tasks:

- *Design a target picture.* The architect creates and maintains the overview, the "big picture" of the solution. This model (or views of the model) must be understood by all stakeholders, from the customer to the engineer. Procedure models for designing this target picture do exist, for instance, TOGAF's

Architecture Development Method. However, in the end, this is an iterative, creative process that integrates the input and repercussions from all forces adjacent to the architect.

- *Communicate and establish "conveyer belts" between stakeholders.* The architect must understand the customer and its requirements, speak the language of the engineers and the builders, have a basic knowledge of technologies (and know which expertise can be left to the specialists), and know the technical state of the art and the available building materials suited for the building site. The architect intermediates between all forces and serves as the interface and translator between them. At the same time, she steers them toward a sustainable, coherent model of the target solution.

These core tasks are also reflected in TOGAF's summary of an Enterprise Architect: "The architect has a responsibility for ensuring the completeness (fitness-for-purpose) of the architecture, in terms of adequately addressing all the pertinent concerns of its stakeholders; and the integrity of the architecture, in terms of connecting all the various views to each other, satisfactorily reconciling the conflicting concerns of different stakeholders, and showing the trade-offs made in doing so (as between security and performance, for example)" (Open Group, 2020a).

Note that the "force" of *technical state of the art* implies that an enterprise architect continuously educates himself, regarding current EAM methods, like TOGAF, but also regarding the digital technologies the architect is responsible for (e.g., identity and access management or data analytics). A leading research and advisory company recently put it like this: "Enterprise Architects are our most avid readers. They have to cover a very broad spectrum of knowledge, though they do not have to know every detail of the individual fields." The force of "building material" in the digital worlds implies that an Enterprise Architect must know the available solutions and vendors in his or her specialization area. The picture deviates in so far that the main task of a house architect ends when the house is built. EAM on the other side is a perpetual task because the enterprise-wide digital ecosystem is never final; it always changes and evolves.

4.2.3   The EAM Process Cube

Different Enterprise Levels Need to Be Architected
In the context of Fig. 2.9, we already established that in large enterprises, the organizational system is structured into circa five hierarchical levels. We also established that on every level we encounter correlated data objects, functions, organizational elements, processes, and IT functions in the granularity specific to that level. Figure 4.5 illustrates this principle regarding the functional dimension, displaying enterprise functions on five levels. Unfortunately, the names (e.g., business unit, segment, domain, department) of the levels change from enterprise to

Depth, i.e., level of detail →

Group-level	Insurance Group
Enterprise level	Property insurance · Car insurance · Health insurance · Industrial insurance
Value chain / segment level	Sales & marketing · Under-writing · Policy management · Claims handling · ...
(Sub-) segment-level	Sales forecasting · Lead management · Customer relationship management · Pricing · ...
Function level	Client data management · Interaction history · Predictive analytics · Activity planning · ...

Fig. 4.5 Business functions on different levels of hierarchy and granularity

enterprise. For the organizational structures on the levels between "enterprise" and "function," we will use the term "segment," as TOGAF does. Other than organigrams, you will find such levels also in the business process modeling method of large enterprises, where often also five hierarchical levels are distinguished.

Now, for every business function, it should be ensured that the digital elements inside this function form a coherent, optimized digital ecosystem. In other words, we could assign an architect to every function. And down to a certain level of detail, that does make sense. To make this more tangible, Fig. 4.6 illustrates typical architecture roles in an enterprise; these differ in the scope of the architected system and in consequence also in the level of architectural detail. These roles are:

- *Enterprise architect:* This role is responsible for the complete enterprise-wide digital ecosystem. However, in practice, usually only the chief enterprise architect really has this broad of a scope, while the other enterprise architects specialize on one part of the enterprise or on one technology. Enterprise architects are part of the Enterprise Architecture capability which, in terms of Fig. 4.5, addresses either the complete group or one enterprise inside the group. In this capability, all aspects relevant for the Enterprise Architecture are addressed. To make this more tangible, the Enterprise Architecture department of the car insurance could comprise eight enterprise architects, each being responsible for a business domain (e.g., sales) and an architecture domain (e.g., data analytics).

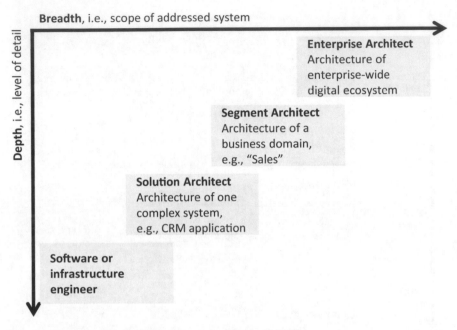

Fig. 4.6 Different roles for different scopes and levels of detail

- *Segment architect:* A segment architect is responsible for a defined business area below the "enterprise" level. This could be one of the functions displayed on the value chain level or the function level of Fig. 4.5. For example, in a large enterprise, it makes sense having a segment architect responsible for the digital ecosystem inside the areas "sales and marketing."
- *Solution architect.* The solution architect is responsible for one complex application or one complex infrastructure element. Take, for example, the Claims Handling Application in an insurance company. This is a centerpiece of the enterprise value chain. Often it is grown via decades, a mixture of legacy and modern components, and extraordinarily complex. The insurance employs a solution architect for this system. Her job is to ensure that this important digital function is reliable, cost-efficient, "future-proof," secure, and of high usability.
- *Software or infrastructure engineer.* The specialized engineers specify, implement, and test the digital functions required for a business application or an infrastructure system. From an architect's perspective, these engineers are important not only because they enable the realization of the digital system but also because of their specialized expertise and feedback toward architectural decisions. In contrast to the solution architect, they focus on one part of the solution, while it is the responsibility of the architect to address the overall solution and dependencies between its components.

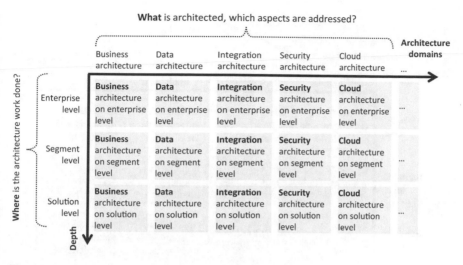

Fig. 4.7   The architecture domains must be addressed on every level

Different Architecture Domains Must Be Addressed

Figure 4.7 introduces another dimension: In every business area that we architect, we have to address the various architectural layers (see Fig. 2.6). In the following, we will use the term of TOGAF, where, instead of "architectural layer," the term *architecture domain* is used. We already described above that the architects on the enterprise level in practice often specialize on different architecture domains. The same happens on the segment level. For example, the segment "sales and marketing" (cp. Fig. 4.5) could have its own architecture department that addresses all architecture aspects relevant for this segment. Thus, one of their segment architects could be assigned to take care of the architecture domain data analytics. Now, complementary to that, the same role could be allocated on other levels of the enterprise, for example, a data analytics architect with the scope of (1) the complete group, (2) the enterprise "car insurance," and (3) the segment "sales and marketing." In large enterprises, at least for such an important capability as data analytics, you will find indeed a responsible data analytics architect on every level, from the level of the group CxO down to large departments.

Obviously, other than the simplified table displayed in Fig. 4.7 might suggest, there is no 1:1 relationship between the higher and the lower levels, but a 1:n relationship (cp. Fig. 4.5). That means that in our example, the enterprise architect for data analytics has four counterparts, each being responsible for data analytics in the respective segment, for instance, sales and marketing, underwriting, policy management, and claims handling.

Architecture Processes Must Address All Dimensions

Comparable to enterprise systems and roles on different hierarchy levels, Fig. 4.8 illustrates that also the architecture processes must be implemented on each level:

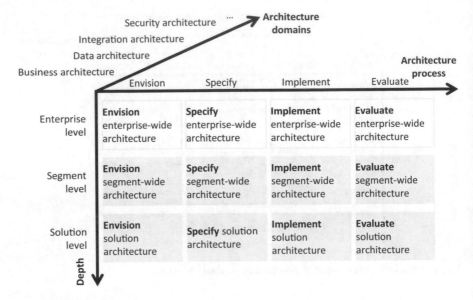

Fig. 4.8 The cube of EAM core processes

The *enterprise* architects envision, specify, implement, and evaluate the architecture of the enterprise-wide digital ecosystem. The *segment* architects execute the same steps on their level, and the *solution* architects on the solution level. As the name Enterprise Architecture Management indicates, the focus of EAM lays on the enterprise level. However, *in practice, EAM is also strongly involved in the levels of segment and solution architecture* since the accumulated systems on these levels in the end constitute the Enterprise Architecture. To make this more tangible: One of the most prominent EAM processes is the evaluation of changes on the solution level, where architecture boards check if a new application or another significant change in the digital landscape is compliant with EAM guidelines and target pictures.

Adding the third dimension of Fig. 4.8, the lifecycle of envision-specify-implement-evaluate is applied to each architecture domain. Take, for example, data architecture or security architecture: both need to be envisioned, specified, implemented, and evaluated on a regular basis. This should happen on the level of an individual solution, on the segment level on the enterprise level. Corresponding examples are the data architecture of a Customer Relationship Management system, the data architecture of the domain sales and marketing, and the data architecture of the complete car insurance.

Processes for Steering, Executing, and Supporting EAM

Figure 4.9 illustrates that EAM processes fall into three categories. The main category comprises the *core processes* of EAM discussed above. In the category below, the core processes are *supported* and enabled by various processes and

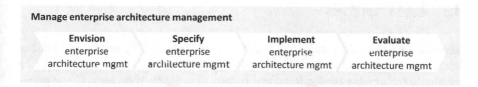

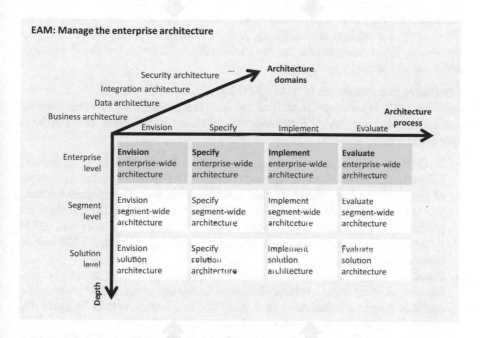

Fig. 4.9 Processes for steering, executing, and supporting EAM

capabilities. The third category is responsible for *steering EAM*; here, the objective of the management activities is not the Enterprise Architecture, but the EAM capability itself.

4.3   EAM Artifacts

The word artifact stems from the Latin word *arte* (skill, craft) and *factum* ("thing made"), meaning an object made or shaped by human hand. In business informatics terminology, artifacts are the input and output of business processes. Correspondingly, EAM artifacts exist for all EAM processes and functions as depicted, for example, in Fig. 4.9. They are objects needed by the EAM capability for envisioning, specifying, implementing, and evaluating the enterprise-wide digital ecosystem. EAM artifacts take the form of catalogs, diagrams (graphical models), matrixes, and textual specifications.

Literature and Standards on EAM Artifacts
Just like for EAM processes, there is no standard that comprehensively describes the artifacts needed for EAM. However, the following publications cover a large spectrum of EAM artifacts:

- *TOGAF* provides a detailed, comprehensive list of artifacts along the phases of the Architecture *Development* Method (ADM). TOGAF distinguishes three types of artifacts: matrixes, diagrams, and catalogs. However, as mentioned before, TOGAF focuses on the *development* of large digital systems. Thus, it does not provide a comprehensive picture of artifacts needed in the complete EAM governance lifecycle. For instance, artifacts for evaluating EA and EAM are not in the focus of TOGAF (cp. Open Group, 2020a).
- Hanschke (2012) describes in detail typical EAM artifacts used in practice. She focuses on diagrams, including business capability maps, application maps, portfolio graphics, information flow graphics, information system lifecycle diagrams, and application landscape roadmap graphics.
- Kurnia et al. (2020) provide a list that covers a good amount of the EAM artifacts used in practice.
- The *California Enterprise Architecture Framework* (CEAF) lists EAM artifacts in five dimensions: strategy, business, information, application, and technology. Like TOGAF, the CEAF also focuses on the *development* of large digital systems. However, as displayed in the choice of their dimensions and in the quality of the artifacts comprised in those, CEAF puts greater weight on the initial two phases, i.e., strategy and business (cp. CEAF, 2021b).

The following sections provide an overview of the most important EAM artifacts. For an exhaustive, detailed list of architecture artifacts, please refer to the publications named above. Note that Sect. 4.6 describes EAM processes in detail, including the artifacts used in the processes.

4.3.1 Baseline, Target, and Reference Architectures

Baseline Architecture, Transition Architecture, and Target Architecture
Imagine you are the enterprise architect responsible for the IT landscape of a worldwide operating cargo airline. Here, the booking engine is an essential system where all flights are booked. Since this booking engine is 30 years old, the CIO asks you to rebuild the engine and to switch from a mainframe-based architecture to a cloud-ready, micro service-based system. Reacting to that, now you first create the as-is picture of the current architecture, to get a thorough understanding of the current situation. In Enterprise Architecture lingo, this artifact is also called the *baseline architecture*. Afterward, you create the *target architecture*, which conveys to the stakeholders how the architecture of the booking engine will look when the change project is completed. Since this project is estimated to take 4 years, you also propose an intermediary picture that will be reached after 2 years. In architecture terminology, this is called a *transition architecture*. For each architecture description, you include the relevant views, for example, on the data, integration, infrastructure, and security aspects of the booking engine. A detailed explanation of how to develop architecture descriptions of complex digital systems is provided foremost by TOGAF and its Architecture Development Method (Open Group, 2020a).

Reference Architecture
In Chap. 2, we defined that a "reference model is a model that can be used as a reference and comparison object in the creation or evaluation of other models or real-world objects. Usually, a reference model has a positive connotation and represents a best practice." Consequently, a reference architecture is an architecture that can be used as a reference and comparison object in the creation or evaluation of other architectures. For example, a reference architecture for IoT applications was created inside the Lufthansa Group. This model provides guidance for solution architects inside the different business units of the group and fosters harmonization of solution blocks as well as communication inside the group. Figure 4.10 shows the structure of the reference architecture model. The architecture has two orthogonal dimensions:

- In the first dimension, the three horizontal views express *where* IoT building blocks and structures are allocated. They can be allocated (a) on the edge layer, for example, in the shop floor of a factory; (b) in the platform layer, e.g., in an integrated IoT platform in the cloud; or (c) in the enterprise application layer, e.g., in an ERP system.
- In the second dimension, the five vertical views indicate *what* must be addressed, i.e., which building blocks. This could be building blocks like "sensor," "actuator," "encryption mechanism," "event streaming platform," "data lake," or "machine learning."

A *target architecture* is dedicated to one specific solution or enterprise area. And usually, it is accompanied by a process, in which the stakeholders agree to a binding roadmap to reach the target picture. Compared to that, a reference architecture is *less binding* and has a *broader scope*; it should be (re)used by many business units. In other words, it leaves more "wiggle room" to the local units for developing their

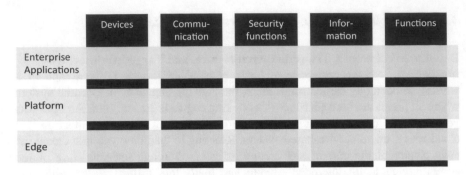

Fig. 4.10 Lufthansa's reference architecture for developing IoT applications. © 2021, Lufthansa Group, reprinted with permission

target architectures. However, the development of a reference architecture requires significant effort since, to serve as a "reference," it must be of high quality. The creators of the reference architecture must be able to abstract from concrete enterprise scenarios while at the same time include practically relevant and modern elements in the reference architecture. Thus, the development of a reference architecture inside an enterprise only makes sense, if there are a high number of potential use cases for the reference architecture and if there is no corresponding reference architecture publicly available coming close enough to the enterprise-specific requirements.

Publicly available reference architectures exist both for business domains and technical domains. For the business domains, industry-specific standardization bodies provide reference architectures; for instance, the IATA (International Air Transport Association) provides reference architectures and standards that describe business processes, capabilities, and documents used in the airline industry. Regarding technical domains, many reference architectures are published from scientists, governmental organizations, and industry standardization bodies. For example, the state of California published reference architectures for the fields of cloud computing, identity and access management (IAM), business intelligence (BI), master data management (MDM), Service-Oriented Architecture (SOA), Enterprise Application Integration (EAI), Enterprise Content Management (ECM), and eGovernment (cp. CEAF, 2021b).

4.3.2 Maps of the Digital Ecosystem

Having in mind that EAM is about steering digital landscapes, it is not surprising that a century-old tool for illustrating landscapes is very prominent in EAM: maps. EAM maps are models that illustrate large collections of homogenous elements of the digital ecosystem. They come in two forms:

1. *Matrixes*, where the elements are sorted along the Y-axis and the X-axis. Examples of this are displayed in Figs. 4.13 4.14.

2. *Cluster maps*, where the elements are grouped into clusters; since these clusters can contain subclusters, these maps often display hierarchies of elements. Figures 4.12 and 4.15 show examples of this type.

Both types of maps are structured simply and focus usually only on one type of element of the digital ecosystem, for instance, on business capabilities or on applications. Due to this simplicity, the maps are easy to understand and can easily be generated by tools based on the entries in the IT asset catalog. These maps are used to address core EAM concerns, like the potential for harmonizing the business landscape, the application landscape, or the infrastructure landscape. Basically, all large enterprises use business capability maps and related EAM maps (cp. also Khosroshahi et al., 2018). EAM maps display selected aspects of the digital ecosystem, usually focusing on one or two of the elements displayed in Fig. 4.11. We already saw in Fig. 2.9 that these core elements exist on different levels of hierarchy, hence the "has-subelements" relationship on most of the elements in Fig. 4.11. In the following, we briefly describe the most important types of EAM maps.

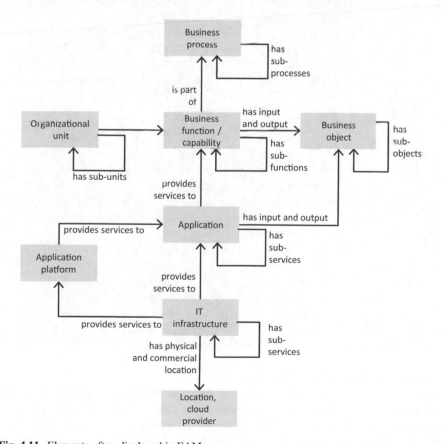

Fig. 4.11 Elements often displayed in EAM maps

The Meaning of Business Capability

In the last years, the rediscovered insight that enterprise digitalization requires a business-driven method brought great interest to "business capability modeling." However, in the context of EAM, the concept of business capability modeling exists at least since the year 2007 (cp. Hanschke, 2012, p. 68). TOGAF defines a business capability as "a particular ability that a business may possess or exchange to achieve a specific purpose." For better or for worse, the term business capability is closely related to the term "business function." The latter is a core concept of business informatics and Business Process Management with the following meaning: *an activity inside a business process that transforms input into output*. Note that both business functions and business capabilities can be classified along the usual architecture dimensions:

- *As-is state and to-be state*, i.e., business capabilities can either depict a current state or envision a future, target state.
- Different *levels of granularity and detail*, i.e., business capabilities exist on various hierarchy levels (cp. Fig. 2.9).
- Different levels of *genericity and specificity*; for example, a generic, enterprise-independent model could display business capabilities used generally in the airline industry. On the other hand, an enterprise-specific model could display the business capabilities used in a particular airline group.

Now, theoretically, there might be differences between the terms "capability" and "function." But, at least in the practice of EAM, *both terms are used synonymously*. Note though that Business Process Management analyzes and optimizes analog or digital business processes. Enterprise Architecture Management, on the other hand, analyzes and optimizes *landscapes* of digital systems. Accordingly, in the context of EAM, business capabilities most prominently appear in *maps*, i.e., in models that provide an overview of large sets of business capabilities in a defined area.

Note that due to their close relationship with business functions, business capabilities belong to the realm of the classic and well-researched field of Business Process Management and enterprise modeling. For example, Scheer (1999) already exhaustively described the relationships between different types of business functions, further business concepts (e.g., processes, data, and organizational elements), and digital concepts (e.g., modules).

Clustered Business Capability Maps

Figure 4.12 shows a clustered map of business capabilities. Referring to the metamodel of Fig. 4.11, this map contains only one element: "business function/capability," i.e., the hierarchy of business capabilities inside one enterprise. The map can be generated automatically from an EAM tool. However, it is often created

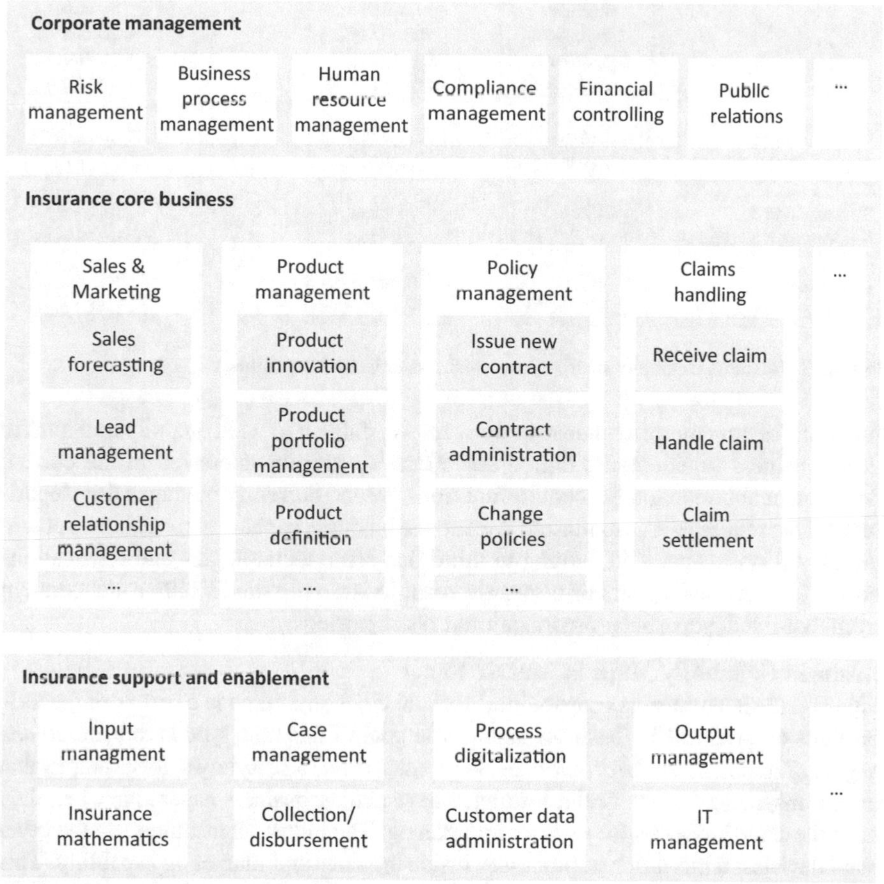

Corporate management

| Risk management | Business process management | Human resource management | Compliance management | Financial controlling | Public relations | ... |

Insurance core business

Sales & Marketing	Product management	Policy management	Claims handling	...
Sales forecasting	Product innovation	Issue new contract	Receive claim	
Lead management	Product portfolio management	Contract administration	Handle claim	
Customer relationship management	Product definition	Change policies	Claim settlement	
...	...	...		

Insurance support and enablement

| Input managment | Case management | Process digitalization | Output management | ... |
| Insurance mathematics | Collection/ disbursement | Customer data administration | IT management | |

Fig. 4.12 Example of a clustered business capability map

manually, resulting in an elaborated slide set that contains the main business capabilities of the enterprise (such a set consists of circa 20 slides, each depicting a map like the one shown in Fig. 4.13, comprising the business capabilities on all hierarchy levels of the enterprise). Due to the imperative of *the structure of the digital ecosystem follows the business structure*, a business capability map is central for EAM. Primarily it is used for structuring the application landscape and is the basis for heat maps, which correlate the individual capabilities in the map with metrics.

On the one hand, the map illustrates the current business functions of the enterprise. On the other hand, it is supposed to be *independent from the actual organizational setting*. Now, why should a business capability model be decoupled from the current organizational chart? A practical reason is that we want to be able to discuss the structure of the digital ecosystem without getting into political quarrels of which organizational unit is responsible for what. Another reason is that here we are interested primarily in a comprehensive ("MECE"; see above) model of business

	Business capability 1 *E.g., sales & marketing*	Business capability 2 *E.g., product management*	...	Business capability 9 *E.g., claims handling*
Business unit 1 *E.g., car insurance*	Business capability 1a	Business capability 2a	...	Business capability 9a
Business unit 2 *E.g., industry insurance*	Business capability 1b	Business capability 2a	...	Business capability 9a
Business unit 3, *E.g., health insurance*	Business capability 1a	Business capability 2b	...	Business capability 9a

Fig. 4.13 Business capability matrix along business units and capabilities

functions of our enterprise, because we want to establish to what quantity and quality these business functions are digitalized. Here we are not interested in the current department abbreviation for certain functions or who currently manages this department. This relates to a third reason: we use the business capability model to structure the digital landscape. And, having in mind that some technologies and applications have lifecycles of 30 years or more, we want to structure the IT rather independent from fast-lived, superficial organizational restructurings.

Business Capability Maps in Matrix Form
Figure 4.13 shows business capabilities' instantiations structured in a matrix of [generic business capabilities] × [business units]. The goal of this map type is to *evaluate the degree of business standardization* inside an enterprise. Here it shows, for example, that the car insurance and the health insurance have similar business capabilities, i.e., they have the same processes for sales and marketing. The industrial insurance on the other hand deviates; it has different processes inside the sales and marketing capability. This insight is important when it comes to the enterprise-wide standardization and technical consolidation of this business capability: It is easy to consolidate the applications of the health insurance and the car insurance, but difficult to integrate the sales and marketing capability of the industrial insurance in the same application.

Application Landscape Maps in Matrix Form and Business Support Maps
As illustrated in Fig. 4.14, application maps can use the same structure as business capability matrixes and visualize an application landscape based on a matrix of [business capabilities] × [business units]. Note that such a map shows which digital solution "supports" which business capability; correspondingly, this kind of map is also called *business support map*.

While the business capability map visualizes the degree of business standardization, the application landscape map visualizes the degree of *technical redundancy* in a digital ecosystem. For instance, based on the map of Fig. 4.14, the insurance group could conclude that currently there are too many redundant applications in the sales and marketing domain. In the next step, they would create a *target picture* where the

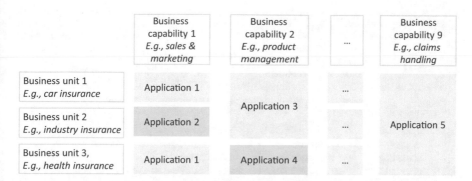

Fig. 4.14 Applications map along business units and capabilities

three business units all use the same application (e.g., the "Application 1" of Fig. 4.14).

Business Object Maps

Figure 4.15 shows a map of business objects that is structured along the clusters of the business capabilities. Business object maps comprise coarse-grained, major business objects; in the nomenclature of Fig. 2.9, this would be the objects allocated at domain or business function level. This map is used, for example, inside architecture decision templates, when the projects must highlight the data objects that they are changing. Another example is the allocation of data *ownership* via the business object map: It is used to assign a data owner to each data object. Note that in large enterprises, data is often managed at various places redundantly, leading to synchronization problems and redundant work. For instance, in large enterprises, you often will find many databases for customer master data. Here, the map helps to establish the *single source of truth* for each data object.

Heat Maps and Other Forms of Assessment Maps

Once the maps have been drawn, you can evaluate the individual elements displayed in them and illustrate the findings. For example, in a so-called heat map, you can mark elements like business capabilities or applications with traffic light colors to indicate if there is high, medium, or low need for changing the elements. However, for evaluating individual, isolated elements of the digital landscape, we do not need maps. The strength of a map is to illustrate cross-element dependencies and patterns. Thus, an important use case of business capability maps (cp. Fig. 4.13) is evaluating the harmonization potential in the application landscape. Further use cases for analyzing the digital ecosystem with EAM maps include:

Capability spanning applications. According to Khosroshahi et al. (2018), a major use case of business capability maps is to analyze if applications are spanning various business capabilities and in that case to change that, e.g., to split an application if it addresses two capabilities. In the spirit of principles like "the IT structure follows the business structure" and "loose coupling of components," that does make sense. It would practically also be bad, if an application has more than one owner, e.g., if it is

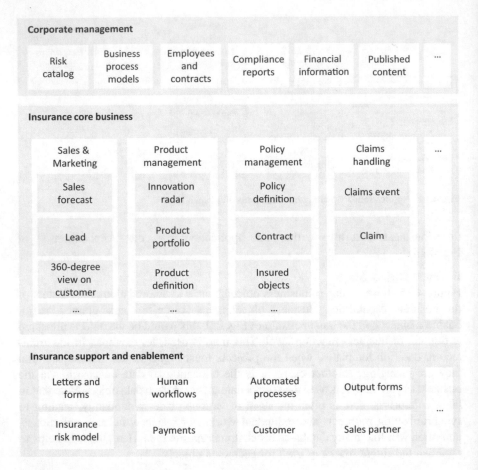

Fig. 4.15 Example of a clustered business object map

owned by two owners of two business capabilities. However, it must be understood that here we are talking of very coarse-grained capabilities in the size of business applications. For example, an application that spans the domains "sales and marketing" and "production" should be revised. But on a more fine-grained level, obviously every application should fulfill various business capabilities. For instance, Fig. 4.5 illustrates various business capabilities fulfilled inside one CRM application.

Physical and logical allocation of systems. There are various use cases where the *location* of the enterprise systems needs to be analyzed. For example, for security reasons, it might be interesting in which country which type of application is hosted and by which vendor this service is provided. Another example is a cloud migration, where the project lead needs to know which applications are allocated already in the cloud and in which type of cloud.

Degree of standardization and customization. For optimizing the cost structure of the IT landscape, a common reflex is to foster highly standardized applications that can be bought "off the shelf." In that context, the map can illustrate if the systems follow cross-enterprise or enterprise-internal standards or if they are heavily customized.

System lifecycle. This point addresses whether we need to replace an application or an infrastructure element soon or if the system is modern and sustainable. This point also relates to costs: If an application is officially not supported by the vendor anymore because the application is beyond its "end of life," we need to pay expensive "extended application support" to the vendor.

Khosroshahi et al. (2018) listed additional use cases for EAM maps. We will come back to the evaluation of individual systems and system landscapes in Chap. 5.

4.3.3   Enterprise Architecture Principles

Criteria for Distinguishing Different Types of EA Guidance
EAM is not about designing one application but about steering landscapes of digital systems. Thus, in EAM, we seldomly use detailed architecture drawings known from traditional architecture, depicting, for example, one large application. Instead, besides highly abstract target pictures and application maps, the *main artifacts for steering the digital ecosystem are principles, standards, and guidelines* that apply for all digital systems. In socio-technical systems, there are many concepts serving as guidance, partially with overlapping realms, like law, commandment, standard, norm, doctrine, paradigm, principle, regulation, rule, guideline, work instruction, code of practice, and policy. Figure 4.16 illustrates that such artifacts for guiding the Enterprise Architecture come in various levels of bindingness and various levels of abstraction. In the context of EAM, we can distinguish different types of guidance by the following attributes:

- *Scope and breadth*: Does the guidance have a broad scope and address, for example, the complete enterprise, or does it have narrow scope and address, for example, only one department?
- *Architecture domain*: Is the guidance related to a specific domain, like business architecture, data architecture, or security architecture?
- *Level of abstraction*: Is the guidance rather a high-level, abstract "north star," or is it a detailed description of how to execute, for example, a certain business process?
- *Change frequency*: How often does the guidance change? For example, is the guidance closely related with fast-changing technologies, or is a technology-agnostic principle that only changes if the business model of the enterprise changes?
- *Level of bindingness*: Is the guidance a strongly binding norm whose non-compliance has legal consequences? Or is it only a "soft" recommendation that is in no way binding? If the guidance is strongly binding, it must be described in a very precise, formal way.

Principles, for instance, have a broad scope, a high level of abstraction, and a high level of bindingness and change very seldomly.

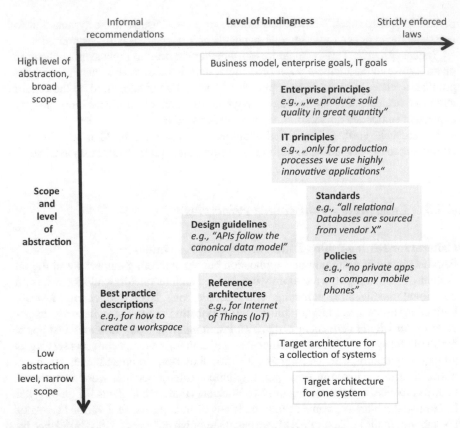

Fig. 4.16 Principles and related artifacts for architectural guidance

Principles Express Core Parameters of the Enterprise Architecture

The word principle stems from Latin principium, meaning "beginning" and "foundation." Principles are fundamental assumptions, describing the general workings of systems. In this vein, the term is also described as follows: "The principles of [...] a system are understood by its users as the *essential characteristics of the system*, or reflecting the system's designed purpose" (Alpa, 1994). Having in mind that architecture also is understood as "the essential characteristics of a system," the close relationship between principles and architecture becomes clear. Here is again the corresponding definition of IEEE 1477 (2007): Architecture is the "fundamental organization of a system, embodied in its components, their relationships to each other and the environment, and the *principles* governing its design and evolution." Note that Enterprise Architecture principles often express the core parameters of the digital ecosystem described in Chap. 2. For instance, principles often address:

- The extent to which systems are *sourced*, e.g., the famous principle "reuse before buy before make."
- The level of *integration*, e.g., "all core business systems must be interoperable with each other."

- The level of *centralization and specialization*, e.g., "all core business system should be based on central platforms."
- The level of *innovativeness*, e.g., "other than in the directly customer-facing systems we pursue a slow-adopter approach and choose rather mature systems."

Principles Are of High Quality and Low Quantity
TOGAF defines that "principles are general rules and guidelines, intended to be enduring and seldom amended, that inform and support the way in which an organization sets about fulfilling its mission" and also states that principles "reflect a level of consensus among the various elements of the enterprise, and form the basis for making future IT decisions" (Open Group, 2020a). However, the examples TOGAF provides for principles primarily resemble high-level, enterprise-wide guidelines, for instance, the guideline "maximize benefit to the enterprise—information management decisions are made to provide maximum benefit to the enterprise as a whole." Khosroshahi et al. (2015, p. 26) conducted a survey where the participants ranked architecture principles according to their relevance; the first entries were:

1. "Compliance with security regulations"
2. "Technology portfolio is based on few technologies"
3. "Reuse of functionality"
4. "Buy before make"
5. "High flexibility, efficiency and modularity of architectural solutions"

Decades ago, Davenport et al. (1989) wrote an article on principles in the context of EAM which seems very up to date; among other things, they wrote: "Most companies need just 20 or 30 principles to capture their approach to technology management. Normally, this approach is deeply rooted in the company's culture, management style, and business strategy, and since those things change slowly, principles should remain valid for a few years." Congruent with this understanding, enterprise-wide or domain-wide principles appear at the top of Fig. 4.16. Such principles are comparable to the *constitution* of a country: They are highly abstract and serve as a guiding north star for specifying more concrete guidance as well as individual applications. Since they have such a strong influence, they have strategic character and are carefully designed to fit to the enterprise and its business model. Also, like the constitution, these principles are strongly binding and seldomly change—even in these agile times. EAM must ensure that the high-level IT principles are based on the business goals and principles.

Principles Connect Business and IT Strategy
Broadbent and Kitzis (2005) proposed principles as a main tool to convey the business strategy into the digital ecosystem; note that instead of "principle," they used the term "maxim." Thus, a chain is formed between business strategy, business principles, IT principles, and IT strategy. They listed six categories of business principles, including cost focus, value differentiation, growth, as well as flexibility and agility of the enterprise. Complementary to that, they define (highest-level) IT

principles as "statements that express how your enterprise needs to design and deploy IT across the enterprise to connect share and structure information." Here, they identified five categories of IT principles:

- The role of IT
- How information and data is managed
- The level of enforcement of IT architectural guidelines and standards
- The extent of communication services
- The nature of IT assets (hardware and software) and how they are made available

Principles for Different Areas and Hierarchical Levels

EAM principles must primarily address the process of forming the enterprise-wide digital ecosystem. However, also the *EAM capability* itself should have principles, like "we foster collaborative problem-solving."

Another distinction often made is that between IT principles and *business principles* (e.g., Broadbent & Kitzis, 2005). Beyond that, every large architecture domain should have specific principles. Figure 4.17 shows a corresponding example: on top of the hierarchy are the enterprise-wide business principles and IT principles. Below that, architecture *domain-specific principles* are illustrated. In this vein, TOGAF states that "sets of principles form a hierarchy," where enterprise-wide business principles, general IT principles, and EAM principles are related with each other (Open Group, 2020a).

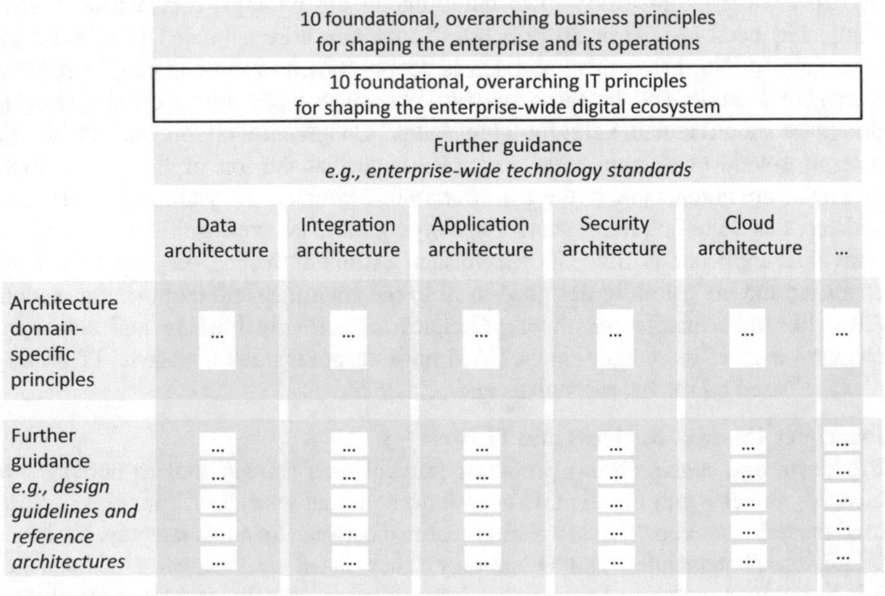

10 foundational, overarching business principles for shaping the enterprise and its operations					
10 foundational, overarching IT principles for shaping the enterprise-wide digital ecosystem					
Further guidance *e.g., enterprise-wide technology standards*					
	Data architecture	Integration architecture	Application architecture	Security architecture	Cloud architecture ...
Architecture domain-specific principles	...	...	...	...	... ...
Further guidance *e.g., design guidelines and reference architectures*	... ...	... ...	... ...	... ...	... ...	... ...

Fig. 4.17 Hierarchy of architecture principles and related guidance

A related question is whether *business units* and enterprises inside a group should have their own principles. In general, this makes sense if the units have different business models and thus also different Enterprise Architectures. For example, inside a large aviation group, separate legal entities exist for "passenger airline," "cargo airline," and "plane maintenance." Each unit has its own enterprise-wide principles. However, to streamline the group-wide digital ecosystems as much as useful, in addition, the group defined overarching principles on top of the unit-specific principles.

Principles vs. Design Guidelines

The transition between high-level, fundamental principles and more operational guidelines is fluent. However, in general, the guidelines on the highest level of an enterprise or a domain are called principles; the more concrete descriptions for shaping the digital ecosystem on the operational level we will refer to as *design guidelines*. Thereby, we combine the term "design instructions" of Greefhorst and Proper (2011, p. 37) with the term "guideline" often found for this type of rules in practice. Design guidelines cover a narrower scope, are of a lower level of abstraction, change more often, and have a lower level of bindingness than principles.

Shaping Principles and Collections of Principles

According to TOGAF, principles must be understandable, robust, complete, consistent, and stable. When creating the principles inside an enterprise, also the overall collection of principles must be guided by some quality attributes, namely:

- *Lean:* The set of principles should be as lean as possible and as exhaustive as necessary. If inside one collection there are more than ten principles, the chance that they will be read and followed is low.
- *MECE:* The principles inside one collection should be "Mutually Exclusive and Collectively Exhaustive." They should be comprehensive and summarize the most relevant design guidelines.
- *Separation of concerns:* One principle should address exactly one concern. On a higher level, the group of principles should address only one concern as well.
- *Homogenous*: Inside one collection of principles, there should be one level of abstraction, scope, and bindingness.

Examples for collections of principles can be found at Greefhorst and Proper (2011, p. 153), Khosroshahi et al. (2015), TOGAF (2020a), and CEAF (2020a, p. 10).

4.3.4   Roadmaps, Strategies, and Standards

Roadmaps

Based on their scope, we can distinguish three types of architecture roadmaps: roadmaps for individual systems, roadmaps for collections of systems, and roadmaps for the complete enterprise-wide digital ecosystem. In all cases, a roadmap describes how a system traverses from its current state (baseline architecture) to a defined target state (target architecture). One way of illustrating a roadmap for an application landscape is to create business capability maps of the as-is landscape (today), a transition landscape (e.g., 1 year ahead), and the target landscape (e.g., 2 years ahead). The roadmap describes the corresponding activities, usually including the costs and the timeframe of the activities. CEAF (2020b, p. 14) provides a short description of a strategic Enterprise Architecture roadmap; for a detailed description of roadmapping complex IT systems, refer to TOGAF (Open Group, 2020a).

Some EAM tools offer the possibility of storing architecture roadmaps: The tool correlates the planned activities with the involved IT systems and business capabilities, which are managed in the same tool. This facilitates a full-circle transparency and enables an automated updating of the roadmap based on its components. Since roadmaps describe investments in the enterprise that require money and human resources, another place for storing roadmaps is a project portfolio management tool.

Strategies

In Chap. 2, we described different types of strategies, i.e., business vs. IT strategy, and ways to describe strategies, i.e., as a set of rules or as goal and a plan to reach the goal. In the latter understanding, a *strategy can be expressed as an architectural target picture and a roadmap* to reach this target. In contrast to tactics, a strategy is about long-term planning and covers a broader scope. Thus, in the context of EAM, a strategy usually addresses the complete enterprise or a large business segment. In addition to that, a strategy can either focus on one architecture domain—for example, a cloud strategy—or it can address the complete digital ecosystem and change fundamental aspects of the IT organization and the digital ecosystem, affecting all architecture domains.

Regarding the timeframe of an IT strategy, the short technology lifecycles and market disruptions of these days make defining an IT target picture difficult. If the target picture lays far in the future and the strategy refers to concrete technologies, the strategy might become obsolete on the way. However, the challenge of creating a comprehensive strategy in a highly dynamic environment is not new to IT: Perks and Beveridge (2003, p. 47) already pointed out that strategies in the context of EAM should rather have a horizon of 2–3 years instead of 4–6 years. The extreme—generally not recommendable—position would be to not have any future IT target pictures: Like finite state machines, the individual elements of the organization would react ad hoc to external events, following a set of rules and principles. Though this might be feasible in some areas, for large socio-technical systems, we need a coherent picture, both in the current and in the future state. The creation of an enterprise-wide cloud strategy is an example: Only if we migrate the complete digital ecosystem into cloud, can we shut down the old, expensive, and inflexible company data center.

Standards

In Sect. 2.5.3, we described the various areas of standardization in the context of EAM. Inside these areas, different artifacts are used:

Business process standards. For the standardization of business processes inside an enterprise, business process models for various enterprise areas are created. These are stored in central Business Process Management suites.

Data and business objects standards. Business Process Management suites usually do not cover only business processes but also the artifacts related to business process, like data objects. Unfortunately, even today, these business-level definitions are often detached from digitalization activities. Thus, in the context of IT, the *integration architecture capability* often manages an enterprise-wide data object catalog, where the syntax of data exchanged between applications is defined. Enterprise-wide integrated data models (IDM) are also produced in the context of *data warehouses*, which need to integrate data from many enterprise areas. Further places for managing enterprise-wide data standards are data catalogs and EAM tool suites.

Standards for business functions and capabilities. From a business perspective, business functions are also managed in Business Process Management suites. As mentioned above, in the context of EAM and digitalization, often the term *business capability* is used instead of business function. A business capability catalog is part of most Enterprise Architecture Management tool suites.

Standards for services and APIs. The technical realization of business functions are services, which are implemented by applications and offered via APIs to other applications. Such service descriptions are stored either in the API management tool suite or in the EAM tool suite.

Application standards. One artifact to harmonize the application landscape is the IT asset inventory, where all applications of the enterprise are described, as well as the products these applications are based on. Related to this are business capabilities maps and application landscape maps, where business capabilities and applications are correlated to each other. Besides that, in practice, "application standard catalogs" are defined. These are simple lists that specify which product must be used for which functionality. For instance, here we can name two CRM applications that in our enterprise might be used for the purpose of "Customer Relationship Management."

Platforms and infrastructure standards. Similar to the list of application standards, here also a central catalog is used; it describes the allowed products and technical standards for various types of platform and infrastructure services in the enterprise. Such infrastructure elements are, for example, servers, databases, firewalls, load balancers, identity and access management tools, cloud landing zones, and process digitalization tools like robotics process automation. TOGAF calls this the "Technology Standards Catalog"; it "documents the agreed standards for technology across the enterprise covering technologies, and versions, the technology lifecycles, and the refresh cycles for the technology" (Open Group, 2020a).

Standards in the context of "IT for IT." IT for IT is as a subsection of the abovementioned platforms and infrastructure standards. The standards listed before aim originally at the IT elements to fulfill the requirements of the "business." Complementary to that, inside the IT service organization, an ecosystem exists for providing the IT services. This includes, for example, a choice of programming languages and DevOps frameworks to be used inside the enterprise.

4.3.5   EAM Artifacts in the Context of Individual Solutions

Let us recapitulate: EAM is about the enterprise-wide digital ecosystem. So why do we care for artifacts in the context of individual solutions? Because the whole is the sum of its parts, and in practice, coaching and reviewing the creation of large individual digital systems is a core part of EAM. Though they fall primarily in the responsibility of solution architects, EAM must ensure the quality of the artifacts described below, because the quality of these artifacts is correlated to the quality of the solutions delivered. Note that here we still focus on artifacts in the context of Enterprise Architecture Management. Naturally, for software engineering, many more artifacts are important, for instance, user stories, epics, and feature lists in the context of agile system development. For a more exhaustive artifact list, refer to TOGAF (Open Group, 2020a), SAFe (2020) or the "Open Agile Architecture" (Open Group, 2020b).

Vision, Solution Sketch, and Architecture Decision Template
When a new digital solution is brought on the way in an enterprise, one of the first artifacts created to depict that solution is a *vision*. A vision is an ambitious, very-high-level target picture description that serves as a "north star" to communicate the purpose and the core functions of the solution. A detailed description of this artifact is described in TOGAF (Open Group, 2020a).

A complimentary artifact is the *solution sketch*. In comparison to a vision, a solution sketch usually is a formal EAM deliverable that must enable the relevant architects to evaluate the proposed way for realizing a digital solution. TOGAF calls this artifact a "solution concept diagram" and states that "its purpose is to quickly on-board and align stakeholders for a particular change initiative, so that all participants understand what the architecture engagement is seeking to achieve and how it is expected that a particular solution approach will meet the needs of the enterprise." In practice, this usually is a presentation of circa 15 slides. This slide set contains the motivation for the new solution, the added value in comparison to the current state, a high-level view on functional and non-functional requirements, and a picture of the envisioned architecture. Normally, it also contains two or three alternative scenarios for architecting the solution and a short evaluation of each scenario. We describe the contents of this evaluation in Chap. 5.

An *architecture decision template* roughly comprises the same contents as a solution sketch. However, while the solution sketch aims explicitly at the early stage of a new solution, the architecture decision template is used for all kind of architectural decisions to be presented in architecture boards. It might seem odd that one template suffices to address all kind of architectural, strategic decisions. However, a short, accurate description of the following points usually does suffice: current situation (baseline), need for changing the current situation (pain points, chances), suggestion for a change, different scenarios for realizing the change, evaluation of the scenarios, and a recommendation for next steps. One example for such an architectural decision is: should we use one central system for access management, or do we pursue a federated approach with different systems?

Architecture and Security Questionnaire
Like the solution sketch, the architecture and security questionnaire is used in the early phases of a solution, usually before the project to realize the solution is initiated. It is a simple way to retrieve standard information on the planned solution, especially useful for smaller projects that do not need a full-scale solution sketch. The format is a short, structured list where essential parameters of a new solution are described. Topics addressed in this questionnaire include generic functional and non-functional requirements, requirements regarding architecture selected domains (e.g., cloud, integration, and data architecture), the need for data protection, and further security measures. Most importantly, it also includes the question "does a similar solution already exist in the enterprise?". An enterprise architect and a security architect support the project in filling out this list. Building on this input, a similar questionnaire can later be used by the procurement capability to contact potential suppliers of the solution.

Architecture Description
When the solution sketch was created and a project is about to implement the proposed change, we need a more detailed architecture description. This is the target architecture that we described above. However, we will still need an up-to-date architecture description when the project delivered the promised system, and the line of business takes responsibility for operating the new system. This architecture description displays the as-is architecture of the system and is needed for further architecturally relevant changes in the system but also in incident situations when a description of the inner workings of the solution is needed. Again, it is the responsibility of the solution architect to create and maintain such an architecture description, but EAM needs it to review the solution.

Architecture Decision Log
Inside large projects, often an architecture decision log is iteratively created. On the one hand, this serves as a to-do list for open architectural decisions—in agile terminology: a *backlog* only for architectural decisions. But primarily it serves as documentation of project-internal decisions and thus complements the architecture description named above. If architecture is understood as the sum of architectural decisions, then this log protocols how the solution architecture "emerges."

4.4   EAM Tools

EAM itself is no exception when it comes to digitalization requirements: it heavily relies on a good choice of digital solutions. In the next sections, we will look in detail at the individual EAM functions and the corresponding digital solutions. In preparation of this, here is a short overview of the EAM tool landscape:

Inventory of Digital Systems

This catalog is the most distinct EAM tool and the backbone of the core EAM processes. Here all applications and all infrastructure elements of the enterprise are described from an EAM perspective. This inventory of information technology assets comprises a short description of each digital system and its essential attributes. Usually, three types of attributes are listed:

- *Core attributes*, like system name, business owner of the system, system owner from the IT site, responsible solution architect, responsible system operator, physical and logical system location, and the vendor the system is sourced from.
- *Architecture documentation*, like business domain the system belongs to, business capability realized by the system, API descriptions, services provided by the system to other systems, technical and business services consumed by the system, as well as the protection and security level of the system. Though this goes beyond a lean catalog, here also documents like the architecture specification or the system's operations manual can be stored.
- *Architecture metrics:* One practically important metric to keep the EAM documentation updated is a "keep alive" attribute; here, the IT owner of the system must acknowledge all couple of months that the documentation of the system is still up to date. Another classic architecture metric describes the *architectural debts* assigned to a system. Beyond that, the metrics for individual systems described in Sect. 5.2 can be used here to assess the need for changing the system. These metrics include the cost of the system—for instance, total cost of ownerships, maintenance costs, and license cost—and the fulfilment of service-level agreements, for example, regarding system response times or system availability.

Tools for Evaluating the Digital Ecosystem and Displaying Architectural Maps

EAM tools that provide an inventory of digital systems usually offer complementary evaluation functions. Based on the abovementioned metrics, the digital systems can be assessed and reports be generated. Different forms of graphics visualize the findings, for example, a matrix that displays the business applications inside one business domain, with "technical fit" on the Y-axis and "business fit" on the X-axis. This is a valuable source for projects that, for example, need information like:

- What is the state of the cloud migration? How many applications inside the domain sales and marking are sourced via an SaaS model?
- What is our most expensive core business application? How do the costs relate to the number of users of the systems?
- In which phase of the technology lifecycle are the applications of the domain sales and marketing? How urgently do we need to modernize that domain?

In a similar vein, EAM tools should support visualizations of *business capability maps*, *business support maps*, and, based on those, *heat maps*. To enable this functionality, among others, the EAM tool needs to store how digital systems relate to business capabilities and how business capabilities relate to each other (for instance, by depicting hierarchies of business capabilities).

Data object maps can also be generated from EAM tools. A comparatively new development in this context are data catalogs. Data catalogs originate from the area of data analytics and aim at improving the enterprise-wide data governance. However, currently data catalogs focus on capturing and publishing the metadata of individual business objects (e.g., lineage, ownership, data quality), while coarse-grained business object maps are left to the EAM tools.

Tools for Managing Further Architectural Content

Many EAM artifacts exist for envisioning, specifying, planning, and evaluating the enterprise-wide digital landscape in the various business and architecture domains. These include as-is and target pictures, gap analysis and requirement lists, roadmaps, architecture principles, architecture guidelines, reference architectures, catalogs of technical standards, and catalogs of logical building blocks. To create, store, and maintain these artifacts, a tailored suite for EAM content management is needed (cp. Ziemann, 2019). A cornerstone of this ecosystem is a Wiki that is easily accessible by the architecture community.

Solution Architecture Modeling Tools

Intuitively, architecture is associated with the creation of elaborated, fine-grained drawings. And as established before, an abstracted representation of complex systems is essential for Enterprise Architecture Management, indeed. However, normally, *the complexities of enterprise-wide digital landscapes cannot be captured in large fine-grained drawings*. Instead, coarse-grained models with a simple metamodel are used, like structured lists, catalogs, or matrixes, for example, Business Capability Maps or heat maps.

Another question is which tool should be used to model individual digital solutions. Since the majority of EAM drawings need to be presented in strategic boards and to be understood easily, often these are created with tools for creating slide decks, i.e., Microsoft PowerPoint or similar. Besides that, a standard for the sole purpose of modeling IT architectures exists: *ArchiMate* (Open Group, 2020c). Several tools are available that support this standard. In a similar vein, various open-source tools offer multi-purpose, fine-grained modeling and support IT modeling standards like the Unified Modeling Language (UML) or the Systems Modeling Language (SysML). A best practice is to use a modeling tool like "Draw.io" that can be embedded in a Wiki; thus, the resulting models do not get lost in a project file share, but have a chance to become part of a living solution documentation.

Tools for Case Management, Communication, and Collaboration

To support and enable their core processes, the EAM capability needs tools for case management, communication, and collaboration: Case management suites are used in IT to track the fulfilment of requests and tasks inside projects, but also to track items, like requirements. In the context of EAM, these are used mostly for tracking the objectives and tasks inside the EAM capability as well as for tracking architecture demands. Besides Wikis today, a bandwidth of other elaborated collaboration tools exists, like Microsoft Teams or Yammer. Such tools are highly valuable to enable the collaborative creation of architectural content inside the architecture community and to get instantaneous feedback on architecture concepts. For the widespread communication of architecture content, further tools are used, like an enterprise-wide intranet for publishing formal architecture statements.

Interfaces to Adjacent Capabilities
As established above, EAM has many touchpoints with adjacent disciplines and incorporates various architecture domains. Since the core functions of managing digital assets are covered by many EAM tools, now vendors improve the quality of the asset inventory by offering automated synchronizations with repositories from adjacent areas. This includes:

Business Process Management. The EAM domain of business architecture overlaps with the discipline of *Business Process Management* (BPM). BPM aims at the optimization of all business processes in an enterprise, both digital and analog. Business architecture (in the context of EAM) on the other hand focuses on business processes that are or should be digitalized. However, the modeling of business goals, processes, functions, data objects, and organizational units and relationships between those is the core functionality of BPM suites. And, as discussed above, these artifacts are also highly relevant for EAM: for example, *business capability maps and business object maps*. Correspondingly, some vendors incorporate functions for modeling business capability maps in their EAM tools.

API management suites also provide a catalog of the services and interfaces of enterprise applications; as mentioned above, these interfaces are usually also described in the EAM inventory of digital assets.

Risk management. Some EAM tools offer an interface to risk management tools, so risks associated with digital system or business capabilities can be evaluated.

IT service management. Not only EAM but also IT service management uses an inventory of IT assets, the so-called configuration management database (CMDB, cp. ITIL, 2019). This database also is a catalog of hardware and software assets being used in the enterprise. However, the EAM asset inventory focuses on data necessary to optimize the enterprise-wide digital landscape. The CMDB, on the other hand, collects the attributes of digital systems for operational, runtime purposes. Thus, the CMDB usually is more fine-grained, technically oriented, and sometimes better synchronized with the actual digital landscape. However, if there already are two decoupled inventories of digital assets, these should at least be synchronized. In this vein, some EAM tools offer an interface to synchronize with CMDB solutions.

Enterprise-independent product catalogs. A large enterprise can have thousands of different digital products, so it is expensive to keep the EAM inventory updated manually. Data that changes often includes lifecycle information—e.g., is the product still supported by the vendor or will it be replaced by a different product soon—security vulnerabilities, and available patches. To reduce the need for manual synchronization, service providers like Technopedia offer current information on digital assets via APIs.

Budget and cost management. EAM has its roots in IT architecture and thus focuses on the creative, proactive aspect of architecting digital landscapes. At the same time, a good architect also ensures an optimal cost-quality ratio and knows the cost positions of the architected system. However, as illustrated in Fig. 3.11 there is a capability dedicated purely to managing IT costs. According to COBIT, this capability—budget and cost management—includes modeling and allocating costs to IT services as well as comparing planned and actual costs. Some EAM tool vendors offer an interface to correlate and synchronize these financial numbers with the IT services listed in the EAM inventory.

Contract and license management. Adding yet another view on digital assets, the procurement capability keeps an inventory of licenses and contracts for the digital systems purchased or rented from third parties.

Tools for project portfolio management and roadmapping. Project portfolio management tool suites describe which projects address which digital system, which business capability, or which technical capability. Thus, on the one hand, the project portfolio tools need to reference the IDs of these elements stored in the EAM inventory (e.g., applications and business capabilities). On the other hand, from an EAM standpoint, it is important to know which projects are currently working on a certain capability or are planned for this capability. Let us take the example of a large insurance group in the year 2020. Not too long ago, the CIO announced the strategy of "cloud first," which set in motion a frenzy of activities all over the enterprise. Now various departments and many projects address the subject of "cloud." To ensure that the projects are complementary and not redundant to each other, it is helpful to have a tool that illustrates which project currently works on which technical aspect of "cloud" (e.g., cloud security, cloud migration framework, SaaS framework) and on the business capability these projects focus on (e.g., car insurance, industry insurance, or group-wide). Closely related to the topic of project portfolio management is the topic of creating *roadmaps* for the development of individual systems or landscapes of systems. A classic functionality of EAM inventories is depicting the lifecycle stage of a digital system, for instance, indicating that the CRM system will only be supported by the vendor for three more years and then needs to be replaced. In the IT project portfolio management system, the planned, future investments for individual systems and landscapes of systems should be visible. It makes sense to synchronize this information toward the EAM inventory, for example, to enable evaluations of the digital landscape.

4.5   EAM Organization and Roles

In this section, we describe the different roles in the context of EAM and the different forms in which the EAM capability of an enterprise can be designed and related to other departments.

4.5.1 EAM Roles

Architectural Roles in Literature
The core architectural roles shown in Fig. 4.6 are well-established and described, for example, by CEAF (2020a, p. 26) and TOGAF (Open Group, 2020a). The Scaled Agile Framework (SAFe, 2020) names similar architectural roles; it also uses the scope and level of abstraction to distinguish between the following roles: (1) an architect for one system, called "system architect"; (2) an architect for a collection of systems, called "solution architect"; and (3) an "enterprise architect," responsible for all systems and collections of systems inside one value stream (i.e., one business domain).

Dimensions of Architectural Roles
In Sect. 4.2.3, we described stereotypical core roles and tasks in the context of EAM. In theory, we could create a role for every architecture task displayed in Fig. 4.9. In practice, architecture roles are cut along the following dimensions:

*   *Organizational scope and level of abstraction,* as shown in Fig. 4.6.
*   *Architecture domain,* e.g., dedicated roles for business architecture, data architecture, and security architecture.
*   *Participation in projects.* Though all enterprise architects need a proximity to projects, the degree of their engagement in projects varies.
*   *Seniority,* e.g., dedicated roles for junior and senior (enterprise) architects. In practice, you can also find dedicated departments consisting only of senior enterprise architects.
*   *Managing and supporting EAM*: The capabilities depicted in Fig. 4.9 in the areas of "managing EAM" and "support EAM" should also be assigned to roles. For example, one role should be assigned to the definition of EAM processes inside the enterprise.

Roles Inside a Typical Department for Enterprise Architecture Management
Coming back to the roles shown in Fig. 4.6, let us have a closer look at the fictive BEI insurance group with 30,000 employees and 6 different business units introduced in Chap. 1. Here, the central EAM department is allocated above the business units, on the group level. It employs ten senior enterprise architects, the chief architect, and its deputy. The two latter roles are responsible for the management of EAM processes (cp. Fig. 4.9), including the specification of EAM processes and the EAM framework in the BEI group. The rest of the processes shown in Fig. 4.9 is distributed over the ten enterprise architects. To enable a collaborative working mode and provide for redundancy during vacations, each process is owned by two enterprise architects: one in the lead and one supporting. Regarding the core processes, the architecture domains are addressed, including enterprise-wide business architecture, data architecture, integration architecture, and cloud architecture. To support a smooth collaboration with the business units, six enterprise architects

are dedicated to each business unit. In a similar vein, currently five architects are also part of large projects with architectural relevance.

Segment Architects

It is important to understand that in large enterprises, EAM is not restricted to one central department but spans many departments. Though there is a dedicated EAM department, the boundaries to adjacent architecture departments are fluent, and tasks are often shared among various departments. In the example of the BEI insurance, inside each of the six business units, another, smaller architecture team exists which mirrors the roles and tasks of the group Enterprise Architecture department. Instead of being responsible for the architecture of the overall group, these teams are responsible for the architecture of their business unit. Though they also address some of the core architecture domains—like integration architecture and data architecture—they focus rather on generic business and IT architecture for the capabilities and departments inside each business unit.

Solution Architects

A solution architect is responsible for the architecture of one large digital system, e.g., a large business application like a CRM system or a large infrastructure element like the Enterprise Service Bus. As mentioned before, each department has usually one large, flagship application. In the example of the BEI group, the architecture of each of these flagship applications and other large digital solutions is managed by 1 out of circa 60 solution architects. The solution architects cannot afford the luxury of focusing only on one aspect of the solution (e.g., the security architecture); instead, they are generalists that address all architecture dimensions relevant for their solution. Note that solution architects can work either inside a *project* at creating a solution or in the *line of business*, when the solution is already operating, but need to be constantly supervised and adapted.

Architectural Roles in the Context of Projects

Staying in close contact with the projects that change the digital ecosystem is of utmost importance to the EAM capability. Now, the classic EAM role in the context of development projects is to understand the requirements of the project, to communicate architectural guidance—like architectural guidelines and reference architectures—and to monitor the compliance of the solutions with architectural standards. Going beyond that, enterprise architects can also take the following roles:

- *Architecture coach:* The IT projects need specialists for architecting complex digital systems and for maneuvering through the oftentimes complex IT processes and decision boards of the enterprise. Thus, the architecture coach "coaches" the project manager and the solution architect regarding Enterprise Architecture guidelines and deliverables. He or she acts both as the project's *attorney*, who knows the enterprise-specific processes and panels, and as a *navigator*, who helps the project to steer through the intricacies of the complex enterprise-wide digital ecosystem. Usually, every strategic project with architectural relevance obtains an architecture coach that it can consult with. The coach also supports the project

in the creation of the slide sets and other documents needed for architecture
decision boards.

- *Solution architect:* The project's solution architect is responsible for creating the
architecture of the digital system addressed by the project. Usually this is a full-
time project member. The idea is that there is an interplay between the solution
architect and the enterprise architect as described in the previous bullet point.
Therefore, these roles normally should be staffed with two separate persons with
different competences; an enterprise architect taking the role of a solution architect should be an exception.
- *Project lead:* In solutions close to Enterprise Architecture, an enterprise architect
can also act as a project lead; examples for such solutions are the introduction of a
new integration solution or a new IT asset inventory.

Note that some enterprises have a dedicated department for "project architecture,"
whose members only work as solution architects inside projects. In the organizational chart, this department must be allocated closely to the EAM department, since
there needs to be an intense, constant exchange of knowledge between solution
architects and enterprise architects.

> **Every Large Project Needs At Least a Solution Architect**
> - Let us highlight again that in any project that builds a complex digital
>   system, there always must be *one dedicated person responsible for the
>   coherent, suitable architecture of this system.* Unfortunately, in practice,
>   due to scarce resources, this is not always the case. If such a role is not
>   staffed, there is a high probability that the architecture (as well as the
>   architecture documentation) will be chaotic piecemeal.
> - Besides an architect being responsible for the overall solution, large pro-
>   jects often staff further architecture roles. These are either *dedicated to
>   selected solution components*, like an architect responsible for the
>   360-degree customer view component (being part of a CRM system).
> - Or, these project roles are *dedicated to architecture layers*, like business
>   architecture, integration architecture, data architecture, security architec-
>   ture, or cloud architecture.

4.5.2   EAM Boards, Communities, and Committees

Figure 4.18 shows major Enterprise Architecture Management boards, communities,
and committees. As the graphic illustrates, generally two types of panels exist:
meetings for *informal exchanges* inside the architecture community and meetings
for *formal decisions* on the Enterprise Architecture. Both informal exchanges and
architecture decisions occur on all levels of the enterprise. Accordingly, these panels
cover the complete range from the CIO steering board down to the architecture of

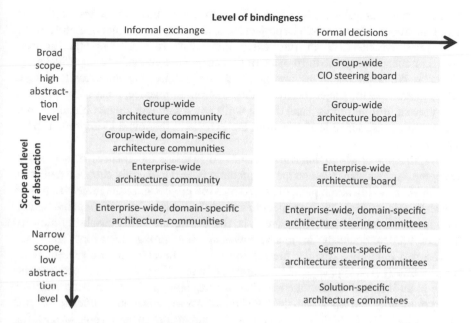

Fig. 4.18   Architecture boards, communities, and committees

individual solutions. Note that the panels shown in Fig. 4.18 are typical for a big consortium with various large business units. This could be, for example, a large aviation group or a large insurance group. The exact instantiation of these panels depends on the size and the structure of a consortium. For example, it could be that not only the complete group has a CIO but also that every large business unit has its own CIO and a corresponding "enterprise-wide CIO steering board."

In enterprises like the fictional BEI insurance, typical panels are:

CIO steering board. The CIO of the overall insurance group meets all 2 weeks with the managers that directly report to him to decide on strategic issues regarding the IT of the overall insurance group. Members of this group include the IT managers responsible for each business unit and the chief enterprise architect. They address only IT architecture topics on the highest abstraction level and only those that could not be decided in the group-wide architecture board.

Group-wide architecture board. The formal architecture board is the flagship panel of the EAM department. It is held every three weeks and usually addresses four topics in 2 hours. Members of this board are the senior enterprise architects of each architecture domain and each business area. The board is led by the chief enterprise architect. Another architect is endowed with the preparation and the post-processing of the meeting, e.g., to distribute the minutes and update the architecture repository with decisions or new guidelines. In this board, the formal decisions are taken that alter the digital ecosystem architecture for all business units. These are, for example, decisions on the group-wide cloud infrastructure or general architecture guidelines and processes. However, the most common topics are current projects and how those relate to the Enterprise Architecture. The architecture board must respond if the solution architecture planned by a project lacks in quality or does not fit to the overall Enterprise Architecture. In this case, the panel can (a) stop the project, (b) recommend changes to the project, or (c) accept the solution but assign "technical debts" to the business unit responsible for the project, i.e., the obligation to change the solution after the project delivered the solution. In practice, most of the projects that present in front of this panel do not walk away with unpleasant obligations but rather with constructive feedback from the experts in the round to improve certain aspects of the architecture.

Preparation of the architecture board. To increase the chances of a positive outcome, various steps precede the architecture board: In the best case, a member of the EAM capability accompanies and coaches the project since the project start. For instance, this *coach* helps the project to create the contents for formal deliverables, like the architecture board template. Via the coach, the EAM capability and the project are continuously in touch, ensuring that strong deviations from the envisioned Enterprise Architecture are improbable. In addition, two presentations in preparatory panels precede the architecture board: First, the project presents the topic in an informal architecture meeting, for example, in the group-wide architecture community. On top of that, the EAM capability organizes an *architecture board preparation panel*, which is a dry run of the architecture board. Thus, at least for important topics, a project already got feedback from various sides before it enters the architecture board. Apart from getting a 360-degree feedback from the various subject matter experts, it is valuable for the project to obtain a formal stamp from the architecture board on the quality of the proposed solution architecture.

The *enterprise-wide architecture board* is the counterpart of the group-wide board. In contrast to that, its scope is only one large business unit, for example, the business unit "health insurance" of the BEI group. The group-wide architecture must focus on the common denominators of the various business units; usually this comprises all architectural domains minus the business architecture. The enterprise-wide architecture board on the other hand focuses stronger on the business architecture and leaves the infrastructure topics to the group-wide architecture board. Other than the scope and the focus on certain architecture domains, it is identical to the group-wide architecture board. However, the members of the enterprise-wide architecture board do not represent the group-wide business units, but the large departments inside one business unit.

Enterprise-wide, domain-specific architecture steering committees. Above we described the architecture board, which covers general Enterprise Architecture topics. Next to that, more focused, topic-specific panels exist, where the experts for one selected architectural domain address architectural issues inside this domain. Examples for such domain-specific architecture steering committees are API steering committees and security architecture boards.

Segment-specific architecture steering committees. In the spirit of a decentralized and "agile" architecture, it might also make sense to have panels for architecture decisions on the segment level. For example, the segment "sales and marketing" of the business unit "car insurance" could have such a panel, where architectural decisions are addressed and recorded in the architecture log.

Solution-specific architecture committees. In general, every solution architect should document architectural decisions regarding his system. Beyond that, large projects that develop complex solutions often have project-internal architecture panels. Here, architectural topics are discussed, decided, and protocoled in the project's architecture log.

Architecture community meetings. Now we come to the left side of Fig. 4.18, where the meetings for *informal exchanges* inside the architecture community are illustrated. They serve to communicate new architectural developments, get early feedback and requirements from all architects of one area, and generally ensure a functioning, beneficial link between the various architecture levels. Since all these activities are essential for the success of EAM, the informal communities are at least equally important to the formal panels. While the formal panels represent the tip of the iceberg, most of the architectural work is already done before, also in the informal meetings. The scope of the informal meetings ranges from group-wide to architecture domain-specific. In the example of the BEI insurance group, a group-wide community meeting would comprise ca. 60 architects that every 3 months discuss ca. 6 topics in a meeting of 3 hours. An example for a more focused meeting is the data analytics community on the enterprise or business unit level, where the respective domain architects meet once a month for a 2 hour meeting.

4.5.3   Allocation of the EAM Capability

EAM Is Decentralized and Allocated Primarily in the IT

It is a classic question whether the EAM department should rather be allocated in the "business" or in the "IT." On the one hand, in enterprises with a highly digital business model, this binary distinction is not possible; here, business and IT are closely interwoven. However, most enterprises today are not that digital, and thus you will often find the distinction between a business and an IT area. The answer to the above-stated question then rests in the purpose of EAM: the management of the enterprise-wide *digital ecosystem*. And the area that holds the people specializing on building and maintaining the digital ecosystem is called "IT." In this vein, an experienced EAM consultant recently stated: "Sometimes EAM departments are allocated at the business-side of an enterprise. However, usually it does not take long before they are moved back into the IT-side." Yet, matters become complicated when it comes to business architecture, which is also a part of EAM. Here, obviously, a high business acumen is required. Luckily, the question of "where is the EAM capability allocated?" does not require a binary answer, because today in large enterprise, EAM is decentralized, i.e., spread over various departments.

The Central EAM Department Is Allocated Closely to the CIO
We already established that enterprise-wide architecture is a highly collaborative, decentralized discipline: EAM is not done by one central EAM department alone but by an ecosystem of architects and architecture departments responsible for all business segments and digitalization areas of an enterprise. However, usually a large enterprise does have an EAM nucleus in the form of a central EAM department responsible for the complete group. Naturally, this central EAM department is allocated in the CIO area, which addresses the IT strategy and the governance of the complete enterprise (cp. Fig. 3.12). How exactly this area is structured varies among enterprises. For example, sometimes, the security architecture department is part of the EAM department in the IT strategy area; sometimes, it is part of the IT security area. Sometimes, the EAM department is allocated directly below the CIO; sometimes, it is part of a strategy department further away from the CIO. Note that the latter position is suboptimal: given the importance of EAM, the chief enterprise architect, which is usually the lead of the EAM department, should report directly to the CIO. Otherwise, the position of the EAM department might be too weak to steer against strong local stakeholders that prioritize their interests higher than reaching an enterprise-wide optimum and following a comprehensive IT strategy. If the business realizes this and is dissatisfied with the enduring chaos in certain architecture domains, a typical reaction is that this architecture domain is moved away from the CIO and allocated under a CxO, who is otherwise responsible for non-IT topics. Besides Figs. 3.11 and 3.12, you can find examples of the allocation of the EAM department and the adjacent organizational structures in TOGAF (Open Group, 2020a), in the 2.0 Version of CEAF (2013), at Ahlemann et al. (2011, p. 101) and at Bente et al. (2012, p. 76).

4.6   EAM Processes and Capabilities

The previous sections covered the general EAM process framework as well as fundamental artifacts, roles, and tools of EAM. Integrating these elements into one view, in the next sections, we describe EAM processes and capabilities. The subsections here follow the classification shown already in Fig. 4.9: *core processes* for managing digital landscapes and individual systems and EAM *support processes* and the *management processes* for steering the EAM capability.

4.6.1   EAM Processes for Managing Digital Landscapes

Addressing the Complete Enterprise or an Enterprise Segment
The EAM core processes consist of the steps envision, specify, implement, and evaluate Enterprise Architecture, applied to either individual digital solutions or solution landscapes. In this section, we will address the latter area, the EAM part,

that addresses *digital landscapes*, i.e., collections of digital systems. If we address digital landscapes, we can either address the complete EAM cube (cp. Fig. 4.8) or slices of it. The following scopes are most important:

1. *Complete enterprise.* Among others, for this scope, high-level IT strategies are created that address all technical domains and all business domains. Since this scope is very broad, this type of strategy is rather abstract.
2. *One architectural domain relevant for all business domains.* For example, here we specify a strategy for the architecture domain "cloud" and define new provisioning models for the digital systems of all business domains in the enterprise.
3. *One business segment.* Here we focus on one large business segment inside our enterprise, like sales and marketing. For this, we envision, specify, and evaluate the target pictures for all architecture domains, including, for example, business architecture, data architecture, integration architecture, and cloud architecture. Note that this task is also assigned to the role "segment architect." However, on the one hand, in practice, the roles of enterprise architect and segment architect often are overlapping. On the other hand, even if these roles are instantiated by different persons in different departments, the EAM department must support and guide the segment architects with this important task.

Now, Fig. 4.19 shows the essential EAM processes regarding digital landscapes but does not distinguish between different scopes. The reason for this is that the core EAM processes for the complete enterprises are very similar to the processes addressing large enterprise segments.

Creating Target Pictures and Roadmaps
In Fig. 4.19, the "processes" area comprises three horizontal rows. The processes in the top row address the concrete shaping of digital landscape with target pictures and roadmaps. Typical artifacts used in these processes are as-is and to-be business capability maps and the respective application landscape maps. An analysis of business opportunities and technical opportunities is useful to prepare the vision for a digital landscape; methods here include a strategic industry analysis or a SWOT analysis. Complementary to this, a so-called technology radar displays new and upcoming technologies. The results of this roadmapping process flow into the demand portfolio or directly into the IT project portfolio. Here, the roadmap items are correlated with funding, resources, and more fine-grained timelines. To evaluate digital landscapes, we use the metrics described in Sect. 5.3. We also use heat maps, to illustrate the findings.

Managing Architectural Guidance and Standards
While the first row addresses concrete roadmaps for future application landscapes, the second row in Fig. 4.19 addresses more abstract guidance on how to generally develop the landscape. The main artifacts here are architectural principles, guidelines and standards, reference architectures, and logical building blocks. Next to the digital ecosystem, also the guidance itself must be evaluated periodically. For example, does the collection of Enterprise Architecture principles meet the quality criteria described, and is it still up to date, lean, and understandable? Do the projects

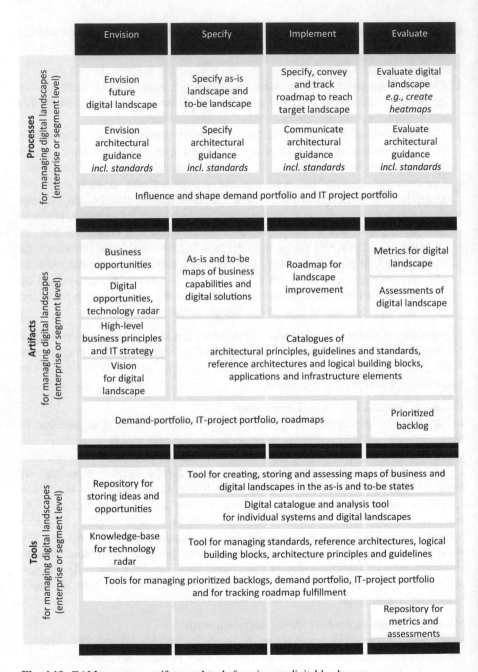

Fig. 4.19 EAM processes, artifacts and tools focusing on digital landscapes

know the guidelines? Are the guidelines integrated into other artifacts, like the architecture board template used in the stage gate process?

Creating High-Level Business Principles and IT Strategies
The artifact "high-level business principles and IT strategy" in Fig. 4.19 refers to the level of what Broadbent and Kitzis called "maxims." An example of such a high-level business principle is "drive economies of scale through best practice." The corresponding IT principles are "we enforce standards of hardware and software selection to reduce costs and streamline resource requirements" and "we centrally coordinate purchasing of IT from major vendors to minimize costs and ensure consistency" (Broadbent & Kitzis, 2005, p. 96). Closely related to such principles is the enterprise-wide *IT strategy that addresses all technical domains and all business domains*. This artifact is published circa once a year by the CIO. It usually addresses the shape of the IT service organization as well as the vision and a high-level roadmap for the complete digital ecosystem. We already established that IT strategy means defining an IT target picture and the way how to reach it. Compared to the finer-grained application landscape maps and roadmaps described above, this overall IT strategy comprises rather coarse-grained decisions like "We will form one central IT service provider for all business units of the enterprise," "We will form exactly one central customer database for the entire group," or "We will achieve seamless interoperability of all business applications via joint standards and central integration platforms."

Influence and Shape Demand Portfolio and IT Project Portfolio
EAM must shape the digital ecosystem already in the early stages of a project and not only serve as a gatekeeper at the end of a project. Therefore, the chief enterprise architect or another representative of the EAM capability must be part of the demand and IT project portfolio management panels. Here, they have the chance to prioritize projects that sustainably improve the overall digital ecosystem, for example, by introducing a new technology that complements the existing portfolio. Another interface from EAM to the demand and project portfolio management is the above-described roadmapping process, where the roadmap activities are transferred into the demand or project portfolio.

4.6.2   EAM Processes in the Context of Individual Solutions

It might be counter-intuitive, but a large part of an enterprise architect's daily life is rather addressed to individual solutions and then to high-level IT strategies that explicitly address the overall landscape. The first row in Fig. 4.20 shows the EAM processes that accompany a new digital system from its idea to its go-live.

Identify Architecturally Relevant Changes in the Portfolios
The first activity in this row is that an enterprise architect scans through the demand and project portfolio to identify projects with architectural relevance. Now, we

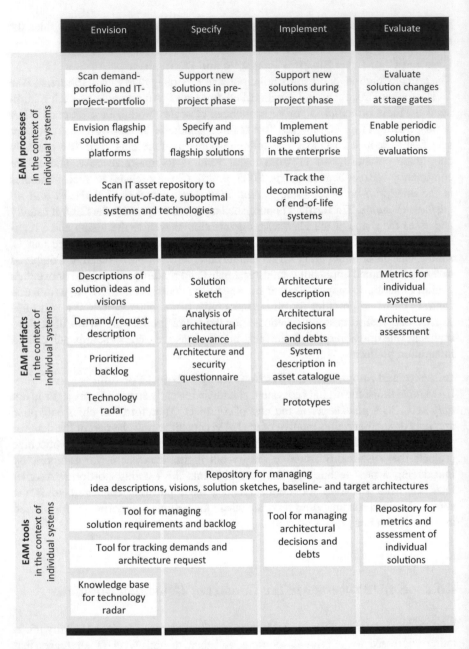

Fig. 4.20 EAM processes, artifacts and tools in the context of individual systems

described above already that EAM generally needs to be part of the demand and project portfolio process. Why do we need to have another look at this portfolio? Because in the practice of large consortiums there are many ways how a project can find its ways to funding. Some projects are directly pushed by a CxO and—for better or for worse—skip process steps; some projects are not on the radar of the EAM capability for other reasons. In practice, in this process, often we scan only those projects that already have been marked by the project initiator as "architecturally relevant." The reason is that often the EAM capability does not have sufficient resources for scanning through the vast number of all new projects of a large group. Instead, EAM needs to rely to some part on the self-assessment of the project stakeholders. Now, based on which criteria do we classify the projects at this point? The short answer is regarding their potential impact on the Enterprise Architecture. An example of one extreme is a small project that implements a standard business functionality that already exists in the enterprise and is realized with a robust technology out of the EAM standards catalog. The other extreme would be a large project that implements a new business function, with a technology that seems to be redundant to a technology already comprised in the portfolio of our enterprise. Typical reactions in this stage gate are:

1. Mark a project as *not architecturally relevant*; in this case, the project will not be accompanied or checked further by EAM.
2. Initiate *basic architecture support*. In consequence, an enterprise architect is assigned to support the project's initiation phase.
3. Assign an *architecture coach* to accompany the project. Due to the limited number of resources, this option is saved only for projects of high relevance for EAM.
4. Recommend *changes or the cancellation* of the project. This can happen, for example, when the proposed technologies contradict the technology strategy of the enterprise. Another example—not unrealistic in large enterprises—is that the solution planned by the project already exists inside the group and does not need to be reinvented.

Refinement and Preparation of Ideas in the Pre-project Phase

Depending on the result of the assessment described above, it can turn out that an enterprise architect supports an idea in the following phase. Now we are in the second process illustrated in Fig. 4.20, "support new solutions in pre-project phase." To refine the idea, here we clarify basic architectural parameters of the solution and make sure the IT strategy and the idea fit together. In practice, the architect helps the stakeholders in creating two artifacts: the *architecture and security questionnaire* and a *solution sketch*.

Building on this input, a similar questionnaire can later be used by the procurement capability to contact potential suppliers. Note that some enterprises also have so-called procurement boards, where plans for purchasing IT services are presented in a panel. An enterprise architect must be part of this panel for at least two reasons:

1. This is another channel for the EAM capability to become aware of new solutions. Now, theoretically the EAM capability should have been involved in the discussion for a new solution before this enters the "purchasing" phase. But as mentioned above, in the practice of large groups, sometimes there are deviations.

2. The EAM capability needs to confirm that this purchase is in line with the strategy for developing the digital ecosystem. For example, it could turn out that a similar solution already exists or that the proposed solution does not follow the technology standards.

Support and Assess Changes to the Digital Ecosystem During Project Phase
During this phase, the three roles described above accompany or steer projects: the architecture coach, the solution architect, and the project lead. The following artifacts are typically produced in this phase:

- *Solution sketch:* If this artifact has not been produced in the pre-project phase, the project should create this now, supported by the architecture coach. This artifact ensures that the project has a comprehensive idea of its solution architecture. It serves as a communication vehicle for various stakeholders inside and outside the project and is a prerequisite to pass architectural stage gates in this phase.
- *Architecture description and architecture log:* This major deliverable is produced by the project architect and should also be a prerequisite to pass architectural stage gates. In parallel, an architecture log is filled.
- *Architecture decision template* and *architectural debts* are used in the context of architecture board decisions.
- *System description in asset catalog.* If a new digital solution is created, a corresponding description needs to be entered in the IT asset catalog. Since this normally is not the top priority of a project's agenda, the creation of this artifact must be obligatory for any solution that goes live and should be checked in a corresponding stage gate. This also serves as an additional sanity check, since the catalog entry comprises essential attributes like "system owner."

Stage Gate Evaluations
We already saw that a solution traverses several phases or "stages." Classic examples for such stages are (1) ideation, (2) specification of requirements and solution architecture, (3) technical specification, (4) implementation, and (5) operations of a solution. In the traditional waterfall model, each stage is followed by a "stage gate" that the project must pass to enter the next phase. For example, a business case is needed to enter the project initialization phase, an architectural solution sketch is needed before entering the implementation phase, and an extensive stage gate test must be passed before the solution can go live and enter the operations phase. Today, following the paradigm of agile software development, the project phases (e.g., concept, implementation, test) are stronger parallelized and produce smaller chunks of working software in many iterations. However, even explicitly agile enterprises often maintain some of the classic stage gates, including a stage gate for verifying the solution architecture in an architecture board. The artifact used here is the architecture decision template.

Post-project Evaluations
On the one hand, every solution owner must monitor the operational performance of his system and make sure that the service-level agreements (SLA) of the system are

met. On the other hand, the strategic performance and the architecture quality of the system need to be checked periodically. The central or local architecture capability should support the solution owners in this task and ensure that the assessment is published in a repository that is accessible by the relevant stakeholders. We will describe the corresponding metrics below.

End-of-Life Management
Next to other strategic attributes, every solution owner must also supervise the sustainability and modernity of her solution. An obvious indicator that the digital product reached its end of life is that the vendor does not support the product anymore. But more subtle indicators should trigger the replacement of the product as well, for instance, too high costs or a bad functional or non-functional performance. However, often the local solution owners are too deeply stuck in the daily operations and do not initiate a big, "disruptive" step of replacing their system. Here, the EAM capability must support a systematic evaluation of the systems and the transition to new systems.

Prototyping Innovative Technologies
An architect must identify gaps in the current digitalization portfolio and foster innovative solutions. Influencing the IT portfolio to trigger the corresponding investments is one way of doing this. However, in the case of new technologies, sometimes the organization needs to be convinced of a larger commitment. In this case, the EAM capability can build prototypes to prove the new concept. This could be, for example, an innovative process digitalization engine or a new cloud-based platform for data analytics.

4.6.3 Processes to Enable and Support EAM

The processes and capabilities described in the following enable and support the EAM core processes during the four lifecycle phases. Figure 4.21 provides an overview of the processes, artifacts, and tools needed in this area. Here we briefly describe the capabilities:

Architecture Request Management
Usually inside a large enterprise, there are many areas of abundant complexity, need for modernization, or, for example, the analysis of complex dependencies in the context of error situations. If the architects in the EAM department have a good reputation, they will be sought after in many areas of the enterprise. In consequence, an EAM department in practice is confronted with a mixture of urgent ad hoc requests and more orderly, long-term engagements. To make a conscious decision which task can be addressed at what time to what extent, it is useful to have a managed, prioritized backlog of EAM requests. Such a list of requests is also valuable for communicating to the demand site of EAM which topics are currently addressed by EAM and which topics will be addressed in the future. Finally, it

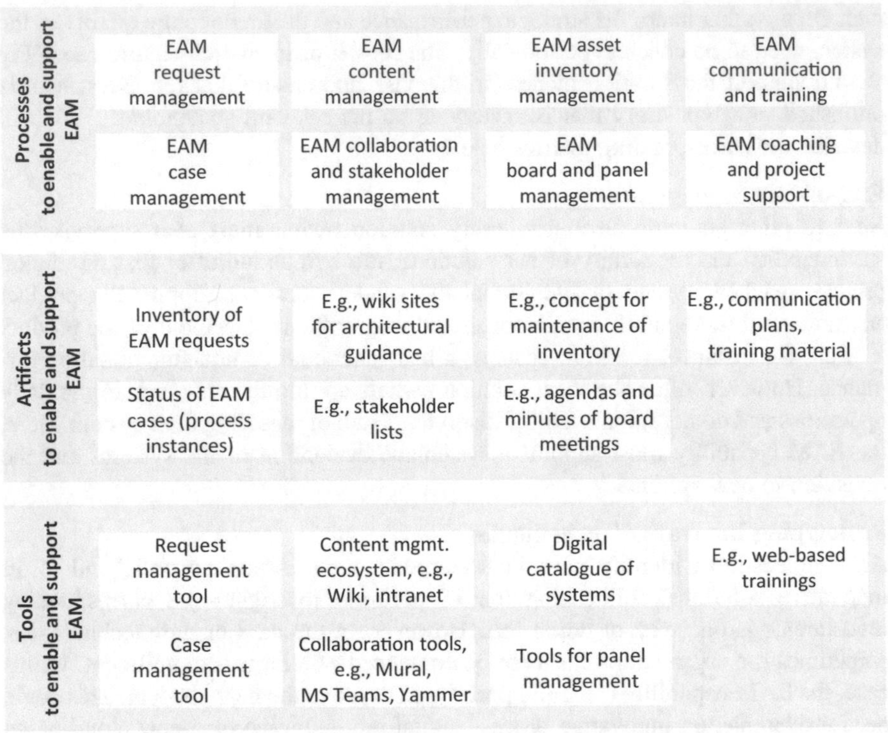

Processes to enable and support EAM			
EAM request management	EAM content management	EAM asset inventory management	EAM communication and training
EAM case management	EAM collaboration and stakeholder management	EAM board and panel management	EAM coaching and project support

Artifacts to enable and support EAM			
Inventory of EAM requests	E.g., wiki sites for architectural guidance	E.g., concept for maintenance of inventory	E.g., communication plans, training material
Status of EAM cases (process instances)	E.g., stakeholder lists	E.g., agendas and minutes of board meetings	

Tools to enable and support EAM			
Request management tool	Content mgmt. ecosystem, e.g., Wiki, intranet	Digital catalogue of systems	E.g., web-based trainings
Case management tool	Collaboration tools, e.g., Mural, MS Teams, Yammer	Tools for panel management	

Fig. 4.21 Supporting and enabling EAM processes, artifacts, and tools

provides transparency to the architects inside the EAM capability: they should not have the impression that they are randomly assigned to tasks of a perpetual chain of ad hoc firefighting missions with questionable results.

EAM Case Management
Closely related to requirements management is the capability for case management. This capability correlates architects with "cases," i.e., the tasks that they currently work on, and enables customers to interact with the architects. Say, for example, the segment architect of the domain Customer Relationship Management of a car insurance needs to know the recommendation for CRM products from the perspective of the overarching insurance group. Thus, she issues a corresponding request to the EAM department via a case management tool. After the EAM lead assigned this request to the responsible enterprise architect, now the requestor sees who is assigned to the task and can track the progress of the case until it is resolved.

EAM Knowledge and Content Management
Architectural content management is about the creation, communication, and maintenance of architectural content. Architectural content comprises all artifacts that describe the current or the to-be state of the Enterprise Architecture, for example, guidelines or reference architectures. Unfortunately, architectural content

management in practice is difficult, and examples of unsuccessful architectural content management are easy to find. For example, a large enterprise, where many groups are addressing a new technology, but lacking transparency—who is doing exactly what, based on what principles and technologies. Another example is the detailed Wiki site on, for example, enterprise-wide integration architecture that is outdated and hence ignored by the organization. Other typical problems are:

- *No single point of entry and truth.* For example, when content is spread over many different tools which are used differently by different departments.
- *Not enough access rights.* It is technically cumbersome to provide access to stakeholders and conceptually hard to find the right balance between making content accessible to everybody and producing stakeholder-tailored content.
- The *binding character and actuality* of the content is unclear, as well as the processes and responsibilities for content maintenance.

To be successful, EAM must be in permanent contact with the organizational stakeholders, e.g., business owners, solution architects, projects leads, and developers. Optimally, the whole organization understands the Enterprise Architecture and the stakeholders are tightly integrated in the creation and maintenance of architectural content. It must be easy for all stakeholders to find, access, and maintain architectural knowledge. Otherwise, a lot of architectural content will be lost, created redundantly, or ignored. As Fig. 4.22 illustrates, usually a great variety of tools is used inside an enterprise to handle architectural content. Each of the tools has different strengths and weaknesses. Based on the desired characteristics like reach, level of formality, level of detail, and level of collaboration required for the different artifacts, the tool chain for architectural content management must be carefully calibrated (compare Ziemann, 2019).

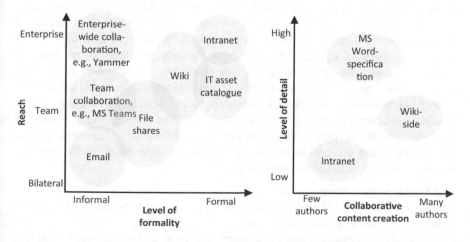

Fig. 4.22 Different forms and functions of EAM content management

Note that here we subsumed the capability of "knowledge management" under the umbrella of "content management." For a description of processes and goals for IT knowledge management, refer also to COBIT (ISACA, 2018).

EAM Asset Inventory Management

As described above, this "inventory of digital system" is a cornerstone of EAM and stores the architectural profiles of all applications and infrastructure elements. Since this information also is "architectural content," we can subsume the process that manages this inventory under the above-described process for architectural content management. However, due to the elevated importance of this process, it should be explicitly listed as an enabling process. In this process, the catalog must be endowed with the needed functional components. However, the main—and practically challenging—task here is to ensure that the information in the catalog it up to date. Reaching this goal can be supported by these points:

- *Efficient decentralization of manual tasks*: Every solution owner must be responsible for updating the information in the catalog. This process should be supported by automated mechanisms, like automatically sending out reminders in case a catalog entry has not been updated for 6 months.
- *Careful selection of content*: To reduce the unpopular burden of documentation, the content in the repository must be carefully selected. It should be rather slim and comprise only essential, core EAM data.
- *Automated updates and synchronizations:* As described in the section on EAM tools, some attributes comprised in the catalog can be retrieved from adjacent systems. Such systems include the CMDB, the API management system, enterprise-independent product catalogs, the Business Process Management tool, and tools for cost and budget management.

EAM Communication and Training

The efficient communication of the envisioned architecture into the organization is essential for EAM; if this "conveyer belt" between the EAM capability and especially the stakeholders on the implementation site is not established, the architectural target pictures will rot in the ivory tower, and the EAM capability will not get constructive feedback regarding their concepts. Partially, the capability of "communication" is addressed by the other enabling processes, foremost content management, architectural collaboration, and EAM boards. However, due to its importance, it should be installed as an explicit, measurable process. Metrics here include: Do the solution architects know the architectural principles and guidelines relevant for them? Do the IT project managers know the architectural processes? Do we publish our EAM success stories efficiently? Do we offer trainings for complex processes, like architecture development?

EAM Stakeholder Management

As expressed in the five forces of architecture (Fig. 4.4), the interaction with various stakeholders makes up the biggest part of the daily EAM operations. And, per definition, the stakeholders are the persons that need to be convinced of EAM.

Like communication, the capability of *stakeholder management* is a cross-cutting capability. Complementary to the other enabling processes, here classic means of stakeholder management are deployed, like creating a list of stakeholders and analyzing their influence and stance toward EAM.

Architectural Collaboration
Architectural collaboration is related to content management, but it addresses the interactive part of communicating and creating architectural content. Naturally, analog architectural collaboration is at the core of the traditional architecture processes. This could be, for example, a sequence of meetings where segment architects, solution architects, and enterprise architects jointly develop the target architecture for the domain "sales and marketing." On the other hand, digital, asynchronous means like Wikis, enterprise-wide collaboration tools (e.g., Yammer), and team-wide collaboration tools (e.g., Microsoft Teams) are an integral part of architectural work. Here content is presented, commented, discussed, and jointly created.

EAM Board and Panel Management
The architecture board is one of the flagship institutions of the EAM capability. Here, the strategic architecture decisions are discussed and formally agreed on, with a high impact on the digital landscape and the involved actors. Corresponding to the importance and formal character of this process, the preparation, execution, and post-processing of the meeting need to be highly professional. Usually, one person from the EAM department is dedicated to preparing, moderating, and post-processing the meeting. Practically, this includes the preparation of the agenda, the sending out of invitations, obtaining the formal approval of the minutes, and the publishing of the decisions made in the panel. As we will see later in detail, usually in one enterprise, a variety of architectural panels exist, corresponding to the various business and technical domains. Often, the same architectural subjects are presented in various panels; in this case, also the sequence of these presentations needs to be orchestrated.

Architectural Coaching and Project Support
The coaching of IT projects is another essential task for establishing a "conveyer belt" between EAM and the implementers of digital systems. We described the corresponding roles and their tasks in Sect. 4.5.1.

4.6.4   Processes for Managing EAM

Figure 4.23 provides an overview of the processes, artifacts, and tools for managing the EAM capability of an enterprise. In a nutshell, the chief architect or the CIO needs to gather their requirements of the business toward EAM, shape an organizational structure that works accordingly, and regularly evaluate if the capability is on track or if the course needs to be adapted. The elements colored in dark gray indicate

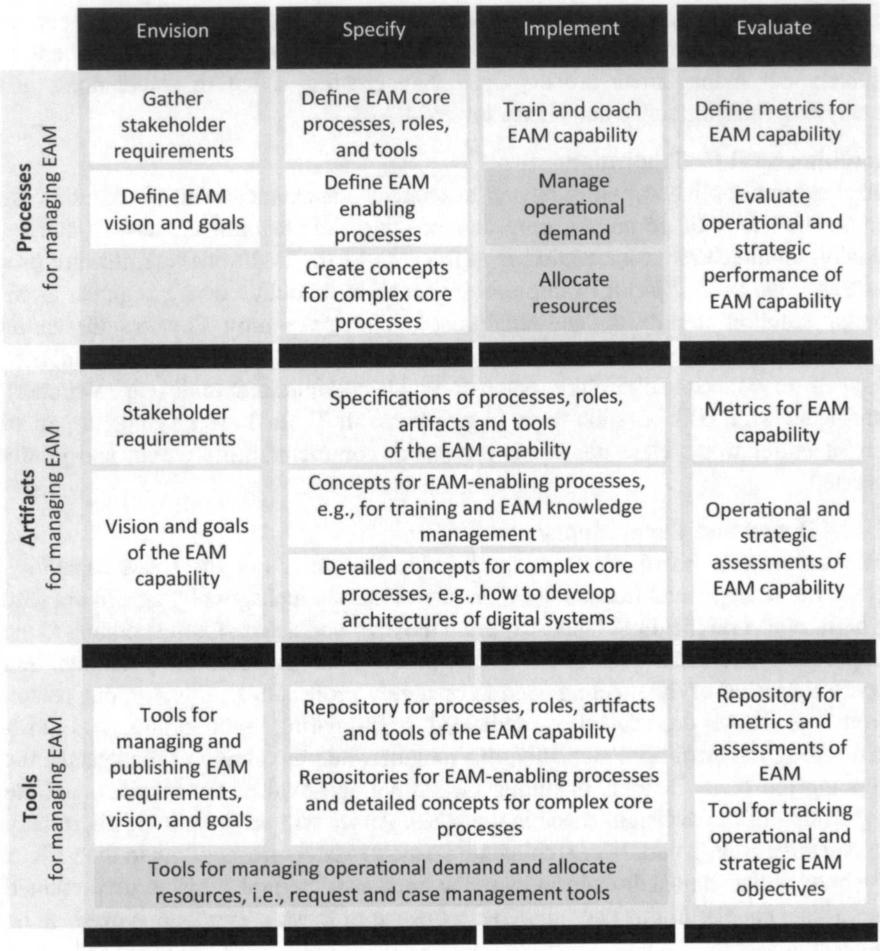

	Envision	Specify	Implement	Evaluate
Processes for managing EAM	Gather stakeholder requirements	Define EAM core processes, roles, and tools	Train and coach EAM capability	Define metrics for EAM capability
	Define EAM vision and goals	Define EAM enabling processes	Manage operational demand	Evaluate operational and strategic performance of EAM capability
		Create concepts for complex core processes	Allocate resources	
Artifacts for managing EAM	Stakeholder requirements	Specifications of processes, roles, artifacts and tools of the EAM capability		Metrics for EAM capability
	Vision and goals of the EAM capability	Concepts for EAM-enabling processes, e.g., for training and EAM knowledge management		Operational and strategic assessments of EAM capability
		Detailed concepts for complex core processes, e.g., how to develop architectures of digital systems		
Tools for managing EAM	Tools for managing and publishing EAM requirements, vision, and goals	Repository for processes, roles, artifacts and tools of the EAM capability		Repository for metrics and assessments of EAM
		Repositories for EAM-enabling processes and detailed concepts for complex core processes		Tool for tracking operational and strategic EAM objectives
		Tools for managing operational demand and allocate resources, i.e., request and case management tools		

Fig. 4.23 Processes, artifacts, and tools for managing EAM

the capabilities for managing the demand and supply of enterprise architects; these capabilities can also be seen as "enabling EAM processes." Thus, Fig. 4.21 also lists capabilities and tools for "case management" and "request management." The following section briefly describes the four phases for managing the EAM capability:

Envision Enterprise Architecture Management

Earlier we described various parameters that influence the shape of Enterprise Architecture Management. This includes, for example, the business model, the size of the enterprise, the type of enterprise digitalization pursued, the organizational structure, and the culture of the enterprise. Based on these parameters and the requirements of the EAM stakeholders in this phase, the EAM management specifies the vision for the EAM capability and its goals.

Specify Enterprise Architecture Management
Based on the input of the previous phase, now the processes, roles, artifacts, and tools for the core EAM processes and for the EAM-enabling processes illustrated in Fig. 4.8 are specified. For more complex capabilities, like EAM content management, dedicated concepts are created. This goes also for complex core processes, like the architecture development of individual systems; often, here, an enterprise-specific version of TOGAFs ADM is used.

Implement Enterprise Architecture Management
In this phase, the concepts specified in the previous phase are implemented in the organization. The EAM capability is staffed with qualified personnel, the envisioned tool chain is implemented, templates for the artifacts are created, and the processes, roles, and artifacts are communicated into the organization, for example, via the enterprise intranet and the architecture Wiki.

Evaluate Enterprise Architecture Management
Based on the goals specified of the first phase, now metrics are specified to assess how efficient and effective the EAM capability works. On a strategic level, these goals are specified and assessed, for example, once a year. On an operational level, fine-grained Objectives and Key Results (OKR), assigned to individual areas and architects, are traced more frequently (e.g., monthly). The next chapter addresses the topic of EAM evaluation in more detail.

Chapter 5
EAM Evaluation

The previous chapters covered the definition, design, and implementation of Enterprise Architecture Management. Now we close the circle by describing how to evaluate EAM in a specific enterprise. The chapter starts by laying out core terminology, like "metric" and "strategic performance measurement system." Afterward, we describe and relate core measuring areas in the context of EA and EAM. Following these areas, the chapter comprises three major sections: (1) evaluating individual digital systems, (2) evaluating the enterprise-wide digital ecosystem, and (3) evaluating the Enterprise Architecture Management capability. For each area, we describe existing measurement systems, like EAM maturity models. Subsequently, we condense and extend the state of the art into a coherent set of metrics. Each set is also illustrated in the form of a comprehensive EAM cockpit.

5.1 Introduction

5.1.1 Basic Terms

Figure 5.1 depicts core terms in the context of evaluating EAM. We will explain those briefly in the following.

Metric
A metric is a value that expresses the quality of a system regarding a specific concern. At least in the context of EAM, metrics are used to measure the fulfilment of *goals* (cp. IEEE, 2019, p. 63). For example, one metric for measuring the quality of a digital enterprise landscape could be "percentage of applications that comply

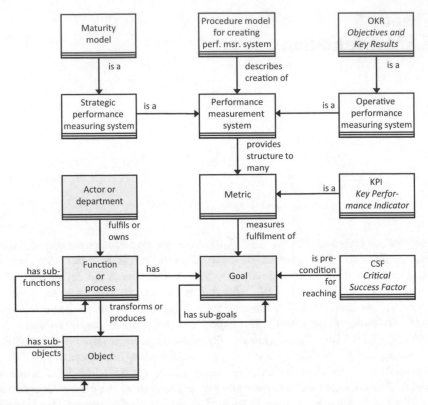

Fig. 5.1 Core terms in the context of evaluating EAM

with architectural standards," where the goal could be "harmonization of the IT landscape," or, more concretely, "80% of the applications should follow architectural standards." A goal is usually related to a function or a process that is responsible for delivering this goal. For describing and structuring metrics, it is important to keep in mind that a *function* is executed or owned by an *actor* and that this function is directed toward an *object*. In the example from above, the function "application standardization" could be owned by the department "Enterprise Architecture Management" and be directed toward the object "application landscape."

Qualitative vs. Quantitative Metrics

For evaluating individual solutions as well as application landscapes, in practice, often simple, qualitative metrics are used, like "technical fit," "functional fit," or simply "need for improvement." Here, subject matter experts can assign values between "very low" and "very high." The advantage of this rather subjective approach is simplicity: instead of collecting many measures over a long period of time, a couple of workshops suffice for the assessment. And often the local experts know well what needs to be improved without having to refer to statistical data.

Naturally, the subjectivity of this approach can lead to biased results. On the other side, in practice, even sophisticated quantitative control systems can be twisted to produce an outcome to the likings of the responsible manager.

However, to obtain a robust source for deriving actions and for being able to present metrics also to critical customers, the aim must be to obtain reliable, reproducible data. Murer et al. (2011) showed for the Credit Suisse that both qualitative and quantitative approaches are used in practice. For example, users were asked to indicate their satisfaction with the architecture on a scale from 1 (very dissatisfied) to 10 (very satisfied). In addition, the Credit Suisse used an elaborated scorecard based on objective data. Here, values like "cost per use case point," "time-to-market for a use case point," and "average number of architecture exceptions per project" were analyzed over the course of several years.

Key Performance Indicator (KPI)

A KPI is a performance metric for a specific business activity. It is a way of measuring a company's progress toward the goals it tries to achieve. Thus, it provides managers with information to analyze and steer the enterprise and its element parts in the right direction (Cambridge, 2021a). In business administration, KPIs refer to the success, performance, or capacity utilization of an enterprise, its business units, or its individual systems. KPIs are used by management and the controlling department to evaluate and steer individual projects or departments. Depending on the perspective taken, different metrics are used as KPI. Internal accounting, for example, is mainly interested in metrics on earnings, profitability, liquidity, or cash flow. General management is more interested in project parameters or quality indicators, while marketing focuses on metrics regarding customer relationships, communication, or price management (Gabler, 2021). In practice, the term is used rather informally to coin any essential metric for measuring quality in any given context, also outside business administration. For example, the OMB (2009) model for assessing the maturity of Enterprise Architecture comprises the KPI "scope of completion," with the explanation: "This KPI is measured by the percentage of the agency enterprise IT portfolio funding amount covered by a completed segment architecture."

Matthes et al. (2012) conducted a literature review on the format of EAM KPIs and suggest several attributes for a KPI, including:

- Title of the KPI, e.g., "compliance with architecture standards."
- Description and unique ID of the KPI.
- KPI owner and consumer, e.g., owner is the group-wide enterprise architecture, and consumer is the CIO and the responsible IT department managers.
- EAM goals supported by KPI, e.g., simple, transparent landscape.
- Calculation description, e.g., percentage of systems compliant with architectural guidance in comparison to all systems.
- Sources, e.g., entries in application catalog.

- Target value of the KPI, e.g., "90% of systems of record and 70% of systems of engagement should be compliant with architectural standards."
- Measurement frequency, e.g., once a year.

Critical Success Factors (CSF)

While metrics in a maturity model measure the degree to which an activity was successfully executed on a scale of, for example, 0–6, Critical Success Factors are *essential preconditions* for executing an activity successfully at all. An example of a Critical Success Factor for EAM is "clarity of mandate" or "CIO support": If the EAM department is not even supported by the CIO, the chances of an Enterprise Architecture Management worth mentioning are low. In the context of EAM, a Critical Success Factor can be seen as a metric of a strategic performance measurement system, like a maturity model. However, in the case of Critical Success Factors, the metric has only two possible values: "metric is fulfilled" and "metric is not fulfilled." Accordingly, in literature, the boundaries between Critical Success Factors for EAM, EAM success factors, and metrics of EAM maturity models are fluent. Since the literature on EAM maturity models and KPIs is more complete regarding EAM metrics, we will not describe Critical Success Factors here further. For a list of CSF in the context of EAM, refer, for example, to Ylimäki (2006), Aier and Schelp (2009), or Jusuf and Kurnia (2017).

Strategic and Operational Performance Measurement Systems

A performance measurement system describes a comprehensive collection of metrics and how they are related to each other. This can be on the metamodel level or at the model level. An example for the metamodel level is the OKR system: The simple method of Objectives and Key Results (OKR) defines the general relationship between "objectives" and a small number of "key results" needed to reach the overarching goal (i.e., the "objective"). The OKR method does not predefine specific objectives, like "redundancy inside application landscape"; thus, it can be used in any context in any industry. An example for a performance measurement system on the model level is an EAM maturity model. Here, specific metrics are defined by the system, like "percentage of standardized applications." Another difference between the OKR system and maturity models is that a maturity model is a *strategic performance measuring system*. The assessment of the maturity of an EAM capability is a laborious task that in practice will happen maybe once a year. OKR, on the other hand, is a *tactical, operative performance measuring system*. For example, the chief enterprise architect could agree with one of its team members on the objective to produce two reference architectures within the next 3 months. Thus, an operational controlling instrument like OKR is applied more often, in smaller time intervals than a strategic controlling instrument like a maturity model.

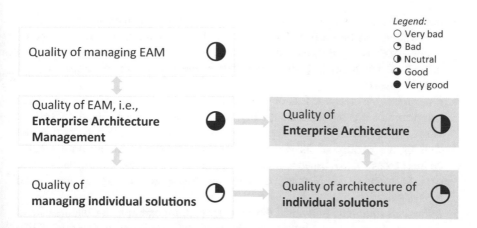

Fig. 5.2 Overview of essential EAM measuring areas

5.1.2 Overview of Measuring Areas and Approaches

Essential EAM Measuring Areas
What are the main areas that a system for EAM metrics should cover? From the perspective of the EAM capability, the most important area addresses the quality of the *enterprise-wide digital ecosystem and the solutions comprised* in it. From the perspective of the CEO, the CIO, and the lead of the EAM capability, the quality of the *management processes* addressing the Enterprise Architecture is of interest, i.e., the quality of Enterprise Architecture Management capability. In other words, both the quality of the processes and the quality of the affected systems need to be measured.

Following this distinction, Fig. 5.2 shows the essential measuring areas in the context of EAM:

1. *Managing Enterprise Architecture Management:* While the area below evaluates the EAM core processes, here we evaluate the *management of the EAM capability*. Metrics in this area address foremost the quality of EAM processes, roles, artifacts, and tools. Note that here we do not evaluate the artifacts on the instance level (e.g., the solution sketch of a concrete CRM development project), but the artifacts on the model level, for example, the quality of the templates for solution sketches.
2. *EAM—managing the Enterprise Architecture:* This area addresses the quality of EAM, i.e., it evaluates how well the Enterprise Architecture Management capability performs. Metrics here follow the individual processes displayed in Fig. 4.8 and goals of EAM. They assess, for example, the quality of the connection to the demand site, the successful creation of architecture visions and architecture specifications, how well the architecture is conveyed to the software engineers, and if the Enterprise Architecture (EA) is systematically evaluated.

3. *Managing individual solutions:* The quality of the management of an individual IT solution can be measured with metrics like availability of critical experts, quality of existing documentation, quality of requirements management, and quality of development plans (for instance, the elaboration of target pictures and roadmaps).
4. *Enterprise Architecture:* It is obvious that the quality of the individual systems comprised in it determines the quality of the enterprise-wide digital ecosystem. However, the quality of the enterprise-wide digital ecosystem is more than the sum of the quality of its elements: Typical Enterprise Architecture metrics address cross-system aspects, for instance, reuse of business components, reuse of infrastructure components, or the complexity and agility of the digital ecosystem.
5. *Individual solutions:* Individual digital solutions, for example, a Customer Relationship Management application, are typically measured with metrics like runtime costs, change costs, stability, availability, modernity ("fit-for-future"), security, standards compliance, as well as usability and solution efficiency.

Existing Approaches for Evaluating EAM

Since ca. 2005, a significant number of systems to measure the quality of EAM have been created. However, as we will detail later, contemporary EAM literature rightfully states that the maturity of existing approaches leaves room for improvement.

Table 5.1 shows a selection of approaches for evaluating EAM. On the top are generic methods like Six Sigma, EFQM, and the Balanced Score Card. Though we can use them to measure EAM processes, these methods are not specific for EAM. Neither is the CMMI maturity model, which is the basis of many EAM maturity models. The most comprehensive systems for assessing EAM are the EAM maturity models from governmental agencies. In addition, various practitioners, researchers, and standardization bodies published similar systems of EAM metrics. Regarding the measurement of the Enterprise Architecture itself, i.e., the quality of the "essential structure" of the enterprise-wide digital ecosystem, fewer literature exists. Among others, Ross et al. proposed a four-stage maturity model for Enterprise Architectures. The quality of the Enterprise Architecture is also addressed by the scorecard from Murer et al. (2011). Zooming deeper into specific areas, several maturity models exist for every architecture domain, like integration architecture or data management. Finally, classic quality measures for individual systems exist, like the ones from ISO/IEC 25010. In the following sections, we will have a closer look at these systems.

Evaluating Different EAM Areas via Generic Process Elements

Above we established that in the context of EAM, there are three major management areas: (1) managing the EAM capability, (2) managing the Enterprise Architecture, and (3) managing individual solutions. Figure 5.3 illustrates that *independent of more specific characteristics of each area, we can dissect each management area into the classic process dimens*ions. Thus, for each of the three management areas, we can assess the quality of the following dimensions:

Table 5.1 Examples for systems of metrics in the context of EAM

Focus area	Exemplary systems of metrics from literature
General enterprise processes	• Six Sigma (Pyzdek & Keller, 2016) • EFQM Excellence Model (EFQM, 2021) • Balanced Score Card (Kaplan & Norton, 1992)
General IT processes	• CMMI maturity model (SEI, 2010)
Enterprise Architecture Management (EAM) *from governmental agencies*	• NASCIO EA Maturity Model (NASCIO, 2003) • Enterprise Architecture Capability Maturity Model (ACMM) from the US Department of Commerce (DoC, 2007) • Maturity model from the US Office of Management and Budget EA Assessment (OMB, 2009)
Enterprise Architecture Management (EAM) *not from government organizations*	• Maturity model from Schekkermann (2006) • Maturity model "DyAMM" (van Steenbergen et al., 2009) • Maturity model from Hanschke (2012) • Metrics provided by COBIT (ISACA, 2018) • EAM "KPI catalog" (Matthes et al., 2011) • Credit Suisse Architecture Scorecard (Murer et al., 2011 p. 214) • Enterprise Architecture Realization Scorecard (EARS) (Prujit et al., 2012) • Metrics in ISO 42020 (IEEE, 2019, pp. 63)
Overall Enterprise Architecture (EA)	• Maturity model from Ross et al. (2006, pp. 69) • Credit Suisse Architecture Scorecard (Murer et al., 2011, p. 214)
Individual architecture domains	• OSIMM maturity model for integration architecture (Open Group, 2016) • Maturity model for data management: CMMI for Data (ISACA, 2021)
Individual systems	• Metrics from ISO/IEC 25010 (ISO, 2011) • Metrics described by McGovern et al. (2003) and Bass et al. (2006) • ATAM method for evaluating system architectures (Bass et al., 2006)

- *Processes and functions:* Here, we evaluate, for example, if the processes are well-defined (e.g., precise, lean, right level of detail), efficient, as well as known and applied by the stakeholders. We also assess if the portfolio of processes and functions in the respective area is complete.
- *Artifacts:* Here, we evaluate if the architectural artifacts are well-defined and if we have the right selection and quantity of artifacts. Further questions are if the stakeholders can easily access the templates for the artifacts and if on the instance level the quality of the used artifacts is good (for instance, the quality of solution sketches within the enterprise).

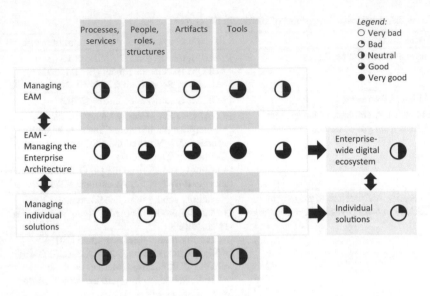

Fig. 5.3 Evaluating EAM based on the EAM process elements

- *Tools:* Here, we ask the following questions: Do we have the right tools for the different areas? Are the tools used efficiently, e.g., are catalog entries filled out completely, do they serve to integrate the stakeholders and enable collaborative content creation, and do they support the automatic analysis of, for example, the application landscape?
- *People, roles, and organizational structures:* This dimension addresses, for example, if the architectural roles are defined in good quality and quantity. It also addresses if the architects are qualified, if an architecture education program and promotion system is established, and if the stakeholder management is effective.

Note that the areas of "enterprise-wide digital ecosystem" and "individual solutions" depicted in Fig. 5.3 address the quality of *objects*, while the areas described before address *processes*.

5.2   Evaluating Individual Systems

5.2.1   Classic Metrics for Digital Systems

It all started in the first century BC with Vitruv, who described the first architecture metrics in his book *De architectura libri decem*. According to him, all buildings should have three characteristics: *firmitas*, *utilitas*, and *venustas*, i.e., firmness/

strength, utility, and beauty. Circa 2000 years after Vitruv, many authors described similar characteristics for digital systems. For instance, the ISO/IEC 25010 standard on System and Software Quality names the following "product quality" character-istics: *functional suitability, performance efficiency, compatibility, usability, reli-ability, security, maintainability*, and *portability* (ISO, 2011). In a similar vein, Bass et al. (2006) named *availability, modifiability, performance, security, usability*, and *testability*. Also referring to Bass et al., McGovern et al. (2003) extended this list and described the following quality attributes of digital systems:

- *Performance* was interpreted only regarding time by Bass et al., i.e., how fast is the system during runtime? As for most of these attributes goes: In real life, the absolute value is only partially helpful; it needs to be related to the required system value, which is usually specified in a service-level agreement (SLA).
- *Availability* is defined as the probability that a system will be operational when needed. It is calculated based on the length of time between failures, as well as by how quickly the system can restart operations after a failure. Based on this definition, availability is closely related to *reliability*: The more reliable a system is, the more available the system will be (cp. also McGovern et al., 2003).
- *Functionality* means that the system offers the needed functions.
- *Usability* refers to the quality of the user interface of a system, making the system easy to understand and to use.
- *Security* refers to the ability of a system to resist unauthorized access attempts and other malicious attacks while still providing services to authorized users.
- *Modifiability* is measured by the effort needed for adding new functions to a system.
- *Portability* means that a system can easily be moved to a different platform. A negative example is a business application that uses many features specific to the database of vendor X. If now the company wants to switch—for example, to an open-source database—it needs to rebuild the application on top of the database, because it relies on the vendor-specific features. Means to enhance portability and vendor independence are, for example, loosely coupled layers that are separated via standardized interfaces or generally the adherence to vendor-independent standards.
- *Reusability* is the ability to reuse parts of the system in other applications.
- *Integrability*, also known as *interoperability*, refers to the effort needed to connect the system with others. Interoperability is enhanced, for example, by following communication standards and good interface design.
- *Testability* refers to the effort for testing a system, e.g., after the system was changed. This is especially important if systems are changed a lot.
- *Subsetability* they define as the ability of the system to run, although not all services of the systems are functioning or implemented. This quality allows to build and execute a small set of features and to add features over time until the entire system is built. In other words, it supports agile system development. The

characteristic also increases stability, when, for example, one micro service of a system crashes but the other services of the system are still working. "Subsetability" is at least closely related to the concept of *modularity*, since it requires *autonomous modules* that are technically and functionally independent from each other.

- *Conceptual integrity* means that there is a clear, concise vision for the overall system where all parts of the system logically fit together. McGovern et al. highlight the importance of one single, *dedicated system architect* responsible for conceptual integrity, even for teams as small as four people. The corresponding proverb is that "too many cooks spoil the broth." Another mechanism to ensure conceptual integrity is the usage of *metaphors*, which provide a common vision and a shared vocabulary for all stakeholders. Conceptual integrity is also related to the principle of *separation of concerns*, in the sense, that—on a selected level—one system should address exactly one concern.

Example: Lacking Conceptual Integrity in a Multi-purpose Data Store
An example for lacking conceptual integrity often found in real-life enterprises is a data store with unclear purposes: To share data across departments, often a so-called operational data store is created. This store is fed by the operational databases from various departments, which replicate their data into the store. Originally it is designed to be only for *analytical* purposes, for instance, to provide a "360-degree view" on customer data. However, at some point, this store is also used for *operational* purposes; for instance, the data is now also used in the new, operational customer portal. Hence, the core concern of the system becomes blurry: is it data analytics, is it transactional data processing, or is it both? And who is responsible for the overall data quality of the store? There is no clear answer to that either. In consequence, the system becomes chaotic and expensive to maintain.

5.2.2 Metrics for Individual Solutions in the Context of EAM

In the previous chapter, we defined EAM goals for different areas. The lower part of Fig. 5.5 shows these goals for individual systems in the form of a dashboard, i.e., the metrics address in how far the goals we defined are met. They cover, on the one hand, the quality of a single, isolated system and, on the other hand, how well the system fits into the digital ecosystem and improves the quality of the overall landscape (for instance, the reduction of complexity by complying to standards). If such metrics are maintained in the IT asset catalogs, an automated analysis of the landscape is possible. Table 5.2 provides exemplary metrics for each goal.

Table 5.2 Metrics for individual IT systems from an EAM perspective

Goals	Exemplary EAM metrics for individual digital solutions
Effective system with high usability	• User efficiency (e.g., time a user needs to fulfill an insurance process with the system) and user satisfaction (e.g., results of a questionnaire)
Functionally adaptable system	• Costs and time for implementing a new function in the system • System has an architecture that fosters adaptability (e.g., modular, decoupled layers, separation of concerns)
Non-functionally adaptable system	• System is scalable and can be used on a pay-per-use basis • Costs and time needed for adapting the system regarding non-functional requirements • Modern architecture, fit for distributed, elastic environments ("cloud-ready" or "cloud-native")
Modern, fit-for-future system	• System is strategically supported by the vendor, no end of life in sight • System is based on modern standards, e.g., for interface descriptions, programming languages, and infrastructure
Cost- and energy-efficient system	• System has good total cost of ownership (TCO), including costs for operating and changing the system, in relation to number of users, implemented functions, and business value of functions • System has low energy consumption
System has optimal sourcing degree	• System follows the sourcing strategy, e.g., commercial off-the-shelf products, from third parties for all non-distinguishing business processes and all IT infrastructure, self-developed systems only for distinctive core processes
Compliant system	• System is compliant with external and enterprise-internal regulations, standards, and architectural guidance • Amount of technical debt assigned to system • System is regularly evaluated regarding compliance and architecture
Secure system	• System complies with external and internal security regulations • Given protection level corresponds to required protection level • Date of last risk assessment, security review, and penetration test
Reliable and performant system	• Service-level agreements are kept (e.g., response times, system downtimes, quantity, and severity of incidents per year) • Measured system reliability corresponds to system criticality
Portable, vendor-independent system	• System is based on modern, vendor-independent standards • System is based on open-source technologies • Modern architecture (e.g., "cloud-native"), separation of concerns
Reusable system	• IT system can technically provide the same service to different consumers • IT system can provide consumer-specific variations of the service
Interoperable system	• Little effort and time required for connecting the IT system technically, syntactically, and semantically to other IT systems • Support of industry- and enterprise-specific interoperability standards

Example: IT Landscape Analysis Based on Application Metrics
The IT landscape of the BEI car insurance had not been evaluated since years. This was mainly due to the managers of the various business departments, who had little interest in this exercise for transparency and enterprise-wide development. The enthusiasm of their counterparts, the local IT managers, was not much higher. One day, the CEO questioned the price-value ratio and the modernity of the digital ecosystem. He was baffled to learn that no strategic overview of the applications landscape maturity existed, neither any report on the enterprise-wide need for application modernization.

Immediately, he ordered the creation of both. Confronted with a challenging deadline to create this material, the local managers were thankful for the methodical support of the central EAM team. Now, instead of EAM having to push concepts into the local departments, the local departments "pulled" the expertise from the EAM capability. A workshop series was organized, where each department analyzed their applications regarding one condensed metric: *need for action*. This final metric was based on other metrics, including business criticality, application performance, cloud-readiness, current costs, stability, and application modernity. It turned out that these fine-grained metrics could not be retrieved from the IT asset catalog. Thus, they were created by expert panels close to the local applications. Finally, for each domain, a business capability map and an application map were created, where the "need for action" of each application was displayed on a scale from 1 to 5.

5.2.3   Metrics for the Management of Individual Systems

Above we described metrics for evaluating individual systems. Beyond the direct qualities of the system itself, in the practice of EAM it also matters how well a system is managed. Table 5.3 lists typical metrics for managing individual systems.

For example, a major source of architectural mischief in large companies is that *systems or collections of systems are not assigned to one single owner*. And if nobody is clearly endowed and responsible for a task, it usually does not get done in good quality. Thus, one simple but important metric is: Is a *business owner* assigned to the system? And is an *IT owner* assigned to the system? In this context, it is best practice to allow a new system only to become productive, if an owner is officially assigned to it.

The need for ownership systems also applies to collections of systems. Say, for example, a large airline company has 20 different CRM systems used in various business units by 20 different departments. Usually, each of the corresponding 20 owners likes her independence, flexibility, and power to directly negotiate with the CRM vendor. Thus, typically instead of having 1 owner for the entire collection of CRM systems, there are 20 owners: each negotiating independently with the CRM

Table 5.3 Metrics for managing individual systems

Quality criterion	Exemplary subgoals and metrics for system management
Assigned responsibilities	• Business owner and responsibilities for changing and running IT systems as well as collections of systems are assigned
Sufficient, current documentation for all stakeholders	• Optimal quantity, quality, and currentness of documentation for business owners, architects, developers, and operations. For example, was the architecture asset repository entry for the respective system updated in the last 6 months?
Process compliance	• Generally needed IT processes implemented, e.g., COBIT, ITIL, and data protection processes • Architecture-specific processes implemented, e.g., for updating the architecture asset repository and for addressing architecturally relevant changes, architectural debts, end-of-life management, and target picture processes

provider, each defining little ornaments for their local requirements. In general, the better solution would be here to have an organization like a "competence center CRM" that logically centralizes and harmonizes the demand for CRM. The next possibility would be the physical centralization of CRM solutions in the company by providing a central CRM platform. In the example of the airline company, the company decided to use the cloud-based CRM system of only one vendor, with different instantiations for the various business units and departments inside the airline. There is another example, from integration architecture: If there is not exactly one person responsible for application interoperability, then every application will use its own standards, and cross-application interactions will be very costly. A third example we already discussed in the context of conceptual integrity: large data stores where nobody feels responsible for the data quality. Thus, positively formulated, having a dedicated owner for a system or a collection of systems has many advantages, including:

- *Improved conceptual integrity,* since one person is responsible for coherent architecture and has oversight of all systems characteristics.
- *Economies of scale:* Having one owner enables the consolidation of systems and the reduction of redundant parts. Before, each of the 20 CRM systems used its own server; now, the infrastructure is consolidated, and only five servers are needed. Moreover, the centralized purchasing enables ordering higher volumes from the vendor. In addition, now a demand-specific allocation of licenses within the enterprise is possible. For example, if department A does not need licenses at a given point in time, department B can use those without having to buy new licenses from the vendor.
- *Economies of scope:* In the example of the integration architecture, the centralized and specialized department for integration architecture gets more practice in integrating systems than the local applications and thus can deliver a better quality.

Another important metric for the management of individual systems is the existence of system *documentation* in the right quality and quantity. To this aim,

EAM tools usually offer a function that indicates if the last documentation update
lies too far in the past. Related to this point, Table 5.3 shows a third metric for
evaluating the management of individual systems: *process compliance*. Generally,
departments in a large enterprise must follow several processes, as defined, for
example, by COBIT and ITIL. Architecture processes closely related to the quality
of the managed system include regularly updating the architecture asset repository,
following the procedures for architecturally relevant changes, managing architectural debts, end-of-life management, and regularly executing system evaluations and
target picture processes.

5.2.4   Evaluating Systems in Architecture Boards

One of the most prominent EAM processes is the evaluation of changes in an
architecture board. Say, for example, our enterprise needs a new CRM application.
Now we start an exploratory study, contact various vendors, and create a long list of
ten viable CRM systems. After a high-level analysis, we narrow down the solution
space to four viable candidates, i.e., a short list of four different CRM systems from
four different vendors. To find out which solution to choose, we gather the requirements of our enterprise and the detailed characteristics of the potential solutions. For
the final evaluation, we use the metrics displayed in Fig. 5.4. The matrix displayed

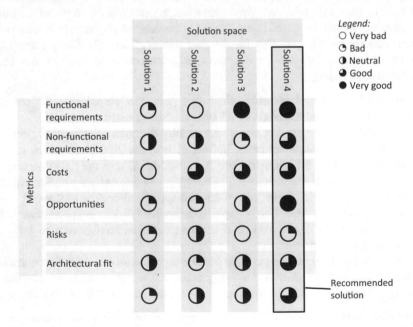

Fig. 5.4 Typical architecture board metrics for comparing solutions

there will also be shown in the presentation in the architecture board, where our findings will be quality-checked. Note that the values here are all qualitative, based on a scale of five values in the range of "very good" and "very bad." The metrics are:

Fulfilment of functional requirements: These are the business functions the application is required to fulfill. In the example of our CRM system, the marketing department names the following core functions: management of customer information, marketing and campaign management, lead management, sales automation, and business intelligence. Since, in our comparison, CRM system A fulfills all requirements, it gets the mark "very good" in this category. CRM system B lacks the function "sales automation." However, the vendor offers to develop the corresponding module in the necessary timeframe for our company. Thus, system B also gets the grade "very good" for functionality. The additional costs for developing the module are considered in the following *cost* assessment, and we also consider the *risk* that with system B, the new developed functionality will not have the quality we could already test in system A.

Fulfilment of non-functional requirements: After consulting with the business and various IT departments, we established the following non-functional requirements: The need for *data protection and security* is very high, since we are storing personal customer information. The need for *availability, scalability,* and *performance* is medium, since the traffic on the system is rather continuous and the system will only be used by employees and not, for example, in a customer web portal. The need for *reliability* and *stability* on the other hand is very high, since the customer data has a very high value to our company. Moreover, the need for *interoperability* is very high, since the CRM system needs to communicate with many other applications.

Costs: Here we establish the initial and the permanent, recurring costs of each solution. This encompasses all costs that occur, from the business specification to software development and operations, from application licenses to infrastructure equipment. After we assembled this number for each solution on one slide of the presentation, we compare the costs of the solutions among each other, as well as with the costs that we generally would expect from such a solution. Based on this absolute numbers, we assign the qualitative values to each solution, for example, "CRM system B is cost-wise very good." During this qualitative assessment, a discussion comes up: Should the qualitative cost assessment be related to the *value* of the respective solution, i.e., representing a cost-value relationship? Or should they represent the absolute amount of money the solution would cost us? Since the value of each solution is already expressed by the other metrics (fulfilment of requirements, opportunities, risks, architectural fit), we choose the second option. Thereby we enable the audience of our presentation to see both the costs and the value of each solution.

Opportunities: One of the products comes with high class, state-of-the-art functions for artificial intelligence. Choosing this product would not only lead to better insight in the CRM area, but we see high chance that we can use the AI knowledge in other areas of our enterprise as well, thus advancing our enterprise-wide analytical skills.

Risks: Since one of the vendors is very large, we see a risk that he will not adapt the product sufficiently to our needs. The vendor of another product is very small, bearing the risk that this company will go out of business. Though the probability of this is not very high, the impact on us would be very high. After some discussion and comparison with the risks of the other solutions, we agree to classify this as a high risk, resulting the grade "very bad" in the risk category.

Architectural fit: While the metrics before addressed the quality of the product in isolation, this metric evaluates if the products fit to the rest of our digital ecosystem and our IT strategy. To use a sports analogy, we identified that a basketball player has great individual skills; now we need to check if he fits in the team and the direction in which we want to develop the team. In the CRM example, in this category, we assigned the highest value to a product that supports our interoperability standards, fits well in our identity and access management landscape, runs on our preferred cloud platform, is cleanly structured into mostly independent Micro Services, enables our internal developers to modify or add functions in their preferred programming language, and supports state-of-the-art functions for artificial intelligence.

5.2.5   Evaluating System Architectures

Complementary to metrics for assessing the quality of digital systems, methods have been defined that describe the process of *evaluating individual architectures*. To be clear, in practice, digital solutions are usually evaluated by the lightweight process and metrics displayed in Fig. 5.4. In contrast to that, the *architecture* of a digital solution is evaluated rather seldomly in isolation. One reason for that is difficulty. It is much more straightforward and easy to assess the costs and benefits of a concrete digital system, optimally in comparison with alternative solutions, than assessing the quality of something as intangible as "the essential structure of a system, comprising its elements and the relationships among the elements as well as the relationships to the environment" (cp. the definition or architecture in Sect. 2.1.1). On top of that, the stakeholders responsible for the assessed system are highly sensitive to the outcome of the evaluation (after all, it judges the essential structure of their system). Another reason for the rarity of such evaluations is that this laborious task is only executed for very large solutions, which (a) are developed in-house and (b) are suspected of having significant architectural deficiencies. Such systems could be, for example, the self-developed contract management system of a car insurance, where the system is suspected of being too expensive. Another example would be the central integration platform of a bank, which is suspected to be too unreliable and outdated.

Tradeoff Analysis Method (ATAM)
One example of such a method is the *Architecture Tradeoff Analysis Method* of the Carnegie Mellon University. According to them, ATAM provides software architects with a means of evaluating technical tradeoffs while newly designing or

adapting an existing system architecture. To this aim, ATAM describes roles, phases, and outputs of an architecture evaluation. The outputs comprise an architecture model and a description of business goals, quality requirements, and usage scenarios correlated with quality requirements, tradeoffs, and risks (compare Bass et al., 2006).

Tradeoffs: Architects Must Decide Between Competing Goals
Tradeoffs are an important concept in the real-life practice of EAM: Usually, it is relatively easy to come up with a long list and short list of visions for architecting a solution. It gets complicated when the one solution from the list must be chosen that finally should be implemented. The solutions in the short list all are feasible— otherwise, they would not be in the short list. Thus, the *strengths, weaknesses, opportunities, and threats (SWOT)* attached to each solution must be assessed, and "tradeoffs" must be made transparent to obtain a conscious decision. A tradeoff means that with one solution, not all goals can be reached to the same degree; reaching goal A must be "traded off" against reaching goal B since the goals compete. Typical examples for tradeoffs in the context of IT strategy and architecture are:

- *Stability vs. flexibility:* For instance, we choose the solution of the largest software vendor because he is the most reliable one with the highest quality. As a tradeoff, we accept the risk that the vendor ignores some of our company-specific requirements and is less open to bargaining.
- *Flexibility vs. stability:* The opposite decision would be that we choose a small start-up company to implement the solution for us. Since we are their biggest customer, they will be rather sensitive to our requirements. As a tradeoff, we accept the risk that the start-up goes bankrupt, leaving our solution without management.
- *Consistency vs. availability vs. partition tolerance:* According to the CAP theorem, in a distributed database, only two of these three characteristics can be guaranteed.
- *Cost vs. time vs. functional scope:* According to the so-called project management triangle, these three goals compete. For example, if the new CRM application must be implemented fast, then the functional scope cannot be large, unless we are willing to have a costly solution (for hiring many software engineers that work in parallel and a project organization able to steer this complexity).

5.3 Evaluating the Enterprise Architecture

5.3.1 Overview of Enterprise Architecture Metrics

Using the Aggregated Metrics of Individual Solutions
In the previous section, we described metrics for the individual solutions that are comprised in the enterprise-wide digital ecosystem. And, as mentioned before, the quality of the Enterprise Architecture is constituted by the sum of the quality

of the individual systems comprised in it. Thus, we can aggregate the metrics of the individual systems described above to obtain metrics for the enterprise-wide digital ecosystem. For example, we could define the metrics to reach the following goals:

- 90% of the core business applications follow enterprise-wide standards for *interoperability*.
- 70% of all digital systems are based on *modern*, "future-proof" technologies.
- 70% of business applications are *sourced* from third-party vendors as software as a service (SaaS).
- 100% are *secure* in the sense that they have a protection level that is adequate to their protection requirements.
- The aggregated *costs* of all business applications are lower than they have been 5 years ago.

Using the Core EA Goals to Obtain Metrics for the Enterprise-Wide Ecosystem
Naturally, we also must address the quality of the "forest" beyond the cumulated quality of its "trees." That is, we must look beyond individual solutions to evaluate the essential characteristics of the enterprise-wide ecosystem. In Fig. 4.2, we illustrated the goals for the enterprise-wide digital ecosystem. Figure 5.5 now shows a

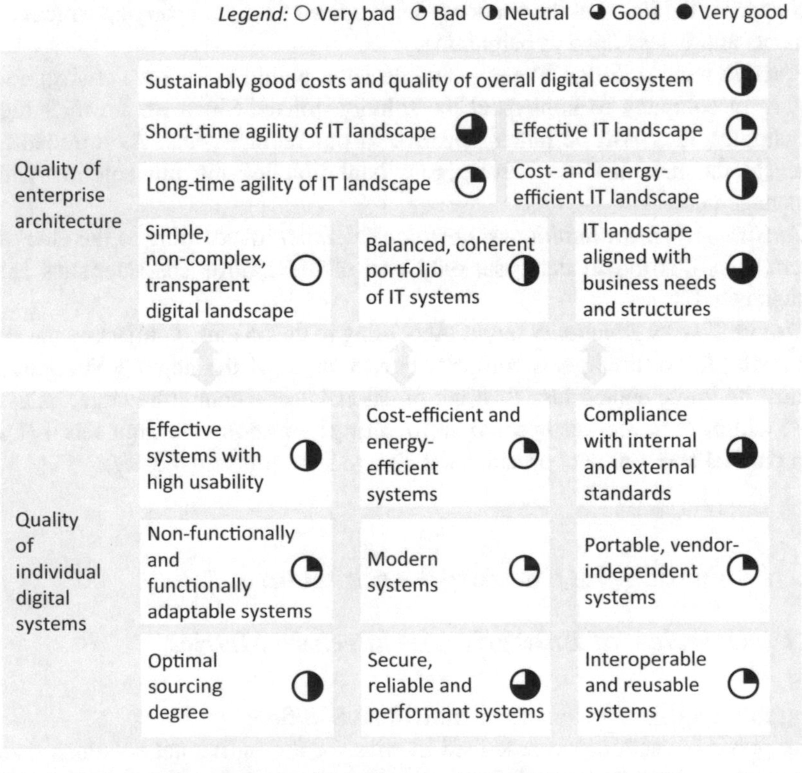

Legend: ○ Very bad ◔ Bad ◑ Neutral ◕ Good ● Very good

Quality of enterprise architecture	Sustainably good costs and quality of overall digital ecosystem ◑		
	Short-time agility of IT landscape ◕	Effective IT landscape ◔	
	Long-time agility of IT landscape ◔	Cost- and energy-efficient IT landscape ◑	
	Simple, non-complex, transparent digital landscape ○	Balanced, coherent portfolio of IT systems ◑	IT landscape aligned with business needs and structures ◕

Quality of individual digital systems	Effective systems with high usability ◑	Cost-efficient and energy-efficient systems ◔	Compliance with internal and external standards ◕
	Non-functionally and functionally adaptable systems ◔	Modern systems ◔	Portable, vendor-independent systems ◔
	Optimal sourcing degree ◑	Secure, reliable and performant systems ◕	Interoperable and reusable systems ◔

Fig. 5.5 Dashboard for core metrics of the enterprise-wide digital ecosystem

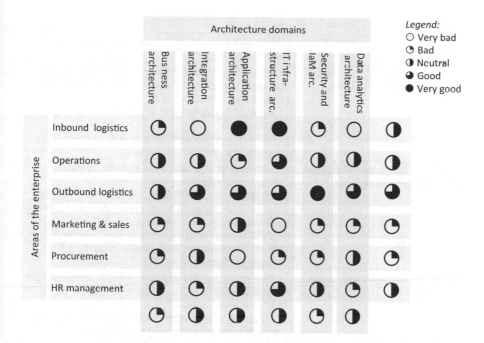

Fig. 5.6 Evaluating the digital ecosystem via the architecture domains

slightly more fine-grained version of the same concepts, displaying the core measuring areas for the overall Enterprise Architecture as a dashboard.

Using the Aggregated Metrics of Architecture Domains
The metrics illustrated in Fig. 5.5 are supposed to reflect the "direct," core goals of stakeholders, including, for example, the CEO of our enterprise. In addition to that, later (cp. Fig. 5.6), we will describe a complementary, more "indirect" approach that assesses the quality of the various *architecture domains* of the enterprise-wide digital ecosystem.

5.3.2 A Closer Look on Selected Metrics

Relating to Fig. 5.5, Table 5.4 provides exemplary metrics for measuring the quality of the enterprise-wide digital ecosystem. In the following, we will have a closer look on prominent Enterprise Architecture metrics:

Optimal Degree of Redundancy and Reuse in the IT landscape
On an abstract level, we can define a redundancy metric as *the amount of (disjoint) technical solutions that fulfill the same function*. For example, having two antivirus products that do the same thing probably does not make sense. However, as

Table 5.4 Exemplary metrics for the core EA goals

Goals	Exemplary metrics for the enterprise-wide digital ecosystem
Digital ecosystem aligned with business needs and structures	• Percentage of applications with high ratings for functional fit; percentage of applications that meet ambition toward innovativeness • Business satisfaction with overall IT services, e.g., questionnaire • Optimal degree of digitalization, e.g., percentage of digitalized repetitive core processes
Short- and long-term effective and efficient digital ecosystem	• Technical fit, e.g., number of systems compliant with architectural guidance • Overall costs, e.g., TCO of IT vs. enterprise revenue, cost for changing the IT vs. cost for running the IT, energy consumption, and other ecological costs • Stability, e.g., severity and number of incidents per month, intermediate time for fixing incidents and for solving problems, and number of SLA breaches
Short- and long-term agile digital ecosystem	• Time-to-market and costs for adding or changing digitalized functions • Percentage of failed IT projects • Optimal degree of interoperability, e.g., percentage of systems supporting interoperability standards
Simple, non-complex, transparent digital ecosystem	• Horizontally and vertically layered digital ecosystem, optimal degree of loose coupling and integration between systems and layers • Effort for understanding dependencies between IT systems, e.g., when integrating a new system, when securing systems, or during problem analysis • Optimal degree of heterogeneity and standardization in the landscape • Optimal degree of componentization, e.g., right granularity of components and comprehensible number of components in one segment or domain
Balanced, coherent portfolios inside digital ecosystem	• Optimal sourcing degree in digital ecosystem, e.g., TCO in-house IT services vs. external IT services • Optimal degree of redundancy and reuse in the landscape, e.g., percentage of applications running on platforms, times an application or an infrastructure element are (re)used by systems, and number of "net new applications" • Optimal degree of centralization (vs. decentralization) and integration (vs. autonomy) of digital services; optimal usage of platforms; optimal degree of economies of scale and scope • Optimal degree of customization of digital services, e.g., percentage of COTS systems vs. bespoke systems, also in relation to business process standardization

discussed in Chap. 2, a certain degree of redundancy in the digital landscape might be useful. When judging a given degree of technical redundancy inside a business unit, we must also relate this to the degree of business standardization in this unit. For example, technical harmonization is difficult when various business units inside an enterprise do require the same function, but in different flavors (e.g., if an insurance group comprises a life insurance and a care insurance, these might use two disjoint policy management systems, because the lifecycle and other core characteristics of car insurance policies differ significantly from those of life insurance policies). Note that redundancy can be measured not only for the business landscape and for applications but also for the other technical dimensions (e.g., data, infrastructure, or development frameworks).

Reuse in the IT landscape can be seen as the antagonist of redundancy. On an abstract level, it can be defined as "the amount of disjoint service consumers that use the same technical solution X to realize one business function Y." For example, the three business units "car insurance," "life insurance," and "health insurance" could all use the service "create new customer entry" of a central CRM system.

"Net new applications" is an interesting metric defined by Murer et al. (2011, p. 211) as "the difference of newly introduced applications minus the number of removed applications in a given time period." This metric seems counter-intuitive in a time of hyper-digitalization and the general feeling of "the more digital functions, the better." However, Murer et al. correctly observe that in the practice of large enterprises, there is a tendency to acquire new applications and a reluctance to remove old applications: "Very often the reason is that a newly developed or bought application covers only parts of the functionality of one or several older applications, so that the older applications cannot be removed. Removing these older applications requires some additional investment, which is difficult to justify because no immediate business benefit is visible. However, the system complexity increases unnecessarily with each redundant application, leading to increased maintenance and operations cost." Naturally, the focus here must be on cleaning up the landscape by shutting down redundant, inefficient systems and not on hindering the digitalization of business functions.

> **The Meaning of "Platform"**
>
> In the context of Enterprise Architecture, *a platform means a set of integrated digital services that are used as a base to develop or to run other digital services.* A traditional example here is an enterprise-specific JEE framework and the corresponding runtime elements: All applications that are developed with the enterprise-specific JEE framework can now run on the application servers specified in the framework and hosted in the data center of the enterprise. In recent years, such platforms are increasingly sourced as cloud services, namely, function as a service (FaaS), platform as a service (PaaS), or infrastructure as a service (IaaS). Besides platforms for application

(continued)

development and infrastructure hosting, further examples are platforms for data analytics, application integration, business process digitalization, and identity and access management. Going beyond the classic understanding of IT infrastructure, also large business application systems that are bought "off the shelf" but need to be heavily customized to enterprise-specific requirements are referred to as "platforms." These are, for instance, Enterprise Resource Planning Systems or large CRM systems. Note that in the context of the "platform economy," a platform is also understood as a global marketplace where, for example, developers offer their apps to consumers (cp. Van Alstyne et al., 2016).

Platform Usage

Platform usage is another classic Enterprise Architecture metric. Why does EAM care for platforms? Because "platform usage" is positively correlated with important Enterprise Architecture principles:

- *Standardization and reuse,* since a platform means that many applications use the same underlying service. The applications are standardized because they need to comply with the interfaces and services provided by the platform. In the example of applications that should run in the cloud, the applications should optimally have a "cloud-native" architecture, or at least they need to be "cloud-ready." There is another example: An extremely feature-rich, SaaS-based Customer Relationship Management application can be seen as a platform as well. If our enterprise uses this CRM platform, it will be encouraged to standardize the processes to comply with the processes already configured in the platform.
- *Centralization, specialization, and efficiency*, since with the platform one central product is used that specializes on selected services, for instance, infrastructure provisioning, application integration, or data analytics. The oftentimes enormous economies of scale of the platform lead to a high efficiency. And the specialization of the platform induces a higher quality than the isolated, one-time development of a system could offer.
- *Integration,* since the platform ensures that the processes, functions, data, rights, and roles offered by it fit together. Thus, a platform realizes a "merging integration" by integrating many elements inside one physical system. An example is an ERP system that offers many integrated functions. In contrast, a product landscape assembled with a best-of-breed approach requires significant integration efforts.
- *Separation of concerns and loose coupling*, since the platform and the applications developed on top of it are separated. This goes at least for infrastructure platforms which act as a decoupled "layer" below an application. Here, developers are forced to leave all infrastructure-specific functions out of their application and to use explicit interfaces and contracts that describe the interaction between application and infrastructure.

Short- and Long-Term Agility of the IT Landscape

As mentioned before, short- and long-term agility of the IT landscape is one of the top EAM goals; most EAM subgoals and activities contribute to reaching and maintaining an agile landscape. In the context of EAM, agility means the ability to change landscapes of digitalized business functions efficiently: changes should have a low time-to-market and be cost-efficient. Metrics to measure this top-level goal include:

- *Costs and time-to-market for implementing new functions.* Measuring the costs and the time of a project or a smaller change is easy, since every project has a budget, a start, and an end. The tricky part is that costs and time must be compared to quantity and quality (business value) of the implemented change. Now, theoretically, every large project should also produce a business case, stating its *business value*. Practically, many IT projects only lead to indirect, supporting improvements that are hard to correlate with, for example, revenue generated. Unfortunately, the size of an application is difficult to measure as well. Classic means include counting the lines of source code (LoC) of an application, function points, or use case points. However, though it might be one indicator, the quantity of the code alone says nothing regarding the quality and usefulness of a digital system. And collecting the number of function points is very laborious and hardly feasible in practice. For more information on this topic, refer to Murer et al. (2011, p. 219), who provide examples of measuring use case points and IT agility in the Credit Suisse. Note that time-to-market is not only a function on money and dynamic project resources but also depends on contextual parameters like infrastructure availability (how long does it take to order the new servers?), IT processes (when is the architecture review done; when is the next window for a production change?), as well as quality and quantity of critical company-internal resources (is the only expert for this system available for the project any time soon?).
- *Percentage of failed IT projects.* The purpose of IT projects is to change the digital landscape. If too many IT projects fail, it shows that the IT landscape is not easy to change, i.e., the digital landscape is not agile. Now the reasons do not necessarily have to lie in the Enterprise Architecture; they could also stem from project faults, like project resources lacking in quality and quantity, or from unclear project goals, unclear expectations, and "scope creep." However, in the case of enduring IT project failures, it must be evaluated if the quality of the Enterprise Architecture contributes to this. Technically, the metric of projects failures/successes should be easy to obtain by the IT project portfolio management.
- *Optimal degree of interoperability.* If applications in the enterprise are generally interoperable, changes in the context of cross-application projects are easy to implement. For example, if all applications follow the same standards for describing and implementing interfaces, a new connection between application A and application B does not cause a lot of effort and is fast to implement. Since establishing interoperability comes with a cost (for preemptively implementing cross-application standards), theoretically, it can be overdone as well, hence the

formulation of "optimal degree" of interoperability. Measures for interoperability could be the number of applications that follow enterprise-wide standards for cross-application communication or the cost for establishing a connection between two applications.

Cumulated Costs of the Enterprise-Wide Digital Ecosystem
The main goal of a typical CIO is to achieve a good price-quality ratio for the IT landscape. As described above, for measuring the quality aspect of the Enterprise Architecture, we need a rather extensive assortment of metrics. Compared to that, obtaining the cumulated costs of the overall IT landscape is easy. Classic metrics in this context include:

- *Costs of changing the IT vs. running the IT.* The idea behind this classic EA metric is that inside the overall IT budget, the *maintenance costs* should be as low as possible. Thus, money for changing the business and implementing new digital functions is left. For sure, it is a worst-case scenario that the complete IT budget must be used to keep the existing systems stable, leaving no resources to adapt or extend the digital ecosystem (cp. also Murer et al., 2011, p. 209). In this context, it makes sense to observe the *maintenance cost of IT over time*, for individual systems, domains, or enterprise-wide. A rise of maintenance cost can be caused by aging technologies, which induce higher licensing fees and make it harder to obtain engineers familiar with the legacy technology. Of course, rising maintenance costs can also be caused by an overly complex landscape, which makes even small adaptions of an application expensive, in case this application must interact with other systems.
- *Total cost of ownership (TCO) of IT in relation to enterprise revenue* is also a classic benchmark. It puts the overall IT costs into perspective and can be used to compare the IT costs with those of other enterprises. To at least have a chance to compare apples with apples, the reference enterprise should be of the same industry—e.g., car insurance—and the same business model, e.g., digital only, direct insurance.

5.3.3   Measuring All Architecture Domains of the Ecosystem

Complementary to the metrics illustrated in Fig. 5.5, Fig. 5.6 shows a simple approach to measure the overall architectural quality of the digital ecosystem: In each enterprise area, we assess the quality of each architecture domain. On the one hand, this matrix provides an impression of the overall Enterprise Architecture quality. On the other hand, the segmentation into enterprise areas helps in identifying in operational detail which areas need improvement.

Note that both the enterprise areas and the architecture domains are only examples, not complete and obviously enterprise dependent. As illustrated, the values can simply range from "very good" to "very bad." However, in the end, the aim of such assessments is to identify "need for action" and to plan where we need to improve the architecture. Therefore, possibly in a second step, the grades could also range from "no improvements needed" to "immediate improvement needed."

The assessment of the architecture domains must be related to the requirements of the respective areas. For example, the area of "HR management" might have lower requirements in respect to integration architecture than the "inbound logistics" area. Thus, the HR area might obtain the grade "no improvements needed" already by fulfilling some basic elements of integration architecture, while "inbound logistics" might have to exhibit a highly elaborated integration architecture.

5.3.4 EA Metrics Must Be Adapted for Each Enterprise

EAM literature has stated for many years that metrics in the context of EAM are challenging. Today, even experienced EAM consultants with good knowledge of a specific enterprise and its industry cannot easily come up with clearly defined metrics for the enterprise-wide digital ecosystem. Now, generally the definition of SMART (specific, measurable, attainable, realistic, timely) goals and corresponding metrics in practice is not trivial. More specifically, Enterprise Architecture metrics are challenging for two reasons:

- *Enterprise- and area-specific goals:* EA goals are highly enterprise-specific, and even inside the enterprise, they vary among the business units. For example, the "optimal degree of digitalization" in a car insurance could mean that 90% of all core processes are automated, while for a reinsurance, already 10% of process automation might be high (a car insurance has more repetitive, simple processes, while a reinsurance has more complex, manual processes). Another example is outsourcing: A typical goal here is that all "non-differentiating digital services" should be outsourced. Now imagine that as an Enterprise Architect you evaluate a business domain (e.g., "customer interaction"), where the domain owner just *insourced* various basic IT infrastructure tasks and thereby gained significant cost savings and reduced the dependency on third parties. This owner will not appreciate a metric that generically declares a high outsourcing degree as the goal.
- *Individual metrics leave room for interpretation.* Some metrics in the context of EA are clearly defined and easy to gather, like "number of business-impacting incidents per year in the enterprise." Other seemingly clear definitions leave room for interpretation. Take, for instance, the metric "Number of business applications sourced as Software-as-a-Services (SaaS)": This requires that the enterprise clearly defined its understanding of "SaaS." For example, does a browser-based software offered by the enterprise's own IT service provider count as a SaaS, or do we count only external services as SaaS? Another example of a complex term is "interoperability": which criteria exactly does an application need to fulfill to reach a certain level of interoperability and which level does it really need?

Similarly, the metric "number of platform-based applications" requires a thorough definition of the term "platform."

In this context, the metrics displayed in Table 5.4 and the explanations above should be seen as a basis and a reference for creating enterprise-specific metrics regarding the quality of the digital ecosystem.

5.4 Evaluating Enterprise Architecture Management

5.4.1 Introduction and Overview

The previous two sections addressed a core concern of the EAM capability: how to evaluate the enterprise-wide digital ecosystem. The coming section now describes how to evaluate the EAM capability itself.

Metrics Help in Optimizing and Communicating the Portfolio of EAM Activities
In its quest of mastering the fatal drive of digital ecosystems toward entropy, the EAM department sits in the middle of many stakeholders and can engage in many useful activities. However, in the complex environment of a real-life enterprise, it is challenging to allocate the scarce pool of enterprise architects to the right activities. For instance, if the EAM department focuses too much on the creation of high-level visions and does not sufficiently convey architecture contents to the organization, EAM will be isolated in the ivory tower. If, on the other hand, the EAM department does not suggest new architectures and strategic roadmaps but instead focuses on working in operational software development projects and on compliance checks, EAM will end up as the guardian of outdated concepts. Thus, to keep the right balance and to make EAM progress transparent to stakeholders, the definition of EAM metrics is useful.

Governance and Management Functions Provide Business Value Only Indirectly
Now, traditionally, IT is a supporting function, providing infrastructure on which business processes can be executed. Thus, for many IT investments, it is difficult to pinpoint in how far they will contribute to increasing enterprise profits. An IT governance function like EAM is even more indirect since it does not provide IT services itself (but steers the overall IT landscape).

The Prevention Paradox
A question comparable to the value of EAM is: how much do we value the state, i.e., the government of a nation, and how much state is needed? This question is hard to answer and has been discussed for centuries. Comparable with many infrastructure elements provided by the state, also for many EAM services goes: They become only visible when they are lacking, not when they function as they should. For example, in a fictional bank, *no central standards for integration architecture exist,*

and all connections are established on a bilateral basis. At the beginning, establishing new connections between applications is amazingly uncomplicated and cheap. However, after some years, managing the plethora of semantical, syntactical, and technical standards and interfaces of only one large application becomes very expensive. In contrast, in a fictional insurance, the integration architecture capability invests a lot of work in keeping the applications interoperable and creating an enterprise-wide standard for data exchange. Now, what the business sees when ordering a new connection between two applications is a large amount of money needed to establish this connection, as well as time spent for creating a new, standard-compliant interface. And the question comes up if the seemingly superfluous process for establishing new, standard-compliant interfaces can be omitted to save time and money. What the customer does not see are the *opportunity costs*, i.e., that without the standardization process in the medium term much higher costs would result.

5.4.2   A Short Review of EAM Maturity Models

Maturity in general refers to the state of being "fully developed" or "complete." It implies an evolutionary progress—from immature to mature—in a specific ability, coming from an initial to a desired end stage (cp. Mettler & Rohner, 2009). Accordingly, EAM maturity models try to assess to which degree the EAM capability of an enterprise is "fully developed" or "perfect." On the top level, EAM maturity models address exactly one metric: the quality of EAM in a specific enterprise. The outcome is a grade, a value usually from 0 to 5, "non-existing" to "perfect." The idea of EAM maturity models is to support the *continuous, iterative development* of EAM in an enterprise. The maturity assessment can also be used as a benchmark for comparison with other enterprises (cp. CEAF, 2020a).

EAM Maturity Models Aggregate EAM KPIs
EAM maturity models are supposed to provide a clear structure for aggregating a complete set of fine-grained EAM metrics into condensed grades. In other words, EAM maturity models represent systems of EAM metrics or EAM KPIs. Accordingly, the EAM maturity model of OMB (2009) explicitly calls the attributes by which the maturity is measured "KPIs." In difference to other EAM KPI systems, the assumption underlying prominent EAM maturity models is that the various fine-granular EAM metrics are strongly correlated with each other. For example, if the overall maturity of the EAM capability inside an enterprise is evaluated as "3—Well-defined program," the values of the individual dimensions constituting the model would be close to "3" as well.

CMMI
Though it was not created specifically for EAM, the CMMI is the basis for many EAM models. It was developed by the Software Engineering Institute (SEI) from the Carnegie Mellon University and provides a framework for developing maturity

models in a wide range of disciplines. The five maturity levels described by it are also the basis for some EAM maturity models. These levels are:

1. *Initial*: Processes are ad hoc and chaotic.
2. *Managed:* Processes are planned and followed mainly locally, inside projects.
3. *Defined:* Processes are defined and understood organization-wide, establishing "consistency across the organization." This set of standard processes is established and improved over time.
4. *Quantitatively managed:* The organization and projects established quantitative objectives for quality and process performance. These objectives are "based on the needs of the customer, end users, organization, and process implementers."
5. *Optimizing:* The organization focuses on continually improving process performance through incremental and innovative process and technological improvements. The organization's quality and process performance objectives are established and continually revised (compare SEI, 2010).

Overview of EAM Maturity Models from Government Agencies
The majority of publicly available EAM maturity models stems from American governmental agencies. The ACMM will be described below; it is noteworthy at least since it is proposed by TOGAF, the most prominent framework in the context of EAM. The NASCIO (2003) model is very similar to ACMM; the metrics of both models are displayed in Fig. 5.9.

ACMM
Figure 5.7 shows the two dimensions of the ACMM. According to the original document (DOC, 2007, p. 3), the ACMM "represents the key components of a productive Enterprise Architecture process." It "delineates an evolutionary way to

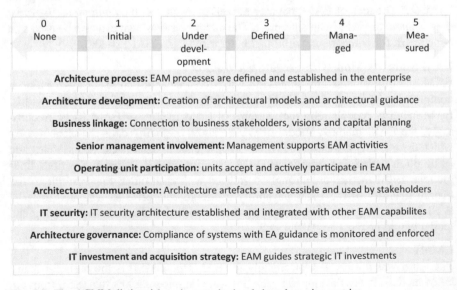

| 0 | 1 | 2 | 3 | 4 | 5 |
| None | Initial | Under development | Defined | Managed | Measured |

Architecture process: EAM processes are defined and established in the enterprise

Architecture development: Creation of architectural models and architectural guidance

Business linkage: Connection to business stakeholders, visions and capital planning

Senior management involvement: Management supports EAM activities

Operating unit participation: units accept and actively participate in EAM

Architecture communication: Architecture artefacts are accessible and used by stakeholders

IT security: IT security architecture established and integrated with other EAM capabilites

Architecture governance: Compliance of systems with EA guidance is monitored and enforced

IT investment and acquisition strategy: EAM guides strategic IT investments

Fig. 5.7 The ACMM distinguishes six maturity levels based on nine metrics

improve the overall process that starts out in an ad hoc state, transforms into an immature process, and then finally becomes a well-defined, disciplined, and mature process." The maturity levels correspond to the CMMI levels described above, plus a level "0" for "no process to speak of." Figure 5.7 names the nine criteria; note that the criterion regarding security architecture sticks out: it is the only concrete architecture domain mentioned in the maturity model; other domains, like integration architecture or data architecture, are not mentioned. The reason could be that in practice the EAM department and the security architecture department often have a distinctively close relationship since both must address the construction and the characteristics of the overall digital ecosystem from multiple perspectives. For a detailed description of the model, refer to DOC (2007) or TOGAF (Open Group, 2020a).

OMB Maturity Model

The ACMM and NASCIO models provide several metrics in a flat list whose completeness is hard to assess. The OMB (2009) model is better in so far that it breaks complexity down by clustering KPIs in three overarching areas:

- *Completion:* This area measures the completion of an enterprise's EA artifacts for all architectural layers. This includes baseline and target architectures as well as transition plans to achieve the defined target states.
- *Use:* Metrics in this category measure how the enterprise has established management practices, processes, and policies for developing, maintaining, and overseeing the Enterprise Architecture. This also comprises how well EAM is connected to and valued by its stakeholders (e.g., the capabilities for strategic planning, IT management, and capital planning and investment control).
- *Results:* Metrics in this category measure how the EAM department measures the effectiveness and value of its own activities.

These clusters do make sense; however, the metrics inside the clusters are highly specific to the OMB agency and hardly can be used as generic EAM metrics.

Non-governmental EAM Maturity Models

There are also several EAM maturity models from non-governmental organizations and authors, both from scientific and practical backgrounds. The model from Schekkerman (2006) again is very similar to the ACMM and the NASCIO model. The same goes for the "Dynamic Architecture Maturity Matrix" (DyAMM) from van Steenbergen et al. (2009). However, instead of the usual five or six maturity levels, they use a rather complex system of a scale from 1 to 10, divided into the three maturity levels a, b, and c. The model from Hanschke (2012) also uses the CMMI maturity levels. In this context, she describes five categories as generally being related to EAM maturity:

- *Content:* Completeness and quality of Enterprise Architecture descriptions
- *Processes:* Completeness and quality of EAM processes
- *Organization:* Completeness and quality of roles, stakeholder management, and EAM bodies

- *Impact:* Extent and scope of EAM influence, extent of EA compliance checks, and extent to which measures for EA, EAM, and stakeholder satisfaction are established
- *Tool support:* Completeness and quality of EAM tools

Interestingly, she argues that a qualitative assessment suffices and a quantitative maturity assessment is not necessary. Fitting to that, she does not stringently correlate the five categories to the five maturity levels.

On the Maturity of EAM Maturity Models

As charming as one scalar metric for the overall EAM capability is, it is difficult to apply existing maturity models to the real-life complexities of EAM. On the one hand, that is because the maturity, i.e., the quality of EAM, heavily depends on the context of a specific enterprise and possibly inside the enterprise again on the specific context of a business unit. For example, the optimal degree of standardization of an *Enterprise Architecture* is enterprise specific. Also, the degree to which the business is involved in *managing the Enterprise Architecture* is enterprise specific: in enterprises with a digital business model, the *IT basically is the business*, while in enterprises with a brick-and-mortar business model, business and IT are rather disjoined disciplines.

On the other hand—the shoemaker's children go barefoot—the current models do not break down the complexity of their measurement models efficiently by using orthogonal dimensions with complementary views that cover all relevant concerns. Instead, they rather randomly correlate a mixture of attributes to certain levels. In a similar vein, CEAF (2013) points at a lacking separation of concerns, stating that existing EAM maturity "models do not present a clear relationship between EA program maturity and the maturity of Enterprise Architecture itself." They also wrote that "a highly mature EA program does not necessarily translate into highly mature Enterprise Architecture." The more recent CEAF (2020a) refined this by stating that "in tandem with program maturity, is the maturity of the organization's Enterprise Architecture. Both the program and organization's architecture maturity are highly intertwined. As the program capabilities mature, the architecture will naturally mature as a result." Also pointing toward limitations of existing maturity models is the development of the *Californian Enterprise Architecture Framework* from 2013 to 2021: CEAF (2013) contained a multi-dimensional maturity model based on the maturity models from Gartner and NASCIO, reasoning that these two models were also used in the state agencies. The model consisted of five maturity levels along eight dimensions: *planning, method, deliverables, communication, compliance, integration, involvement,* and *administration.* Instead of attempting to quantitatively assess EAM maturity based on various dimensions, in the newer version, CEAF (2021a) only lists one simple qualitative metric: the *perceived value* of EAM. This has four possible levels "1. noisy," "2. useful," "3. trusted," and "4. influential."

Bente et al. (2012, p. 134) neither shed a too positive light on EAM maturity assessment models: These would have the tendency to be subjective, academic, manipulative, bureaucratic, superfluous, and misleading. Instead of using EAM maturity models, they propose using EAM "dashboards" with selected metrics.

However, this criticism is not specific for EAM maturity models, but rather applies to the general difficulty of objectively evaluating socio-technical systems. The difficulty of creating holistic (in contrast to one-sided), unambiguous (precise), and helpful (constructive) metrics is indicated by the proverb "I only believe in statistics that I doctored myself." Unfortunately, that stands in contrast to the other famous proverb: "you can only control what you can measure." Nevertheless, it surely is helpful to measure the EAM quality inside an enterprise and to show a development path as indicated by rising maturity levels to enable an iterative, continuous improvement. And existing EAM maturity models at least provide valuable hints which metrics can be used to measure EAM.

5.4.3   Process- and Capability-Oriented Evaluation of EAM

Evaluating EAM Based on Its Individual Capabilities

A simple way to measure the quality of EAM is to assign values to the specific EAM processes and capabilities. Figure 5.8 shows a corresponding dashboard where each process is judged on a scale from "very good" to "very bad." Again, in the end, these values are the basis for initiating changes in the EAM capability. Thus, possibly in a second step, they could also range from "no need for change" to "immediate improvement required." *One possibility for deriving the values of each capability is using the four process dimensions described above, i.e., to check if the processes, artifacts, tools, and people for each capability are efficient* (cp. Fig. 5.3). Another possibility is a stakeholder questionnaire regarding their satisfaction with the outputs of each process area. Note that the dashboard shown in Fig. 5.8 is based on the process overview shown in Fig. 4.9. If a more fine-grained analysis is needed, the previously shown detailed capability maps of the individual EAM areas can be used:

- EAM processes focusing on the enterprise-wide digital ecosystem (cp. Fig. 4.19)
- EAM processes focusing on individual solutions (Fig. 4.20)
- Supporting and enabling EAM processes (Fig. 4.21)
- Processes for managing EAM (Fig. 4.23)

Correlating the Metrics of the Maturity Model to the EAM Processes

Figure 5.9 illustrates that the EAM maturity model metrics can easily be clustered along the areas of Fig. 5.8. Interestingly, the metrics of NASCIO and ACMM focus on the core EAM processes (envision, specify, implement, evaluate EA), while the DyAMM metrics focus on the "Management of EAM" area.

More specifically, Fig. 5.9 displays the metrics used by the ACMM, and by the NASCIO maturity model, it also illustrates 15 metrics of the DyAMM (we omitted three of DyAMM's metrics because in today's practice of EAM, they would not be used anymore). The description of the six maturity levels in Fig. 5.9 stems from NASCIO. Here, they only serve to illustrate the idea of metrics with varying values across different maturity levels (ACMM uses very similar levels, while DyAMM

Legend: ○ Very bad ◐ Bad ◑ Neutral ◕ Good ● Very good

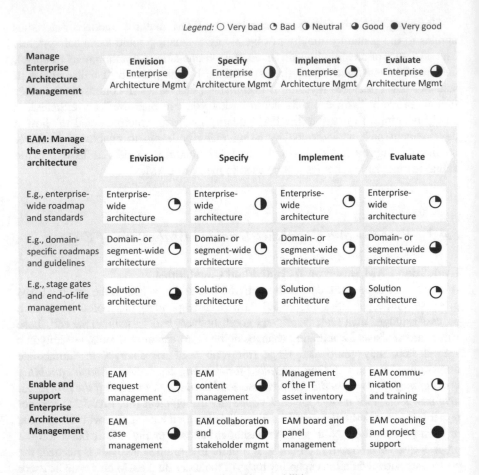

Fig. 5.8 Evaluating EAM based on the quality of its capabilities

uses a scale from 1 to 10). Note that some of the NASCIO metrics are identical with the ACMM; we left them in the table anyway to display the focus areas.

5.4.4   Further Metrics for Evaluating EAM

Do Good and Talk About It: Communication as EAM Quality Criterion
The metrics above addressed the stakeholder's trust and support for EAM. Trust also comes with successful EAM initiatives or, more precisely, with *EAM success stories that reach the stakeholders*. Related to that, Broadbent and Kitzis (2005, p. 20) describe the "credibility lifecycle" of a new CIO: When she enters her new job, she gets initial credibility. If she makes bad use of her resources, she might enter a downward spiral of failures, loss of credibility, and more failures. If, on the other hand, she uses the resources well, she builds credibility and can enter an upward spiral, i.e., a virtuous cycle.

Legend: Metrics from a: ACMM, b: NASCIO, c: DyAMM	0 No program	1 Informal program	2 Repeatable program	3 Well-defined program	4 Managed program	5 Continuously improving, vital program

Manage EAM

Architectural tools: Architects are supported by tools[c]

Framework: Processes and templates used for enterprise architecture[b]

Use of an architectural method: An architectural method is used[c]

Administration: Governance roles and responsibilities are defined[b]

Roles and responsibilities: Architectural responsibilities are efficiently allocated[c]

Architectural roles and training: Architectural roles are supported and respected[c]

Consultation: Structured communication among architects and with stakeholders[c]

Maintenance of architectural process: Process is actively maintained and improved[c]

Architecture process: EAM processes defined and established in enterprise[a]

Integration: Touch-points of management processes to EAM[b]

IT security: IT security arc. established and integrated with other EAM capabilities[b]

Quality management: Quality management for the EAM department established[c]

Budgeting and planning: Architectural activities are sufficiently budgeted and planned[c]

Envision Enterprise Arch.

IT investment and acquisition strategy: EAM guides strategic IT investments[a]

Business linkage: Connection to business stakeholders, visions and capital planning[a]

Alignment with business: Processes and deliverables are aligned with business[c]

Specify Enterprise Arch.

Blueprint development: Collection of the actual standards and specifications[b]

Architecture development: Creation of architectural guidance and models[a]

Planning: EA program road map and implementation plan[b]

Implement Enterprise Arch.

Communication: Education and distribution of EA and blueprint detail[b]

Architecture communication: EA artefacts are accessible and usable[a]

Coordination of developments: Architecture is involved in relevant projects[c]

Evaluate Enterprise Arch.

Architecture governance: Compliance with EA guidance is monitored and enforced[a]

Compliance: Adherence to EA standards and tracking of those standards[b]

Monitoring: Standards-compliance of projects is checked[c]

Enable and support EAM

Maintenance of architectural deliverables: Architectural deliverables are up-to-date[c]

Senior management involvement: Management supports EAM activities[a]

Alignment with development: EAM is aligned with systems development[c]

Alignment with operations: EAM is aligned with operations and maintenance[c]

Operating unit participation: Units accept and actively participate in EAM[a]

Involvement: Support of the EA Program throughout the organization[b]

Commitment and motivation: Commitment is attained from the organization[c]

Fig. 5.9 Clustered metrics of prominent EAM maturity models

Example: EAM Success Story "Cloud Application Development"
Yesterday, the implementation of our new flight booking engine was presented in the format of a "System Demo": 3 Agile Release Trains (ART) showcased the core components of our engine in front of 60 stakeholders from business and IT. *The EAM department was proud that the centrally architected cloud infrastructure, architectural guidelines, and patterns for developing cloud-native applications based on micro-services could successfully be used by the project architects and engineers.* Following the Scaled Agile approach, central architects were also part of the teams, fostering and connecting local innovations and specialized central knowledge. Instead of re-inventing the wheel, the use of central patterns and tools greatly increased the development efficiency. And instead of having to hire consultants, internal architects for specialized subjects like data analytics, security, and application integration helped to address these topics.

The teams were also satisfied that the experiences they made were not lost but could contribute to our enterprise-wide body of knowledge for architecting modern, cloud-based applications: their valuable architectural knowledge was harvested and can be reused in future projects.

Acceptance and Awareness of EAM Inside the Enterprise

Weiss and Winter (2012) described a set of metrics that address how well EAM is integrated within the organization and among non-architects. Therefore, they described eight categories:

1. *Legitimacy*: How many "social," personal benefits does an individual gain by supporting Enterprise Architecture?
2. *Efficiency:* In how far does EAM induce a more efficient system development that makes the stakeholder using EAM look good?
3. *Multiplicity:* How well does EAM cope with the different directions, strengths, and synergies of interacting stakeholder claims?
4. *Grounding:* How well is EAM supported and accepted by stakeholders from the demand site (business) and the supply site (IT)?
5. *Goal consistency:* Are the goals of EAM congruent with the goals of individual stakeholders, such as project managers?
6. *Content creation:* Are processes for creating and reviewing architectural guidance established? Are the necessary stakeholders involved in the process?
7. *Diffusion:* Is EA content efficiently communicated to stakeholders? Do stakeholders, including non-architects, approve of the content?
8. *Trust:* Do stakeholders, especially non-architects, trust the EAM department to be competent and to have the right values?

In a similar vein, Murer et al. (2011, p. 206) described in detail how an architecture survey was conducted in the Credit Suisse for measuring the *acceptance* of EAM inside the organization. Van der Raadt et al. (2007) proposed a model, where *awareness* is one of the key metrics to measure the effectiveness of EAM.

Next to the supporting processes described above—e.g., communication, collaboration, and content management—naturally also the quality of the EAM core processes is related to the perception of EAM by the stakeholders: If the EAM processes are of low quality, the stakeholder acceptance will sink. If the quality of the core processes is high, it generally can be expected that the stakeholder satisfaction is high. And clearly, in practice, it is highly important that EAM is accepted by a broad spectrum of stakeholders. In an ideal scenario, all stakeholders engage in *architectural thinking*, and it is ingrained in the hearts and minds of all architects and software engineers how to efficiently develop sustainable systems optimally for the overall enterprise.

However, it is the fate of EAM that it cannot satisfy all stakeholders equally, because sometimes the optimization of the global enterprise-wide system goes against local interests. Thus, regarding the abovementioned fifth point, "consistency between personal and EA goals," Weiss and Winter wrote that "even if the top management directive was to maximize the benefit for the whole organization, this will be difficult to achieve without additional incentives. As repeatedly experienced with industry partners, a project manager will be reluctant to spend \$10 M more, even if it would save another unit \$20 M."

5.5   Chapter Summary

This chapter covered the three main areas of evaluating EAM: evaluating individual digital systems, the enterprise-wide digital ecosystem, and evaluating Enterprise Architecture Management itself.

The first section, *EAM-related evaluations of individual digital solutions*, started with laying out classic quality attributes for digital solutions, like functional suitability, performance efficiency, usability, reliability, security, and maintainability. In a second step, we described similar metrics for individual solutions, however, now focusing on attributes relevant from an EAM perspective. These include, for instance, standards compliance, cost-efficiency, modernity, interoperability, and the right sourcing degree. Next to the quality of the solutions, also the quality of the capabilities that manage the systems is important. Metrics here include assigned responsibilities, process compliance, and documentation quality. Architecture metrics are also part of a core EAM process, in which architecturally relevant changes are presented in front of the architecture board. There, a small set of high-level metrics is used to evaluate and compare solutions. In addition to metrics for assessing the overall quality of digital systems, we addressed methods for *evaluating the architecture* of a solution. A prominent example of such a method is ATAM, the Architecture Tradeoff Analysis Method.

The second section, *evaluating the enterprise-wide digital ecosystem*, distinguished three approaches: *First*, to obtain metrics for the enterprise-wide digital ecosystem, we can aggregate the metrics used already for the individual systems. Thus, we can assess how many solutions in the digital ecosystem are compliant with architecture standards and how many are cost-efficient, are modern, and have the

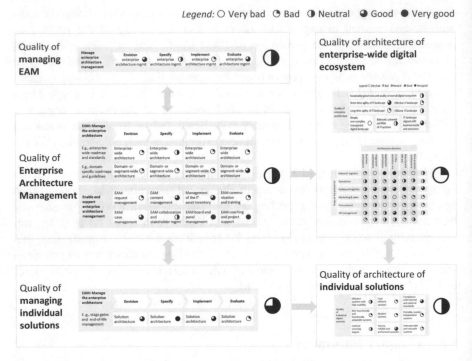

Fig. 5.10 Synopsis of core EAM measuring areas and dashboards

right sourcing degree. *Second*, to assess the essential characteristics of the enterprise-wide ecosystem beyond the aggregation of individual solutions, we referred to the EAM goal pyramid. This comprises cross-cutting goals like the complexity, transparency, agility, and complementarity of the digital landscape. *Third*, complementary to measuring the fulfilment of the "direct," high-level EA goals, we described an approach that assesses the quality of the various *architecture domains* of the enterprise-wide digital ecosystem.

In the final section, *evaluating the EAM capability*, we first laid out the need for a systematic EAM evaluation approach. Afterward, we reviewed existing EAM maturity models; from the multitude of such models, we had a closer look at ACMM, NASCIO, and DyAMM. Though EAM maturity models are hard to apply in the reality of large enterprises, they do provide useful hints for EAM metrics. Thus, in the next section, we correlated these metrics to the process framework, which also serves as a frame for structuring the EAM measuring areas. Finally, we highlighted additional topics that are important for a successful EAM capability: successful communication of EAM and further factors influencing the acceptance of EAM inside an enterprise.

Returning to the framework for clustering EAM measuring areas laid out in Fig. 5.2, Fig. 5.10 summarizes the dashboards and concepts explained in this chapter.

References

Ahlemann, F., Stettiner, E., Messerschmidt, M., & Legner, C. (Eds.). (2011). *Strategic enterprise architecture management. Challenges, best practices, and future developments.* Springer.

Aier, S. (2014, February). The role of organizational culture for grounding, management, guidance and effectiveness of enterprise architecture principles. *Information Systems and e-Business Management 12*(1).

Aier, S., & Schelp, J. (2009). A reassessment of enterprise architecture implementation. In A. Dan, F. Gittler, & F. Toumani (Eds.), *ICSOC/service wave 2009, LNCS 6275* (pp. 35–47). Springer.

Aier, S., & Schönherr, M. (2006). Evaluating integration architectures – A scenario-based evaluation of integration technologies. In D. Draheim & G. Weber (Eds.), *TEAA 2005, LNCS 3888* (pp. 2–14). Springer.

Aier, S., Riege, C., & Winter, R. (2008, August). Unternehmensarchitektur – Literaturüberblick und Stand der Praxis. *Wirtschaftsinformatik 50*(4).

Aier, S., Winter, R., & Wortmann, F. (2012). Entwicklungsstufen des Unternehmensarchitekturmanagements. In *HMD Praxis der Wirtschaftsinformatik* (Vol. 49). Springer.

Al-Debei, M., & Avison, D. (2010). Developing a unified framework of the business model concept. *European Journal of Information Systems, 19*(3), 359–376.

Alpa, G. (1994). *General principles of law.* Annual Survey of International & Comparative Law, Vol. 1: Is. 1, Article 2. Golden Gate University School of Law. Cited from Wikipedia, "Principle". Accessed June 2021, from https://en.wikipedia.org/wiki/Principle

Asprion, P. & Knolmayer, G. (2021). IT governance. In *Enzyklopädie der Wirtschaftsinformatik – Online Lexikon.* Accessed April 2021, from https://www.enzyklopaedie-der-wirtschaftsinformatik.de/wi-enzyklopaedie/wi-enzyklopaedie/lexikon/is-management/Systementwicklung/lexikon/daten-wissen/Grundlagen-der-Informationsversorgung/ITgovernance/index.html

Barnett, G., Leganza, G., Hecht, A., & Lynch, D. (2021). *The Forrester wave: Enterprise architecture management suites, Q1 2021.* Forrester Research.

Bass, L., Clements, P., & Kazmann, R. (2006). *Software architecture in practice* (2nd ed.). Addison-Wesley.

Beese, A., & Haki, K. (2016). *Drivers and effects of information systems architecture complexity: A mixed-methods study.* ECIS.

Beimborn, D. (2021). Standardisierung und Homogenisierung der Softwarelandschaft. In *Enzyklopädie der Wirtschaftsinformatik – Online Lexikon.* Accessed January 2021, from https://www.enzyklopaedie-der-wirtschaftsinformatik.de/wi-enzyklopaedie/lexikon/is-

© The Author(s), under exclusive license to Springer Nature Switzerland AG 2022   205
J. Ziemann, *Fundamentals of Enterprise Architecture Management*, The Enterprise
Engineering Series, https://doi.org/10.1007/978-3-030-96734-5

management/Management-von-Anwendungssystemen/Beschaffung-von-Anwendungssoftware/Standardisierung-und-Homogenisierung-der-Softwarelandschaft

Bente, S., Bombosch, U., & Langade, S. (2012). *Collaborative enterprise architecture: Enriching EA with Lean, Agile, and Enterprise 2.0 practices.* Morgan Kaufmann.

Booch, G., Rumbaugh, J., & Jacobson, I. (1999). *The unified modeling language user guide.* Addison-Wesley.

Broadbent, M., & Kitzis, E. (2005). *The new CIO leader – Setting the agenda and delivering results.* Harvard Business School Press.

Buckl, S. (2011). *Developing organization-specific enterprise architecture management functions using a method base.* Dissertation Thesis, Technical University Munich.

Cambridge. (2021a). *Key performance indicator. Cambridge advanced learner's Dictionary & Thesaurus.* Cambridge University Press. Accessed February 2021, from https://dictionary.cambridge.org/de/worterbuch/englisch/kpi

Cambridge. (2021b). *Culture. Cambridge advanced learner's Dictionary & Thesaurus.* Cambridge University Press. Accessed August 2021, from https://dictionary.cambridge.org/de/worterbuch/englisch/culture

CEAF. (2013, August 01). *California Enterprise architecture framework.* Version 2.0. California Department of Technology.

CEAF. (2020a). *California enterprise architecture framework – Program.* California Department of Technology.

CEAF. (2020b). *California enterprise architecture framework – Portfolio.* California Department of Technology.

CEAF. (2021a). *California enterprise architecture framework – Digest.* California Department of Technology..

CEAF. (2021b). *California enterprise architecture framework views.* California Department of Technology.

Chandler, A. D. (1962). *Strategy and structure: Chapters in the history of the American Industrial Enterprise.* MIT Press.

CISR. (2021). *Classic topics – Enterprise architecture.* MIT Center for Information Systems Research. Accessed January 2021, from https://cisr.mit.edu/content/classic-topics-enterprise-architecture

Conway, M. (1968). How do committees invent? *Datamation, 14*(5), 28–31.

Davenport, T. H., Hammer, M., & Metsisto, T. J. (1989). How executives can shape their company's information systems. *Harvard Business Review, 67*(2), 130–134. https://doi.org/10.1225/89206

Dern, G. (2009). *Management von IT-Architekturen. Leitlinien für die Ausrichtung, Planung und Gestaltung von Informationssystemen* (3rd ed.). Vieweg + Teubner.

DOC. (2007, December). *Enterprise architecture capability maturity model.* Version 1.2. United States Department of Commerce Enterprise Architecture Program Support.

EFQM. (2021). *EFQM model.* Accessed February 2021, from https://www.efqm.org/index.php/efqm-model/

Evans, E. (2004). *Domain-driven design: Tackling complexity in the heart of software.* Addison-Wesley.

Feess, E. (2021). *Komplexität. Gabler Wirtschaftslexikon.* Accessed January 2021, from https://wirtschaftslexikon.gabler.de/definition/komplexitaet-39259

Frese, E., Graumann, M., Talaulicar, T., & Theuvsen, L. (2019). *Grundlagen der Organisation – Entscheidungsorientiertes Konzept der Organisationsgestaltung* (11th ed.). Springer.

Gabler. (2021). *Key performance indicator (KPI). Gabler Wirtschaftslexikon.* Accessed February 2021, from https://wirtschaftslexikon.gabler.de/definition/key-performance-indicator-kpi-52670#references

Gartner. (2021a). Bimodal. In *Gartner glossary.* Accessed April 2021, from https://www.gartner.com/en/information-technology/glossary/bimodal

Gartner. (2021b). IT governance. In *Gartner glossary*. Accessed December 2021, from https://www.gartner.com/en/information-technology/glossary/it-governance

Gillenkirch, R. (2021). *Definition system. Gabler Wirtschaftslexikon*. Accessed January 2021, from https://wirtschaftslexikon.gabler.de/definition/system-50117

Greefhorst, D., & Proper, H. (2011). *Architecture principles – The cornerstones of enterprise architecture*. Springer.

Hafner, M., & Winter, R. (2008). *Processes for Enterprise application architecture management*. In 41st Hawaii International Conference on System Sciences (HICSS), Los Alamitos, CA, p. 396. IEEE Computer Society.

Hall, D. J., & Saias, M. A. (1980). Strategy follows structure! *Strategic Management Journal, 1*(2), 149–163.

Hanschke, I. (2012). *Enterprise architecture management – einfach und effektiv: Ein praktischer Leitfaden für die Einführung von EAM*. Hanser.

Hesse, M. (2017, October 14). *Verzettelt und verzwergt*. Der Spiegel, 42/2017, Germany.

Heutschi, R., Österle, H., Winter, R., & Brenner, W. (2007). *Serviceorientierte Architektur – Architekturprinzipien und Umsetzung in der Praxis*. Springer.

Hoogervorst, J. (2009). Enterprise governance and enterprise engineering. In J. Dietz, E. Proper, & J. Tribolet (Eds.), *The enterprise engineering series*. Springer.

IEEE. (2007). *Systems and software engineering – Architecture description*. ISO/IEC/IEEE 42010: 2007. Cited from Open Group, TOGAF 9.1. Accessed August 2021, from https://pubs.opengroup.org/architecture/togaf91-doc/arch/chap02.html

IEEE. (2011). *Systems and software engineering – Architecture description*. ISO/IEC/IEEE 42010: 2011(E).

IEEE. (2019). Software, systems and enterprise – Architecture processes. *ISO/IEC/IEEE, 42020, 2019*.

ISACA. (2018). *COBIT 2019 framework: Governance and management objectives*.

ISACA. (2021). *Data Management Maturity (DMM) model*. Accessed March 2021, from https://cmmiinstitute.com/data-management-maturity

ISO. (2011). Systems and software engineering – Systems and software quality requirements and evaluation (SQuaRE) – System and software quality models. *ISO/IEC, 25010*, 2011.

ITIL. (2019). 5 ITIL management practices. In *ITIL foundation, ITIL 4 edition*. TSO (The Stationery Office).

Johnson, S. (2001). *Emergence: The connected lives of ants, brains, cities*. Scribner.

Jusuf, M., & Kurnia, S. (2017). Understanding the benefits and success factors of enterprise architecture. In *Proceedings of the 50th Hawaii International Conference on System Sciences, HICSS*.

Kaplan, R., & Norton, D. (1992). The balanced scorecard – Measures that drive performance. *Harvard Business Review, 1992*, 71–79.

Keller, W. (2012). *IT-Unternehmensarchitektur: Von der Geschäftsstrategie zur optimalen IT-Unterstützung* (2nd ed.). dpunkt.

Khosroshahi, P. A., Hauder, M., Schneider, A., & Matthes, F. (2015, November). *Enterprise architecture management pattern catalog – Version 2.0*. Software Engineering for Business Information Systems. Technische Universität München.

Khosroshahi, A., Matthes, F., Gerngroß, M., Hauder, M., & Volkert, S. (2018). Business capability maps: Current practices and use cases for enterprise architecture management. *In 51st Hawaii International Conference on System Science (HICSS), Waikoloa Village, Hawaii, USA*.

Korhonen, J., Lapalme, J., McDavid, D., & Gill, A. (2016). Adaptive enterprise architecture for the future: Towards a reconceptualization of EA. In *2016 IEEE 18th Conference on Business Informatics (CBI)*.

Kosiol, E. (1964). *Betriebswirtschaftslehre und Unternehmensforschung: Eine Untersuchung ihrer Standorte und Beziehungen auf wissenschaftstheoretischer Grundlage*. Cited from Thomas, O. (2006). Das Referenzmodellverständnis in der Wirtschaftsinformatik: Historie,

Literaturanalyse und Begriffsexplikation. In Veröffentlichungen des Instituts für Wirtschaftsinformatik. ISSN 1438-5678.

Kotusev, S. (2016). The history of enterprise architecture: An evidence-based review. *Journal of Enterprise Architecture, 12*(1), 29–37.

Kotusev, S. (2020). *What is agile enterprise architecture?* British Computer Society (BCS). Accessed August 2021, from https://www.bcs.org/content-hub/what-is-agile-enterprise-architecture/

Kurnia, S., Kotusev, S., Taylor, P., & Dilnutt, R. (2020). *Artifacts, activities, benefits and blockers: Exploring enterprise architecture practice in depth.* In Proceedings of the 53rd Hawaii International Conference on System Sciences I HICSS 2020.

Lange, M., Mendling, J., & Recker, J. (2016). An empirical analysis of the factors and measures of enterprise architecture management success. *European Journal of Information Systems, 25*(5), 411–431. https://doi.org/10.1057/ejis.2014.39

Mack, R., & Frey, N. (2002). *Six building blocks for creating real IT strategies.* Gartner.

Mangi, L., Swanton, B., & Van Der Zijden, S. (2017). *What is Gartner's pace-layered application strategy and why should you use it?* Gartner.

Mason, R. (2017). *Have you had your Bezos moment? What you can learn from Amazon.* CIO.com. IDG Communications. Accessed August 2021, from Https://www.cio.com/article/3218667/have-you-had-your-bezos-moment-what-you-can-learn-from-amazon.html

Matthes, F., Monahov, I., Schneider, A., & Schulz, C. (2011). *EAM KPI catalog v 1.0.* Technical University Munich. Accessed July 2021, from https://wwwmatthes.in.tum.de/pages/19kw70p0u5vwv/EAM-KPI-Catalog

Matthes, F., Monahov, I., Schneider, A., & Schulz, C. (2012). Towards a unified and configurable structure for EA management KPIs. In S. Aier et al. (Eds.), *TEAR 2012 and PRET 2012, LNBIP 131* (pp. 268–283). Springer.

McGovern, J., Ambler, S., Stevens, M., Linn, J., Sharan, V., & Jo, E. (2003). *A practical guide to enterprise architecture.* Pearson.

Mell, P., & Grance, T. (2011). *The NIST definition of cloud computing (technical report).* National Institute of Standards and Technology, U.S. Department of Commerce. Accessed May 2021, from NIST SP 800-145, The NIST Definition of Cloud Computing

Mettler, T., Rohner, P. (2009). Situational maturity models as instrumental artifacts for organizational design. In *DESRIST'09: Proceedings of the 4th International Conference on Design Science Research in Information Systems and Technology.*

Müller-Stewens, G., & Gillenkirch, R. (2018). *Strategie. Gabler Wirtschaftslexikon.* Accessed January 2021, from https://wirtschaftslexikon.gabler.de/definition/strategie-43591/version-266920

Murer, S., Bonati, B., & Furrer, F. (2011). *Managed evolution – A strategy for very large information systems.* Springer.

NASCIO. (2003). *NASCIO Enterprise architecture maturity model – Version 1.3.* National Association of State Chief Information Officers (NASCIO).

Niemann, K. (2006). *From enterprise architecture to IT governance – Elements of effective IT management.* Vieweg.

Nilsson, L., & Gil, J. (2019). The signature of organic urban growth: Degree distribution patterns of the City's street network structure. In L. D'Acci (Ed.), *The mathematics of urban morphology, modeling and simulation in science, engineering and technology.* Springer.

OECD. (2015). *G20/OECD principles of corporate governance.* OECD. Accessed April 2021, from https://doi.org/10.1787/9789264236882-en

OMB. (2009, June). *Improving agency performance using information and information technology (Enterprise architecture assessment framework v3.1).* Executive Office of the President of the United States.

OMG. (2011). *Business process model and notation (BPMN) – Version 2.0.* OMG. Accessed from http://www.omg.org/spec/BPMN/2.0

Open Group. (2016). *The open group service integration maturity model (OSIMM). Version 2.* Accessed March 2021, from http://www.opengroup.org/soa/source-book/osimmv2/

Open Group. (2017). *Open Group IT4IT Reference Architecture, Version 2.1.* Accessed May 2021, from https://pubs.opengroup.org/it4it/refarch21/index.html

Open Group. (2020a). *Open agile architecture. A standard of the open group.* Accessed July 2021, from https://pubs.opengroup.org/architecture/o-aa-standard-single/

Open Group. (2020b). *ArchiMate 3.1 Specification.* Accessed December 2020, from https://pubs.opengroup.org/architecture/ArchiMate3-doc/toc.htmlHttps://pubs.opengroup.org/architecture/ArchiMate3-doc/chap03.html

Open Group. (2020c). *The TOGAF Standard. Version 9.2.* Accessed December 2020, from https://pubs.opengroup.org/architecture/togaf9-doc/arch/

Op't Land, M., Proper, E., Waage, M., Cloo, J., & Steghuis, C. (2009). *Enterprise architecture. Creating value by informed governance.* Springer.

Osterwalder, A., & Pigneur, Y. (2010). *Business model generation – A handbook for visionaries, game changers, and challengers.* Wiley.

Patig, S. (2021). IT-Infrastruktur. In *Enzyklopädie der Wirtschaftsinformatik – Online Lexikon.* Accessed May 2021, from https://www.enzyklopaedie-der-wirtschaftsinformatik.de/wi-enzyklopaedie/lexikon/daten-wissen/Informationsmanagement/IT-Infrastruktur

Perks, C., & Beveridge, T. (2003). *Guide to enterprise IT architecture.* Springer.

Porter, M. E. (1985). *Competitive advantage – Creating and sustaining superior performance.* The Free Press.

Prahalad, C. K., & Hamel, G. (1990). The core competence of the corporation. *Harvard Business Review, 68*(3), 79–91.

Pruijt, L., Slot, R., Plessius, H., Bos, R., & Brinkkemper, S. (2012). The enterprise architecture realization scorecard: A result oriented assessment instrument. In S. Aier et al. (Eds.), *TEAR 2012 and PRET 2012. LNBIP 131* (pp. 300–318). Springer.

Pyzdek, T., & Keller, P. (2016). *The six sigma handbook: The complete guide for greenbelts, blackbelts, and managers at all levels* (5th ed.). McGraw-Hill.

Rao, P., Reedy, A., & Bellman, P. (2018). *Certified enterprise architect all-in-one exam guide.* McGraw-Hill.

Rosemann, M. (1996). *Komplexitätsmanagement in Prozessmodellen – Methodenspezifische Gestaltungsempfehlungen für die Informationsmodellierung.* Gabler.

Ross, J., Weill, P., & Robertson, D. (2006). *Enterprise architecture as strategy: Creating a foundation for business execution.* Harvard Business Review Press.

Ross, J., Beath, C., Mocker, M. (2019). *Designed for digital. How to architect your business for sustained success.* MIT Press.

SAFe. (2020). *Scaled Agile Framework (SAFe) 5.* Accessed January 2020, from https://www.scaledagileframework.com

Sanger, D., Perlroth, N., & Barnes, J. (2021). *As understanding of Russian hacking grows, so does alarm.* The New York Times.

Scheer, A.-W. (1984). *EDV-orientierte Betriebswirtschaftslehre – Grundlagen für ein effizientes Informationsmanagment* (1st ed.). Springer.

Scheer, A.-W. (1999). *ARIS – Business process frameworks* (3rd ed.). Springer.

Scheer, A.-W. (2000). *ARIS – Business process modeling* (3rd ed.). Springer.

Scheer, A.-W. (2016). Nutzentreiber der Digitalisierung. Ein systematischer Ansatz zur Entwicklung disruptiver digitaler Geschäftsmodelle. *Informatik-Spektrum, 39,* 275–289.

Scheer, A.-W., Thomas, O., Seel, C., Martin, G., & Kaffai, B. (2004). Geschäftsprozessorientierte Software-Architekturen: Revolution auf dem Software-Markt? In P. Dadam & M. Reichert (Eds.), *Informatik 2004 – Informatik verbindet: Band 1: Beiträge der 34. Jahrestagung der Gesellschaft für Informatik e.V. (GI)* (pp. 2–13). Springer.

Schekkerman, J. (2006). *Extended enterprise architecture maturity model support guide – Version 2.* Institute for Enterprise Architecture Developments.

Schneider, W. (2021). *Standardisierung. Gabler Wirtschaftslexikon.* Accessed January 2021, from https://wirtschaftslexikon.gabler.de/definition/standardisierung-42240

SEI. (2010, November). *CMMI for development. Version 1.3.* Software Engineering Institute, Carnegie Mellon. Accessed from https://resources.sei.cmu.edu/asset_files/TechnicalReport/2010_005_001_15287.pdf

Sinz, E. (2002). Architektur von Informationssystemen. In P. Rechenberg & G. Pomberger (Eds.), *Informatik-Handbuch* (3rd ed., pp. 1055–1068). Hanser.

Stachowiak. (1973). *Allgemeine Modelltheorie.* Springer.

Tamm, T., Seddon, P., Shanks, G., & Reynolds, P. (2011). How does enterprise architecture add value to organisations? *Communications of the Association for Information Systems, 28,* 10.

Van Alstyne, M., Parker, G., & Choudary, S. (2016, April). Pipelines, platforms, and the new rules of strategy. *Harvard Business Review.*

Van der Raadt, B., Slot, R., & van Vliet, H. (2007). *Experience report: Assessing a global financial services company on its enterprise architecture effectiveness using NAOMI.* In 40th Annual Hawaii International Conference on System Sciences (HICSS'07), p. 218b. https://doi.org/10.1109/HICSS.2007.217

Van Steenbergen, M., Schipper, J., Bos, R., & Brinkkemper, S. (2009). The dynamic architecture maturity matrix: Instrument analysis and refinement. In A. Dan, F. Gittler, & F. Toumani (Eds.), *Service-oriented computing. ICSOC/ServiceWave 2009 Workshops. ServiceWave 2009, ICSOC 2009* (Lecture Notes in Computer Science) (Vol. 6275). Springer.

Weiss, S., & Winter, R. (2012). Development of measurement items for the institutionalization of enterprise architecture management in organizations. In S. Aier et al. (Eds.), *TEAR 2012 and PRET 2012, LNBIP 131* (pp. 268–283). Springer.

Wirtz, B. (2018). *Digital business models – Concepts, models, and the alphabet case study.* Springer.

Wöhe, G. (1996). *Einführung in die Allgemeine Betriebswirtschaftslehre* (19th ed.). Vahlen.

Ylimäki, T. (2006). *Towards critical success factors for enterprise architecture. Project report.* Information Technology Research Institute, University of Jyväskyla. Accessed March 2021, from https://jyx.jyu.fi/bitstream/handle/123456789/41413/1/Report_CSFs_for_EA.pdf

Zachman, J. (1987). A framework for information systems architecture. *IBM Systems Journal, 26*(3), 276–292.

Ziemann, J. (2010). *Architecture of interoperable information systems. An enterprise model-based approach for describing and enacting collaborative business processes.* Logos.

Ziemann, J. (2019). Architectural content management in agile times – Challenges, requirements and solutions identified in a large enterprise. In C. Draude, M. Lange, & B. Sick (Eds.), *Informatik 2019 Workshops, Lecture Notes in Informatics (LNI).* Gesellschaft für Informatik.